COMPUTER-AIDED TECHNOLOGIES - APPLICATIONS IN ENGINEERING AND MEDICINE

Edited by **Razvan Udroiu**

Computer-aided Technologies - Applications in Engineering and Medicine
http://dx.doi.org/10.5772/62618
Edited by Razvan Udroiu

Contributors
Piotr Cheluszka, Francisco J. Martínez-Murcia, Juan Manuel Górriz, Javier Ramírez, Behnaz Ghoraani, Prasanth Ganesan, Mark Sterling, Steven Ladavich, Hiroshi Honda, Ren Gui, Yu-Chen Lo, Jorge Torres, Andrea Corrado, Wilma Polini, Kristina Wärmefjord, Rikard Soderberg, Björn Lindau, Lars Lindkvist, Samuel Lorin, Razvan Udroiu

Published by InTech
Janeza Trdine 9, 51000 Rijeka, Croatia

Publishing Process Manager Martina Usljebrka
Technical Editor SPi Global
Cover InTech Design team

First published December, 2016
Printed in Croatia

Additional hard copies can be obtained from orders@intechopen.com

Computer-aided Technologies - Applications in Engineering and Medicine, Edited by Razvan Udroiu
p. cm.
Print ISBN 978-953-51-2787-1
Online ISBN 978-953-51-2788-8

For EU product safety concerns:
IN TECH d.o.o., Prolaz Marije Krucifikse Kozulić 3, 51000 Rijeka, Croatia,
info@intechopen.com or visit our website at intechopen.com.

Meet the editor

Dr. Razvan Udroiu is an associate professor in the Department of Manufacturing Engineering and serves as the head of Aerospace Engineering at Transilvania University of Brasov, Romania, since 2009. He received a BSc degree (5 years) in Aerospace Engineering in 1995 and then an MSc degree in Mechanical Engineering in 1996 from Transilvania University of Brasov. He obtained his PhD (cum laude) in Industrial Engineering field from the same university, in 2003. He is the research director of the Industrial Innovative Technologies Laboratory within PLADETINO's interdisciplinary technological platform since 2007. R. Udroiu is the author/coauthor for 9 books and more than 60 research papers within journals and international conferences and coauthor for 2 patent proposals. He participated in 13 research projects with companies (director) and 14 research-development-innovation grants (team leader or team member). His main competences are related to the field of computer-aided design and manufacturing, advanced manufacturing technologies, additive manufacturing, aircraft and helicopter engineering, and composite materials technologies. He is a member of the international professional associations, IAENG Society of Industrial Engineering, IAENG Society of Mechanical Engineering, and Academic Association of Manufacturing Engineering.

Contents

Preface IX

Section 1 Introduction 1

Chapter 1 **Introductory Chapter: Integration of Computer-Aided Technologies in Product Lifecycle Management (PLM) and Human Lifecycle Management (HUM) 3**
Razvan Udroiu

Section 2 Computer-Aided Technologies in Engineering 17

Chapter 2 **Computer-Aided Manufacturing of Working Units for High-Performance Mining Machines 19**
Piotr Cheluszka

Chapter 3 **Joining in Nonrigid Variation Simulation 41**
Kristina Wärmefjord, Rikard Söderberg, Björn Lindau, Lars Lindkvist and Samuel Lorin

Chapter 4 **Computer-Aided Techniques for Geometry Assurance 69**
Andrea Corrado and Wilma Polini

Section 3 Computer-Aided Technologies in Medicine 89

Chapter 5 **Computer-Aided Clinical Decision Support Systems for Atrial Fibrillation 91**
Prasanth Ganesan, Mark Sterling, Steven Ladavich and Behnaz Ghoraani

Chapter 6 **Computer-Aided Biosensor Design 121**
Yu-Chen Lo, Ren Gui, Hiroshi Honda and Jorge Z. Torres

Chapter 7 **Computer-Aided Diagnosis in Neuroimaging 137**
Francisco J. Martínez-Murcia, Juan Manuel Górriz and Javier Ramírez

Preface

The aim of this book is to present the latest applications, trends, and developments of computer-aided technologies in engineering and medicine. Computer-aided technologies are the core of product lifecycle management (PLM) and human lifecycle management (HUM). This book has a total of seven chapters and is divided into two sections: "Computer-Aided Technologies in Engineering" and "Computer-Aided Technologies in Medicine." The first book section treats the different aspects of the product lifecycle management, including design, simulations and analysis, manufacturing, production planning, and quality assurance. Computer-aided technologies in medicine are used to extend and improve human life, reduce patient's pain, diagnose infections, treat diseases, make medical interventions, and make research on diseases affecting humans. Computer-aided technologies play a key role in a variety of engineering and medical applications, bringing a lot of benefits in product life cycle, extending and improving human life.

Dr. Razvan Udroiu
Associate Professor
Department of Manufacturing Engineering
Faculty of Technological Engineering and Industrial Management
Transilvania University of Brasov
Brasov, Romania

Section 1

Introduction

Introductory Chapter: Integration of Computer-Aided Technologies in Product Lifecycle Management (PLM) and Human Lifecycle Management (HUM)

Razvan Udroiu

Additional information is available at the end of the chapter

http://dx.doi.org/10.5772/66202

1. Introduction

The major objectives of computer-aided technology (CAx) are to simplify and to improve human's work (engineer, architect, physician, surgeon, etc.), by using the computer as an indispensable tool to solve a problem in a certain field (engineering and production, medicine, architecture, business, teaching, economy, etc.) [1].

The advanced computer-aided technologies (CAx) are focused on solving specific problems by increasing human's creativity and innovation obtained through collecting, using, and sharing information between interdisciplinary teams.

Computer-aided technologies in X field are general terms to define a technology, from a specific field of work, which is computed-aided. The substitute for X includes engineering (CAx-E), medicine (CAx-M), natural science (CAx-S), education (CAx-Ed), etc.

Nowadays, computer-aided technologies are not islands of automation, being integrated in general context of **Lifecycle Management in X field**. The concepts used to define the lifecycle management in engineering and medical field are the following (see **Figure 1**):

- **Product lifecycle management (PLM)** in the industry field
- **Human lifecycle management (HUM)** or **health management across the human lifecycle**

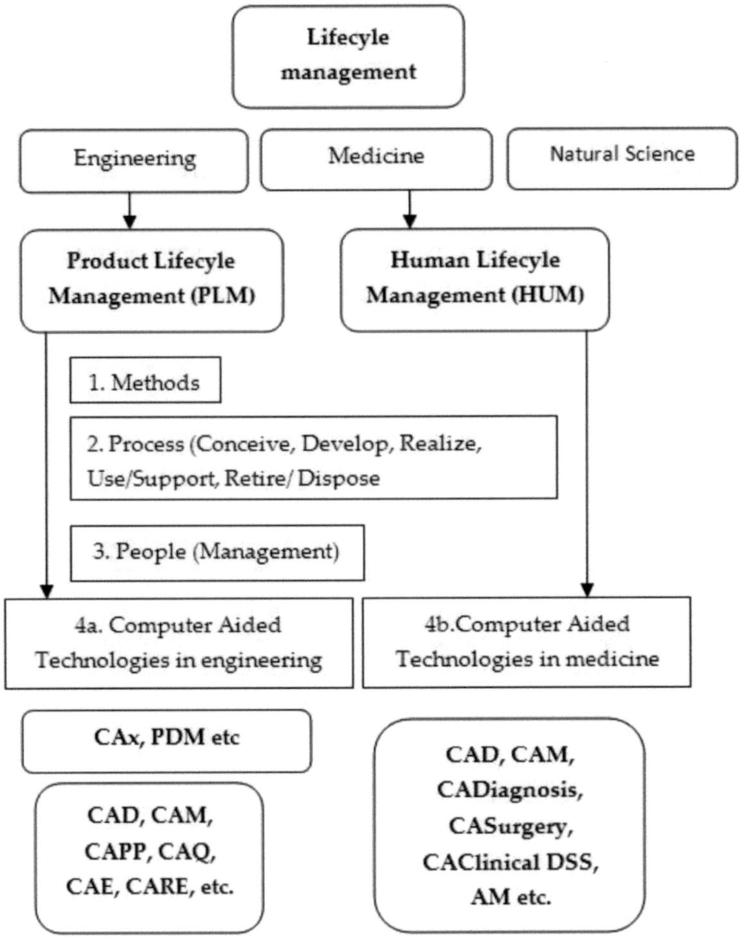

Figure 1. Schematic representation of lifecycle management in industry, medicine, and natural science.

2. Computer-aided technologies in product lifecycle management

Product lifecycle management (PLM) is the process of managing the entire lifecycle of a product including conception, design, manufacturing, quality control, use, service, and disposal of products, having integrated people, data, methods, CAx tools, processes, and business systems [2, 3]. PLM is a digital paradigm, products being managed with digital computer, digital information, and digital communication [3].

The main benefits of product lifecycle management (PLM) for the industry field are faster time-to-market, improved productivity, better product quality, decreased cost of new product introduction, improved design review, and approval processes, identifying potential sales opportunities and revenue contributions and reducing environmental impacts at end-of-life.

PLM emerged from tools such as CAD, CAM, and PDM, being viewed as the integration of these tools with innovative technologies (e.g., additive manufacturing, reverse engineering), methods, people, and the processes through all stages of a product's life [4].

To improve the product lifecycle management, a lot of methods and techniques are used [3] such as concurrent engineering, bottom-up design, top-down design, both-ends-against-the-middle design, design in context, design for X (DFX), TRIZ, lean production, design for six sigma (DFSS), total quality management (TQM), and failure mode effects analysis (FMEA).

Concurrent engineering [5, 6] or simultaneous engineering is a workflow that, instead of working sequentially through stages, carries out a number of tasks in parallel.

The most used design for X method is design for manufacture and assembly (DFMA) that is the combination of two methodologies: design for manufacture (DFM) and design for assembly (DFA), which mean the design of the parts for ease of manufacturing and the design of the product for ease of assembly.

Product data management (PDM) is the business function often within product lifecycle management (PLM) that is responsible for the management and publication of product data.

The tools used to access the information and knowledge regarding the product data are the computer-aided technologies (CAx). Computer-aided technologies (CAx) [7, 8] are the use of computer technology to aid in the design, analysis, production planning, manufacture of products, etc.

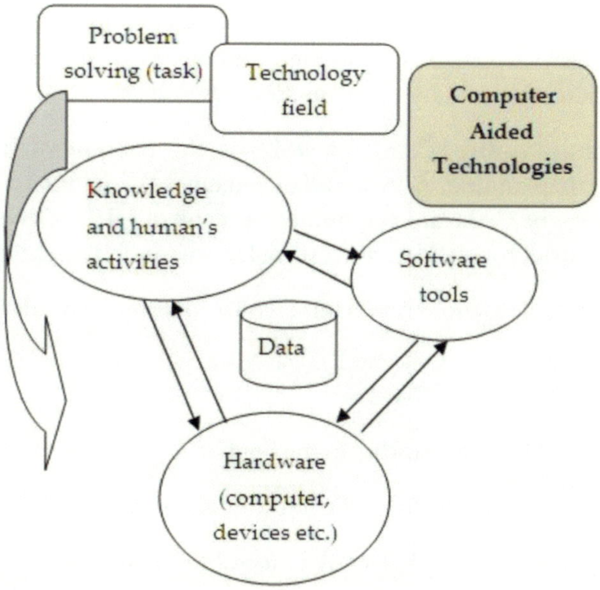

Figure 2. The main components of computer-aided technologies (CAx).

A CAx system can work like an "island of automation" or it can be integrated in the PLM system, interacting with other "islands of automation". Thus, the advanced CAx tools merge many different aspects of the product lifecycle management, including design, manufacturing, etc. CAx can be integrated, also, with other computational systems of management and planning of trials and output, such as MRP (material resource planning), ERP (enterprise resource planning), EDM (electronic document management), and PDM (product data management).

A CAx system may be defined, in generally, having the following main components (see **Figure 2**):

- Hardware component consisting in computer and interactive devices
- Software packages
- Data
- Knowledge and human's activities

Computer-aided design (CAD), computer-aided engineering (CAE), computer-aided manufacturing (CAM), computer-aided process planning (CAPP), and computer-aided quality assurance (CAQA) are the most known and mature computer-aided technologies.

Computer-aided design [1, 6, 9–12] is the computer-aided technology that involves the computer to assist in the creation, modification, analysis, and optimization of a design and design documentation.

Computer-aided engineering (CAE) [6, 9–12] is the computer-aided technology that involves the computer to analyze, simulate, and optimize the CAD geometry. CAE tools are available for a wide range of analyses: stress analysis, deformation, heat transfer, fluid flow, magnetic field distribution, kinematics, and dynamic analysis, etc.

Computer-aided manufacturing (CAM) [6, 9–12] is the computer-aided technology that involves the computer in planning, control, and management of manufacturing of any product. The most mature areas of CAM are the numerical control (NC) of the machine tools and programming of industrial robots that perform tasks as assembly, welding, etc.

The following are the most known commercial software tools for computer-aided technologies:

- CATIA by Dassault Systemes, Creo by PTC, NX by Siemens, PowerShape/ PowerMill by Delcam etc., in the field of CAD/CAM
- Materialise Magics and Netfabb Studio, in the field of 3D-printing/ additive manufacturing
- RapidForm and Geomagic in the field of computer-aided reverse engineering
- Ansys, Abaqus, COMSOL Multiphysics, Adams, LMS Virtual.Lab are focused on CAE

The computer-aided technology tools used in the engineering field are presented in **Tables 1** and **2**.

http://dx.doi.org/10.5772/66202

Computer-aided technologies	Remarks
CAx in engineering field	X=design, analysis, process planning, manufacturing, quality, innovation, etc.
CAD	Computer-aided design [6, 9–12].
CAM	Computer-aided manufacturing [6, 9–12]. *Software to control machine tools and related machinery in the manufacturing of workpieces.*
CAPP	Computer-aided process planning [9–12] *system is the bridge between CAD and CAM.*
CAE	Computer-aided engineering. *Software to aid the simulation of mechanical, strength, temperature, pressure, etc.*
FEA	Finite element analysis *is the practical application of the finite element method (FEM), which involves the use of numerical methods in structure analysis, dynamics, thermal analysis, etc.*
CFD	Computational fluid dynamics *uses numerical analysis and algorithms to analyze problems that involve fluid flows.*
MBDS	Multibody dynamics simulations.
CAQ	Computer-aided quality.
CAQA	Computer-aided quality assurance.
CAInsp	Computer-aided inspection.
CAI	Computer-aided innovation [13] *is an emerging domain in the array of computer-aided.*
CARE	Computer-aided reverse engineering [14] *has the aim to capture the geometry of an existing physical model, through digitization, and to create a 3D virtual model that is used then in different applications.*
CATAM	Computer-aided technologies for additive manufacturing. *Supporting the design, simulation and process planning for additive manufacturing.*
RapidX	RapidX [15, 16] *is a generic term for rapid technologies, e.g., rapid prototyping (RP), rapid tooling (RT), and rapid manufacturing* (*RM*) [17].
CADComposite	Computer-aided design in composite material technology.
CAMComposite	Computer-assisted manufactured composite [18].
CAMT	Computer-aided manufacturing technologies.
CAPE	Computer-aided production engineering [19].
CAMaintenance	Computer-aided maintenance.
CAMSE	Computer-aided manufacturing system Engineering [20]. *CAMSE is defined as the use of computerized tools in the application of scientific and engineering methods to the problem of the design and implementation of manufacturing systems.*
CAT	Computer-aided techniques for tolerance analysis computer-aided tolerancing [21].
CAAD	Computer-aided architectural design

Computer-aided technologies	**Remarks**
CAID	Computer-aided industrial design [22].
CAW	Computer-aided welding.
CAWFD	Computer-aided welding fixture design.
CAFD	Computer-aided fixture design [23].
CAMAP	Computer-aided mechanical assembly planning.

Table 1. Computer-aided technologies in engineering – terminology 1.

Integrated Cax in engineering field	**Remarks**
CADM	Computer-aided design and manufacture.
CAD/CAM/CAQ	Integrated CAD/CAM/CAQ system.
CIM	Computer integrated manufacturing [9–12] *has the purpose to tying "the separate islands of automation" together, including the computer-aided design, computer-aided planning, computer-aided manufacturing, and computer-aided quality assurance into an efficient system.*

Table 2. Computer-aided technologies in engineering – terminology 2.

The most known standards used in the product data exchange between computer-aided technologies systems are presented in **Table 3**.

CAD geometry translator standards	The neutral file format allows to exchange files containing 2D/3D product data models between different CAx software: **STEP** (standard for the exchange of product model data) is an ISO 10303-21 standard IGES (initial graphics exchange specification) DXF (drawing exchange format) **STL** (stereolithography, standard triangle language, or standard tessellation language) VRML (virtual reality modeling language) AMF (additive manufacturing file format) is an ISO/ASTM52915 standard [24]

Table 3. Standard exchange of product data used in computer-aided technologies.

Some terms, connected to computer-aided technologies, are shown in the **Table 4**.

Concepts	Remarks
PLM	Product lifecycle management [2, 3].
PDM	Product data management [2, 3].
PPLM	Product and process lifecycle management.
ERP	Enterprise resource planning.
DM	Digital manufacturing.
DF	Digital factory *is the foundation of the factory of the future, consisting in a digital mock-up of the factory.*
MPM	Manufacturing process management.
CPD	Collaborative product development.
DMU	Digital mock-up *is a concept that allows the description of a product, usually in 3D, for its entire life cycle.*
ICT	Information and communication technologies.

Table 4. Processes of managing and terms connected to computer-aided technologies.

3. Computer-aided technologies in health management across the human life cycle (human lifecycle management)

Medical technology is the type of technology which is used to extend and improve human life. Medical technology is used to diagnose infections, treat diseases, and to make research on diseases affecting humans. Computer-aided technologies play an important role in health management across the human life cycle. The main applications of computer-aided technologies in the medical field are the following:

- Computer-aided design (CAD)
- Computer-aided detection and diagnosis
- Computer-aided medical interventions or computer-aided surgery
- Computer-aided clinical decision
- Computer-aided simulation

CAD systems play an important role in medical applications, allowing to simulate and analysis, prosthesis design, surgical implant design, blood flow analysis, preoperative planning for surgical operations, and computer-assisted surgery [25].

Virtual reality (VR) enables physicians and surgeons to interact, manipulate, and simulate the geometric 3D CAD models of anatomical structures directly in a virtual environment, with 3D displays and haptic devices.

Rapid prototyping (RP), 3D printing (3DP), and additive manufacturing (AM) technologies allow us to obtain a real copy of anatomical structures, before a medical implant is inserted or a surgical procedure is performed.

The computer-aided technology tools used in the medical field are shown in **Table 5**.

Computer-aided technologies	Remarks
CAx in medical field	X=design, diagnosis, detection, surgery, manufacturing (RP, 3D printing), etc.
CADMF	Computer-aided design in medical field [25–27].
CAMD	Computer-aided manufactured devices [26–28].
CAL	Computer-aided learning [29].
CADiagnosis	Computer-aided diagnosis [30].
CADetection	Computer-aided detection *is a technology designed to decrease observational oversights of physicians interpreting medical images* [31].
CAMS	Computer-aided modeling and simulation.
CAClinical DSS	Computer-aided clinical decision support systems [32].
DSS	Decision support systems.
CAMI	Computer-aided medical interventions.
CASurgery	Computer-aided surgery [33] *is focused on surgical planning and simulation, and for guiding or performing surgical interventions.*
CAOSurgery	Computer-aided orthopedic surgery [29].
CATSurgicalG	Computer-aided technology of surgical guide.
CATE	Computer-aided tissue engineering or computer-aided technologies in tissue engineering *applies many CAx techniques including computer-aided design, medical image processing, reverse engineering, finite element analysis, computer-aided manufacturing, and additive manufacturing for multiscale biological modeling, biophysical analysis and simulation, and design and manufacturing of tissue and organ substitutes* [34].
CAO	Computer-aided orthodontics.
CAR	Computer-aided reconstruction.
AM	Additive manufacturing [15].
RP	Rapid prototyping [11, 15, 17].
CARE	Computer-aided reverse engineering.
CT	Computed tomography.
MRI	Magnetic resonance imaging.
PET	Positron emission tomography.
SPECT	Single photon emission computed tomography.
CAT	Computerized axial tomography.

Table 5. Computer-aided technologies in medicine – terminology.

Table 6 shows some computer-aided technology tools used in other fields.

Computer-aided technologies	**Remarks**
CAx in other fields	
CAS	Computer-aided technology in sport training [35] *is such a scientific training method that will improve athlete's training level when it is applied in athletics training.*
CAT3DAnim	Computer-aided technology applied in 3D animation.
CATDecorD	Computer-aided technology applied in decoration design.
CATArt	Computer-aided technology in art.

Table 6. Computer-aided technologies in other fields – terminology.

4. Conclusion and new trends

Nowadays, some computer-aided technology systems have reached the maturity, especially in engineering, and other CAx systems in medicine field are areas of research. The future of computer-aided technologies is focused on their integration in the smart factory, which is part of the fourth industrial revolution, Industry 4.0 [36] (**Figure 3**). The fourth industrial revolution supposes the introduction of the Internet of Things and Services into the manufacturing environment [37]. A sketch of Internet of Things is shown in **Figure 4**. The new concepts related to Industry 4.0 are presented in **Table 7**.

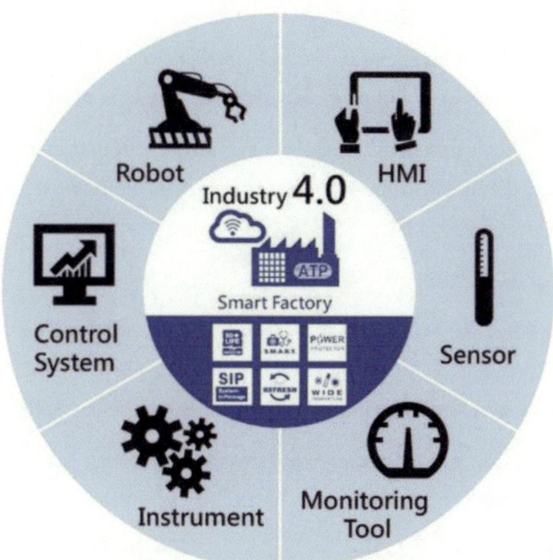

Figure 3. A generic Industry 4.0 [37].

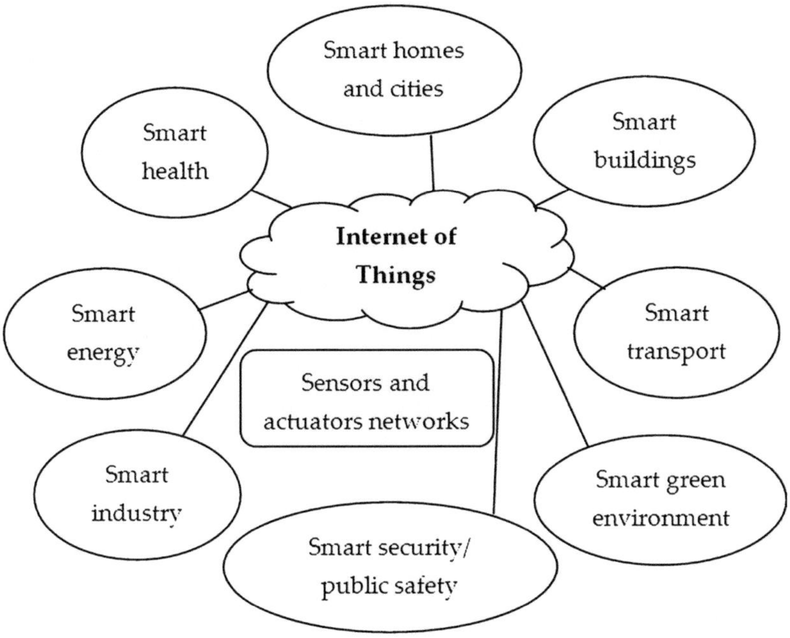

Figure 4. Internet of Things.

New concepts	
Virtual reality (VR)	Virtual reality [39] *refers to computer technologies that use interactive software and hardware to generate a realistic and immersive simulation of a three-dimensional environment controlled by movement of the body.*
Virtual enterprise (VE)	Virtual enterprise *consists in "a group of people who work together on a project, communicating mainly by phone, e-mail, and the internet, rather than regularly going to a central office to work providing operations as competitive as those in a traditional enterprise"* [40].
Factory of the future	Factory of the future *is the combination of virtual and real in order to get a full view of the complete value chain that it will allow factories to produce more rapidly, more efficiently and with greater output using fewer resources* [41].
Smart factory	Factory of the future.
Industry 4.0	Industry 4.0 *or the fourth industrial revolution* [37, 42] *creates a virtual copy of the physical world called "smart factory" including cloud computing, cyber-physical systems that communicate and cooperate with each other and with humans in real time, via the Internet of Everything and Services.*
Cloud computing	Cloud computing *store, manage, and process data, rather than a local server or a personal computer by using a network of remote servers hosted on the Internet.*
CMfg (Cloud manufacturing)	Cloud manufacturing [43] *uses cloud computing, the Internet of Things, service-oriented technologies, and high performance computing for solving manufacturing applications.* *CAx software can be supplied as a service on the* Manufacturing cloud (MCloud).

New concepts	
Cyber-physical production systems	Cyber-physical production systems *"comprise smart machines, warehousing systems, and production facilities that have been developed digitally and feature end-to-end ICT-based integration, from inbound logistics to production, marketing, outbound logistics, and service"* [37].
IoT (Internet of Things)	Internet of Things *comprises an intelligent interactivity, via Internet, sensors and actuators, etc., between human and things to exchange information and knowledge.*
IoTS (Internet of Things and Services)	Internet of Things and Services [38] *comprises the infrastructure, technologies, and applications that connect the real world and the virtual world. IoTS interconnects via the Internet, human, things, and services.*
IoE (Internet of Everything)	Internet of Everything joins *people, process, data, and things.*
Industrial Internet	Industrial Internet *"is the integration and linking of big data, analytical tools, and wireless networks with physical and industrial equipment, or otherwise applying metalevel networking functions to distributed systems"* [42].

Table 7. New concepts.

Author details

Razvan Udroiu

Address all correspondence to: udroiu.r@unitbv.ro

Department of Manufacturing Engineering, Transilvania University of Brasov, Brasov, Romania

References

[1] Li, Y., Hedlind, M. and Kjellberg, T. Usability evaluation of CADCAM: State of the art. Procedia CIRP. 2015;36:205–210.

[2] Kurkin, O. and Januška, M. Product Life Cycle in Digital factory. In Knowledge management and innovation: a business competitive edge perspective. Cairo: International Business Information Management Association (IBIMA). 2010; pp. 1881–1886.

[3] Stark, J. Product Lifecycle Management. Volume 1, 21st Century Paradigm for Product Realization, Springer International Publishing Switzerland, 2015, DOI 10.1007/978-3-319-17440-2.

[4] Teresko, J. The PLM Revolution. Industry Week, 2012.

[5] Udroiu, R. Concurrent systems engineering. Acad JManuf Eng. 2005;3(1):69–74.

[6] Udroiu, R. Integrated CAD/CAM system the core of concurrent engineering. Bull Transilvania Univ Braşov. 2004;11(46):161–168.

[7] Fagali De Souza, A. and Bodziak, S. Advanced Free Form Manufacturing by Computer Aided Systems—Cax. In: Mechanical Engineering. M. Gokcek (Ed.), InTech, Rijeka, Croatia, 2012, p. 555–586, DOI: 10.5772/36324.

[8] Werner Dankwort, C., Weidlich, R., Guenther, B. and Blaurock, JE. Engineers' CAx education—it's not only CAD. Comput Des. 2004;36(14):1439–1450.

[9] Chang, T.C., Wysk, R.A. and Wang, H.P. Computer Aided Manufacturing. Pretince Hall, Upper Saddle River, New Jersey, 1998.

[10] Kalpakjian, S. and Schmid, R. Manufacturing Engineering Technology. Pretince Hall International, London, New York, Tokio, Paris, 2001.

[11] Lee, K. Principles of CAD/CAM/CAE Systems. Addison Wesley Longman, Inc., USA, 1999.

[12] Groover, P.M., Enrory, W. and Zimmers, J.R. CAD/CAM Computer Aided Design and Manufacturing. PTR Pretice Hale, Englewood Clifts, New Jersey, 1984.

[13] Noel, L. Computer Aided Innovation. Comput Industry. 2009;60(8): 539–550.

[14] Bere, P. and Neamtu, C. Methodology for evaluate the form deviations for formula one nose car. Cent Europ J Eng. 2014;4(2):148–154.

[15] Udroiu, R. and Nedelcu, A. Optimization of Additive Manufacturing Processes Focused on 3D Printing. In: Rapid Prototyping Technology—Principles and Functional Requirements. M. Hoque (Ed.), InTech, Rijeka, Croatia, 2011, p.1–28, DOI: 10.5772/21433.

[16] Udroiu, R. and Ivan, N.V. Rapid-X using 3D printers. Supliment Acad J Manuf Eng. 2008;2:199–205.

[17] Udroiu, R. Rapid Prototyping and Rapid Manufacturing Applications at Transilvania University of Braşov. Bulletin of the Transilvania University of Brasov-Series I: Engineering Sciences, 2010.

[18] Udroiu, R. Composite materials. Technology and application in aviation. Transilvania University Press, Braşov, 2006.

[19] Novak-Marcincin, J. and Kuzmiakova, M. Computer aided production engineering. Proc Int Conf Manuf Syst–ICMaS. Bucuresti, 2009;4, p.311–314.

[20] McLean, C. Computer-aided manufacturing system engineering, in `Proceedings of the IFIP TC5/WG5.7 International Conference on Advances in Production Management Systems, APMS '93, 1993.

[21] Anselmetti, B. and Mawussi, K. Computer aided tolerancing using positioning features. J Comput Inf Sci Eng. 2003;3(1):15.

[22] Dönmez, S. Computer aided industrial design software selection in industrial product design education at Turkey using expert choice program. Procedia-Soc Behav Sci. 2013;106:682–689.

[23] Wang, H., Rong, Y. (Kevin), Li, H. and Shaun, P. Computer aided fixture design: recent research and trends. Comput Des. 2010;42(12):1085–1094.

[24] ISO/ASTM52915-16, Standard Specification for Additive Manufacturing File Format (AMF) Version 1.2, ASTM International, West Conshohocken, PA, 2016, www.astm.org [Accessed: 2016:09:20].

[25] Knopf, G.K. and Johnson, J.A. Computer Aided Design. Wiley Encyclopedia of Biomedical Engineering, 2006.

[26] Bilgin, M.S., Baytaroğlu, E.N., Erdem, A. and Dilber, E. A review of computer-aided design/computer-aided manufactures techniques for removable denture fabrication. Eur J Dent. 2016;10(2):286–291.

[27] Rustemeyer, J. Reconstruction of Maxillofacial Osseous Defects with Computer-Aided Designed/Computer-Aided Manufactured Devices, In: A Textbook of Advanced Oral and Maxillofacial Surgery Volume 2, Prof. Mohammad Hosein Kalantar Motamedi (Ed.), InTech, Rijeka, Croatia, 2015, p.733–746, DOI: 10.5772/58955.

[28] Lee, K.H., Yeo, I.S., Wu, B.M., Yang, J.H., Han, J.S. and Kim, S.H., et al. Effects of computer-aided manufacturing technology on precision of clinical metal-free restorations. Biomed Res Int., 2015. 5p, Hindawi Publishing Corporation, DOI: 10.1155/2015/619027.

[29] Rosenberg, H., Posluns, J., Tenenbaum, HC., Tompson, B. and Locker D., Evaluation of computer-aided learning in orthodontics. Am J Orthod Dentofacial Orthop. 2010;138(4):410–419. DOI: 10.1016/j.ajodo.2008.11.030.

[30] Li, Q., Nishikawa, R.M. Computer-Aided Detection and Diagnosis in Medical Imaging, CRC Press, Taylor & Francis Group, 2015, 454p.

[31] Castellino, R.A. Computer aided detection (CAD): an overview. Cancer Imag. 2005;5(1): 17–19.

[32] Holstiege, J., Mathes, T., and Pieper, D. Effects of computer-aided clinical decision support systems in improving antibiotic prescribing by primary care providers: a systematic review. J Am Med Informatics Assoc. 2015;22:236–242.

[33] Ellis, E. Computer-aided surgical planning for orthognathic surgery. J Oral Maxillofac Surg. 2016;74:1302–1303.

[34] Sun, W., Starly, B., Nam, J., and Darling, A. Bio-CAD modeling and its applications in computer-aided tissue engineering. Comput Des. 2005;37(11):1097–1114.

[35] Lai, C. The application of computer aided technology in the sport training (CAS). Appl Mech Mater. 2014;644–650:5753–5755.

[36] Hermann, M., Pentek, T. and Otto, B. "Design Principles for Industrie 4.0 Scenarios," 2016 49th Hawaii International Conference on System Sciences (HICSS), Koloa, HI, 2016, pp. 3928–3937. DOI: 10.1109/HICSS.2016.488.

[37] Kagermann, H., Wahlster, W. and Helbig, J. Recommendations for implementing the strategic initiative Industrie 4.0: Final report of the Industrie 4.0 Working Group. 2013.

[38] Langnau, L. Tips on designing for the Internet of Things. 2015, Available from: http://www.designworldonline.com/tips-on-designing-for-the-internet-of-things/#_ [Accessed: 2016:09:26].

[39] Virtual reality, 2016. Available from: http://www.dictionary.com/browse/virtual--reality [Accessed: 2016:09:26].

[40] Virtual enterprise, 2016. Available from:http://dictionary.cambridge.org/dictionary/english/virtual-enterprise [Accessed: 2016:09:28].

[41] Factory of the future, White Paper, International Electrotechnical Commission, Geneva, Switzerland, 50p., Available from: http://www.iec.ch/whitepaper/pdf/iecWP-future-factory-LR-en.pdf [Accessed: 2016:09:26].

[42] Techopedia, Industrial Internet, 2016. Available from: https://www.techopedia.com/definition/30044/industrial-internet [Accessed: 2016:09:26].

[43] Zhang, L., Luo, Y., Tao, F., Li, B. H., Ren, L., Zhang, X., Guo, H., Cheng, Y., Hu, A. and Liu, Y. Cloud manufacturing: a new manufacturing paradigm. Enterprise Inform Syst. 2014;8(2):167–187.

Section 2

Computer-Aided Technologies in Engineering

Chapter 2

Computer-Aided Manufacturing of Working Units for High-Performance Mining Machines

Piotr Cheluszka

Additional information is available at the end of the chapter

http://dx.doi.org/10.5772/65039

Abstract

Mining machines (roadheaders, long-wall shearers, continuous miners, milling machines and others) are the key mechanised systems used in mining works—in underground and surface mining and in civil engineering (tunnelling). Rock cutting is carried out with working units fitted with cutting tools (most frequently picks mounted in pickboxes welded to side surfaces). It is important to appropriately arrange and position such tools in order to adapt them to the operating conditions (rock workability). This will guarantee very high efficiency of the cutting process. For this reason, such parts are designed with dedicated software. Designing is based on the simulation of the cutting process according to which the solution established is accepted. A prerequisite ensuring that the working process is performed highly efficiently by mining machines is to guarantee the high manufacturing quality of working units, especially with regard to the placement of cutting tools on the working unit side surface according to technical documentation. Robotised technologies are helpful here. Due to a large variety of solutions, utility programmes for robotised production sockets are developed with software for designing and simulating the operation of robotised stations.

Keywords: mining cutting machines, working unit, computer-aided design, computer-aided manufacturing, quality control, reverse engineering

1. Introduction

Mining machines create a broad group of heavy-working machines designed for mining natural materials such as soils and rocks with different petrography, and composite materials —concrete or bituminous masses. Although the mining industry is the key area of application for such machines, they are also employed extensively in civil engineering—for the construction of transportation tunnels using trenchless methods (road, railway, metro tunnels), sewage collectors, underground tunnels and networks (microtunnelling), or underground engineering structures (water channels in hydropower plants, garages, etc.). Cutting machines with their construction and working principle similar as in the mining sector are utilised in road engineering—for cutting (milling) concrete and asphalt surfaces during construction and for road surface renovation.

Mining cutting machines (roadheaders/shearers) are multifunctional machines enabling the full mechanisation of the basic activities in mechanised technologies for drilling dog headings and tunnels and excavation of minerals in underground and surface mining. Among the many other activities, rock cutting or cutting other materials such as concrete, asphalt, and so on is the most important activity performed by such machines. A mechanical cutting process may be carried out in various ways depending on the properties of the medium being handled—by cutting, using static pressure or a stroke. Mining by way of cutting is the most popular method of those mentioned. In such case, cutting machines are equipped with working units most often in the form of rotating bodies, on which pickboxes are positioned. Picks acting as cutting tools are attached on the pickboxes. A cutting process of the medium being cut is carried out when the picks are travelling along a trajectory which can be either a straight line or a curved flat or spatial line.

Machines that are mined by way of cutting are used in underground mining for hard coal, salt and other materials. They are used in opening and preparation works (for drilling of dog headings—roadheaders—**Figure 1**) and for excavation of minerals (including, among others, shearers and coal ploughs). They are used in surface mining for extracting deposits of certain

Figure 1. Boom-type FR 160 roadheader designed for drilling dog headings in underground mines and tunnels in civil engineering [6].

rock resources, coal, salt, lime, bauxite, iron ore, phosphorus, bituminous shale and kimberlite. They are even used in subaqueous mining—for extracting the deposits of mineral resources from the bottom of inland water reservoirs and sea areas and oceans (e.g. polymetallic sulphides of copper and gold) [1].

Mining practice and the results of theoretical and experimental studies conducted for decades in many research institutions acting in the field of mechanical rock cutting show that the system of picks (the number and method of arranging and setting the pickboxes spatially on the side surface of the working unit of the mining machine) has a substantial effect on the performance and efficiency of the cutting process carried out. It is essential from the user's viewpoint because it translates into drilling progress (in case of drilling dog headings and tunnels), the output (for operating works), energy consumption and the wear of picks per worked material unit, which is conditioning the economic profitability of conducting such type of mining works. It is therefore not possible to develop a universal system of picks for the working units of cutting machines ensuring the efficient cutting of rock and other materials with varied mechanical properties.

The aspect of computer aid should be approached—in relation to the elements considered here—in an area encompassing: design – production – quality control. It covers a number of activities based on the use of a graphical environment and simulation models (virtual reality). The computer tools used for this purpose represent a so-called virtual-manufacturing system [2–4]. Such a system, already at the stage of process preparation, delivers information about the product itself (at the stage of product design and optimisation), as well as about the progress of the manufacturing process. A virtual-manufacturing system is centred on product design (aided design), production (optimisation of production process implementation) and control (utility programmes are created for real production lines) [4, 5].

A manufacturing process of the working units of mining cutting machines consists of a number of successive stages. The sequence of such events can be considered in terms of the project lifecycle. In a classical approach, the cycle consists of the four basic phases: initiation, planning, execution and completion (implementation). Those phases encompass a whole spectrum of activities associated with organisation and management, economic analysis and analysis of technical activities, which are aimed at achieving the set objective according to the adopted time, cost and efficiency criteria [7–9]. Technical requirements are defined by the user at the stage of project initiating by focussing on the technical aspect of the process considered in this paper (**Figure 2**). In terms of the implementation of cutting process, the basic information for a designer of the considered working units is to identify technical conditions for mining machine operation, for which working units are to be designed and produced, including mechanical properties of the worked rocks. As pick systems on working units of mining machines lack universality, they are designed using state-of-the-art computer techniques for specific applicational conditions. Apart from standard computer-aided design (CAD) software for preparing the components of technical documentation, dedicated programmes are utilised enabling the optimisation of pick systems and their verification based on a computer-simulated working process [10–14]. Computer aid at the stage of designing a pick system for the complex operating conditions of a cutting machine is meant to deliver information to the designer allowing to assess the suitability of the created solution being a basis for its acceptance or rejection (modification). The number and method of arranging and setting the picks spatially on the side surface of the working unit of the cutting machine is selected (optimised) according to a number of criteria (objective functions) ensuring the achievability of the expected functional and operating features, while satisfying the condition of a given solution's technical feasibility.

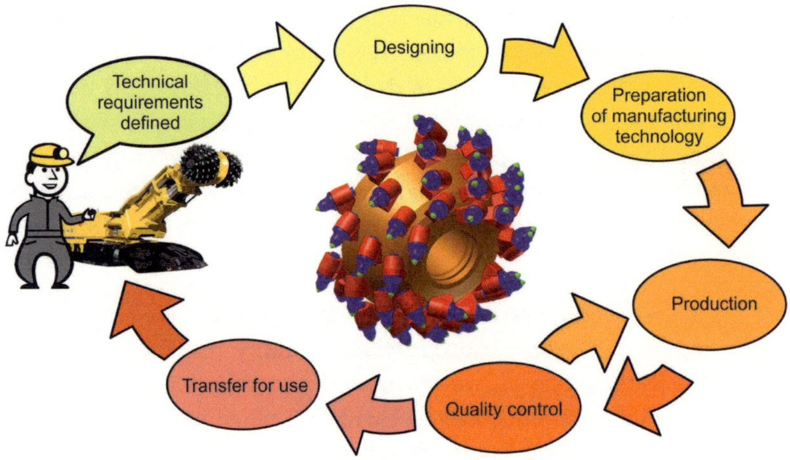

Figure 2. Manufacturing process of the working units of mining cutting machines—project lifecycle.

Technical documentation becomes a starting point in developing a manufacturing technology of the working units of mining machines. The efficient work of the working units considered in the paper is not possible without ensuring their high manufacturing quality and repeatability. This applies especially to the accurate representation of the position of pickboxes in compliance with the established technical documentation. A solution guaranteeing the fulfilment of such requirements is the use of robotised technologies, especially at the stage of the preliminary installation (attaching) of pickboxes to a working unit's side surface. As particular pickboxes are set differently and considering their, often, large number, a robotised station-programming process should be aided with computer tools intended for offline programming. When such operations are robotised, utility programmes are generated at the stage of technology development, controlling the work of the automated production sockets.

Quality control is an inherent part of each manufacturing process—even this, utilising robotised techniques. Quality control for working units of cutting machines consists of, in particular, establishing whether the actual location of pickboxes is compliant with the technical documentation. The stereometry of working units in mining machines should be measured after the completion of two stages, during which pickboxes are mounted—after the completion of pickbox placement, and after final welding. As large-size welds have to be made, which guarantee the high strength of welds between pickboxes with the working unit side surface, there is a risk that post-welding deformation will occur. Such deformations may be a reason for the displacement of pickboxes, as a result of which deviations may occur in the actual values of stereometric parameters describing the spatial arrangement and position of individual pickboxes in relation to the values defined in the design. Product compliance confirmation is fundamental for transferring a product to the user for utilisation. If inadmissible dimensional deviations are identified, a working unit is again transferred to the production department to make the necessary modifications.

Computer-aided design of working units of mining cutting machines is based on the use of various software and computer modules, which form an integrated system CAD/CAM/CAQ (computer-aided design/computer-aided manufacturing/computer-aided quality). These modules are grouped according to the tasks they have to fulfil in successive stages of the process (**Figure 3**). The (uni- and bidirectional) exchange of information between the individual modules of the software enables the efficient creation of the components of technical documentation (at the stage of design), the development of technology (at the stage of manufacturing preparation) and the control of the progress of the manufacturing process of cutting machines working units having optimally designed parameters. An example of such system is presented in the following chapter.

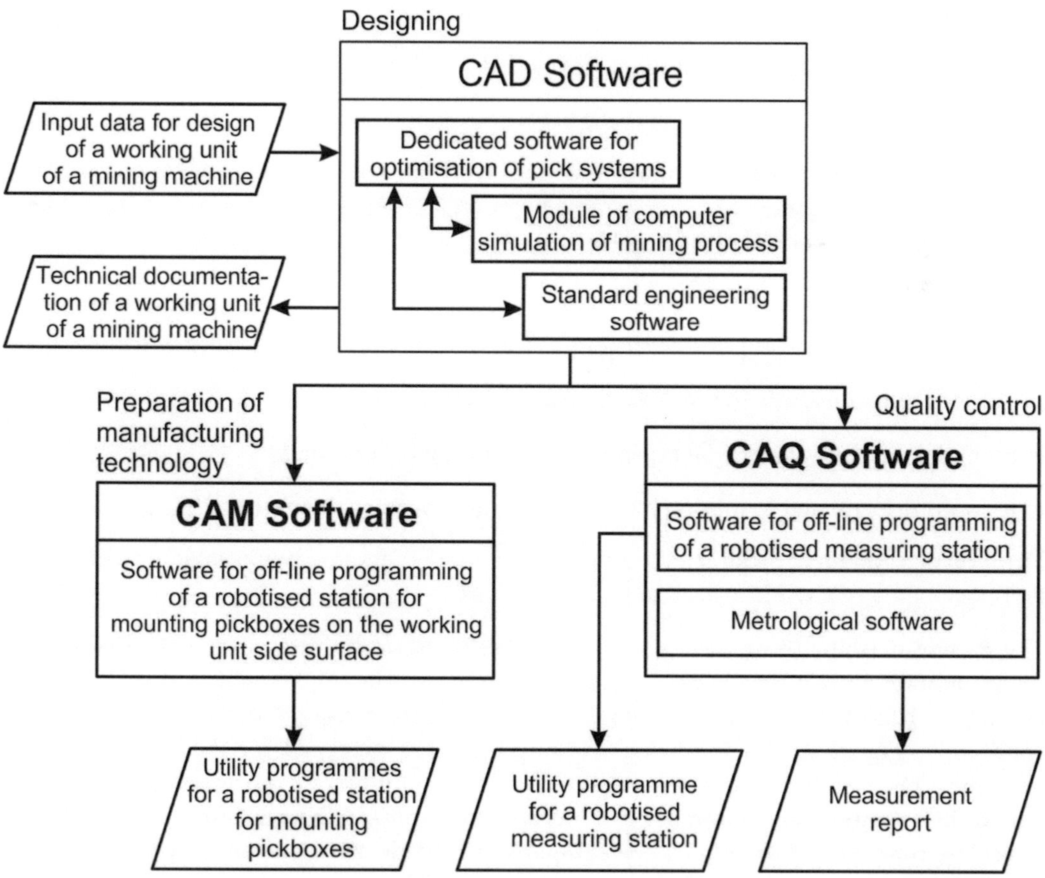

Figure 3. The integrated system of the computer-aided design of mining machines working units.

2. Computer-aided design of the working units of mining machines

The underlying functional requirement of the software intended for the computer-aided design of pick systems in working units of cutting machines is the possibility of generating rapidly alternative solutions creating a field of possible solutions for an optimisation task. The solution can be selected manually or with automatic optimisation methods and tools. A computer-simulated cutting process is the basis for seeking an optimum solution in both cases. It is executed using experimentally verified mathematical models.

The theoretical and experimental investigations of roadheaders and shearers were fundamental for determining evaluation criteria (objective function) for the suitability of solutions of mining machines working units in complex mining and geological conditions. These include [15, 16]:

- the minimum criterion of the average cutting picks load;
- the minimum criterion of dynamic load in the cutting system;
- the anti-resonance criterion;
- the criterion of maximum cutting efficiency and
- the minimum criterion of cutting energy consumption.

The computer-aided design of mining machines working units mostly consists of specifying the advantageous (optimum) picks' arrangement on their side surface ensuring the achievement of a feasible technical objective [16]:

- high rock cutting efficiency;
- reduced energy consumption of cutting and wear of picks;
- reduced dynamic loads in the cutting heads drive;
- limitation of excessive output crushing in the cutting process and
- reduced risks related to mining machine operation, such as dusting, sparking, and so on.

The term of a system of picks is understood as the number and method of spatial arrangement and positioning of a working unit at the side surface.

The mining machine (type, size, power, etc.) is selected in the first place when designing a mechanisation system for the performance of mining works during which mechanical rock cutting is carried out for the defined parameter values characterising the mining and geological conditions—**Figure 4**. The following working units are designed for the selected mining machine. This usually consists of generating a pool of solutions for the systems of picks with varied configuration. The particular variants are then evaluated based on the adopted criteria (objective functions). Solutions were compared based on the evaluation with scores and weight. A general evaluation of a given solution is in this case a weighted average of partial scores corresponding to particular criteria. The solution with the highest score is considered to be adopted for implementation. Further design works are carried out for such a design, the outcome of which is the established detailed documentation.

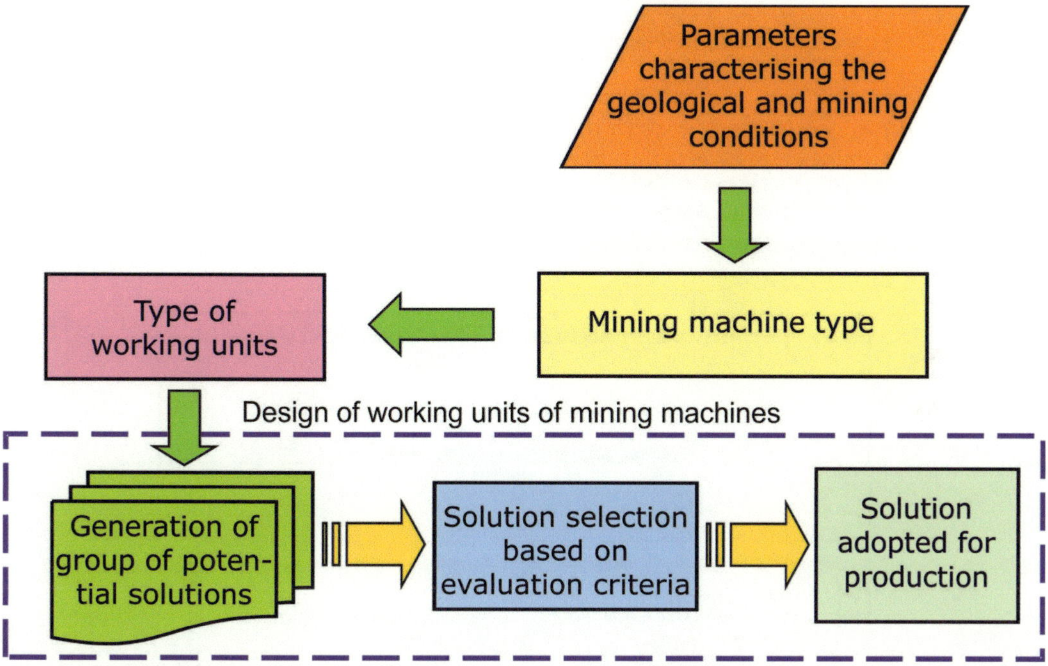

Figure 4. Designing of mechanisation system—stage of selecting a mining machine for the set operating conditions and designing of working units for the machine.

The best configuration of picks on the side surface of the mining machine working unit for the specific operating conditions is searched with a set of solutions which are technically feasible, differing in the number and method of picks arrangement and positioning. For such a procedure, different pick systems have to be generated rapidly to be evaluated technically. This is possible by using dedicated computer software for the aided designed process of such type of elements. Such a computer tool is exemplified by *KREON* software developed by the Institute of Mining Mechanisation, Faculty of Mining and Geology, Silesian University of Technology in Gliwice, Poland, for the computer-aided design of boom-type roadheader cutting heads. The software is employed by internationally recognised Polish manufacturers of mining machinery (Famur S.A. and Kopex Machinery S.A.) for computer-aided design, selection and approval of boom-type roadheader cutting heads. The software provides multiple functionalities to the designer, in particular [14]:

- a system of picks is generated manually or automatically on a cutting head;
- the generated solution is exported to CAD software;
- the cutting process is simulated and the so-produced results are visualised;

- scripts are generated automatically in Python programming language for the purpose of offline programming of a robotised station for mounting pickboxes on the cutting head side surface.

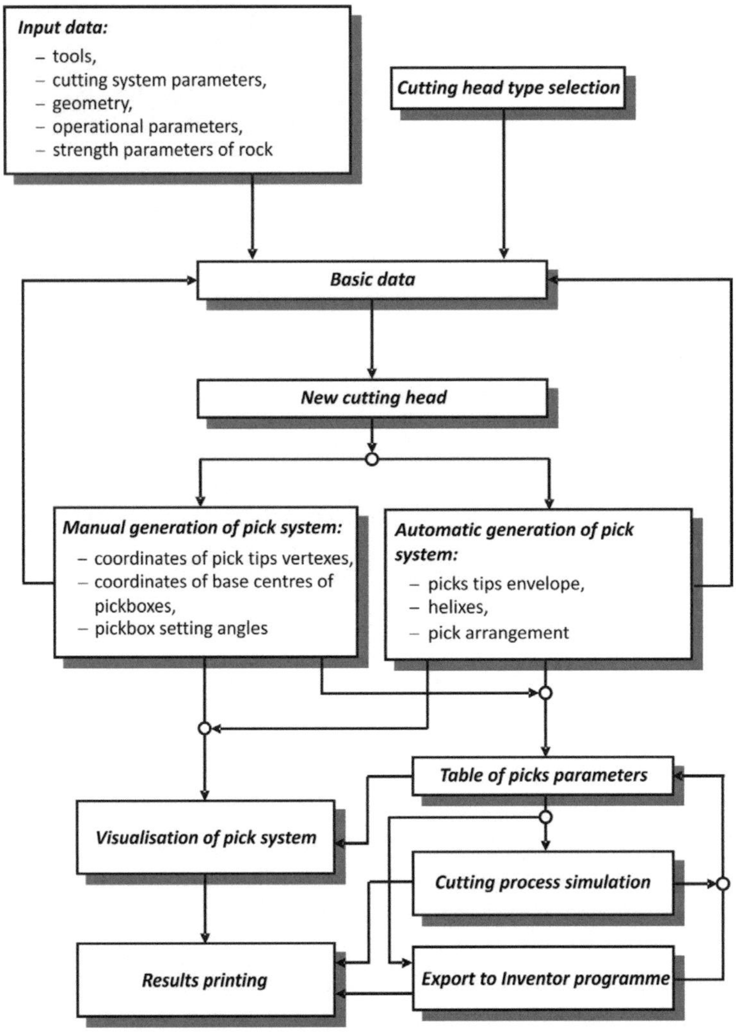

Figure 5. Algorithms for procedure of computer-aided design of cutting heads of boom-type roadheader in *KREON* software.

Cutting heads designing in the *KREON* environment begins by entering input data identifying the mining machine for which working units are designed (cutting heads here) and cutting process implementation conditions (**Figure 5**). The type of the designed cutting head is being determined at this stage (transverse/longitudinal) and information is entered about its dimensions and number of picks it is to be equipped with (basic data). A system of picks is generated after entering all the necessary data. This can be done manually (which is useful especially for analysing the operation of existing heads) or automatically. In the second of the listed methods, the shape of the picks tips envelopes is designed, the way of arranging picks on helixes is chosen (the number of helixes, twisting angle, etc.) and the method of setting picks in the space is defined along with the corresponding pickboxes. The shape of the picks tips envelopes may be modelled here either manually, automatically or drawn using the available drawing tools (**Figure 6**). The output-generated pick system is visualised graphically and the values of parameters describing it are listed in a table (**Figure 7**). A pick system, further in the design process, after the solution established has been accepted, can be exported to Autodesk Inventor® software to create detailed documentation of the designed cutting head. Corrections to the pick system can be made by analysing the technical feasibility of the given solution by editing the table of parameters for picks.

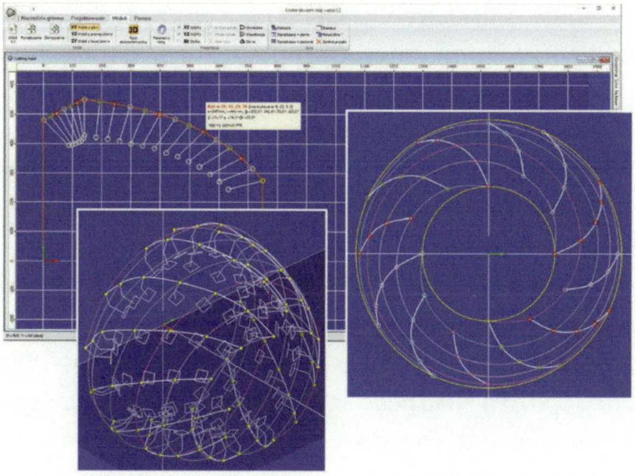

Figure 6. Generation of pick system on the side surface of boom-type roadheader cutting head in *KREON* environment.

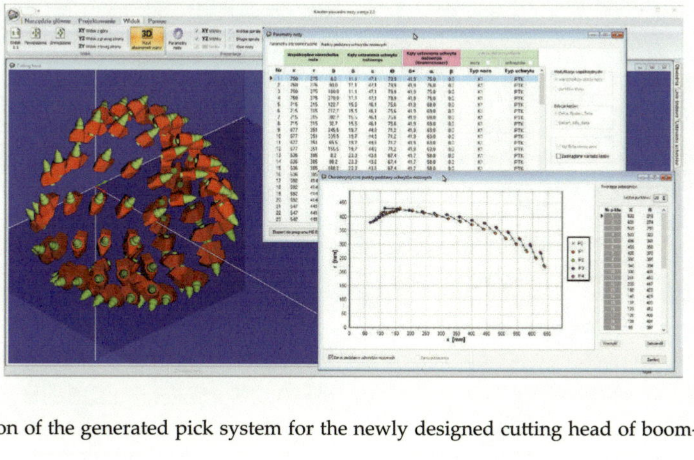

Figure 7. Visualisation of the generated pick system for the newly designed cutting head of boom-type roadheader in *KREON* software.

In order to establish the most advantageous configuration of picks for the set roadheader operating conditions, the designer generates a certain number of solutions differing in the number of picks and their arrangement and the method of positioning on the cutting head side surface with assumed dimensions. A certain shape of the cutting head side surface is usually assumed at the design stage for different systems of picks, with such a shape being adapted to the roadheader cutting system design (the way a cutting head is mounted to an output shaft of the gear in the cutting system, the gearbox shape in cutting heads or the way the water inflow to the spraying system is solved). The shape can be further modified depending on the final setting of pickboxes in the aspect of welding technology optimisation for such holders to the side surface of the cutting head (*KREON* software delivers data on the location of characteristic base points of pickboxes based on which a beneficial shape of the cutting head side surface can be determined—**Figure 7**).

At the decision-making stage, a system of picks is chosen from the created group of potential solutions according to the evaluation criteria adopted. A computer-simulated cutting process is a tool that can provide information allowing to select and accept a specific system of tools (**Figure 8**). The tool enables to establish characteristics for the cutting process of the heading face surface with a cutting head, including, in particular, projections of cuts and a load curve of the cutting heads drive and boom-deflection mechanisms. A dog-heading outline is also generated for the defined cutting system geometry (boom length, turntable dimensions and ranges of boom-deflection angles in the plane parallel and perpendicular to the floor), which can be performed from one roadheader setting with the designed cutting heads. With the dimensions and shape of the outline, the size of the heading cross section can be judged to be tunnelled with a specific type of a roadheader equipped with the designed cutting heads. This information, especially the size of the heading cross section, is given in technical specifications of each roadheader designed for drilling dog headings and tunnels.

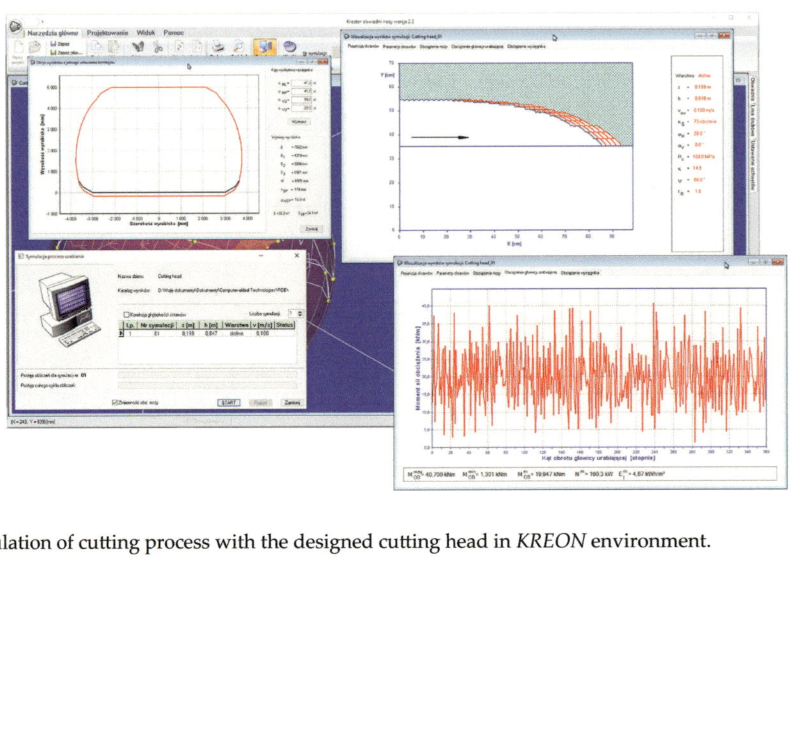

Figure 8. Simulation of cutting process with the designed cutting head in *KREON* environment.

3. The use of offline programming for the purpose of robotisation of the manufacturing process of the working units of mining machines

In a manufacturing process of the working units of mining machines, the individual pickboxes are basically fitted to their side surface in a way resulting from the technical documentation prepared at the design stage (activities for constructing the side surface itself are omitted here). The process covers basically two stages: pickboxes are arranged on the cutting head side surface and are finally welded to such surface. In the first of the mentioned stages, an appropriately positioned pickbox is initially mounted with a joint weld to the side surface of the mining machine working unit. This is a very time- and work-intensive process. It requires considerable attention and concentration from the operator. The same operations have to be repeated in the pickbox installation process (the number of repetitions results from the number of pickboxes the mining machine working unit is to be equipped with). Each of the pickboxes is set, however, differently, according to the way of arranging and positioning the related picks. For this reason, the robotisation of the pickbox installation process is the right direction.

Utility programmes controlling the work of industrial robots executing main assembly operations are prepared at the stage of developing a manufacturing technology of mining machines working units, and in such assembly operations: the individual pickboxes are collected from the magazine, they are transferred to the set position and attached to the side surface of the mining machine working unit. Software dedicated to the configuration and simulation of operation of robotised stations supplied by manufacturers of industrial robots is used to generate programmes for controlling the work of robots. Robots are programmed here outside the working environment of robots (offline) based on the data generated in the design-aided software of the working units considered in this work (**Figure 9a**). The so-created utility programme has to be recorded in a form acceptable by the robot's operating system into which it is entered (in the implemented programming language). An important part of offline programming is a possibility of testing the so-created control programmes and to introduce modifications. **Figure 9b** shows an interface of an example of a programme created in RAD Studio environment for testing the operation of a programme controlling the work of the IRp-60 robot on an experimental station at the laboratory of the Institute of Mining Mechanisation of the Silesian University of Technology for testing potential automatisation of the discussed assembly process. Free GLScene graphical libraries created in OpenGL technology were used for visualising the operation of this station [17]. Professional offline software delivered by a manufacturer of industrial robots has to be used for the automated assembly of pickboxes on the side surface of the mining machines working units at an industrial scale. An example of such a solution is *KUKA.Sim Pro* software dedicated to offline programming of KUKA Roboter GmbH robots. The software was used for programming KUKA KR 16-2 and KR 5arc robots installed on a test station created in a laboratory of the Institute of Mining Mechanisation of the Silesian University of Technology. Pickboxes can be installed at this station on the side surface of the roadheader and longwall shearer working units in the actual size (at the geometric scale of 1:1). The KR 16-2 robot is designed for positioning pickboxes on the working unit side surface, and the KR 5arc robot is equipped with a welding machine pipe and simulates the installation of such pickboxes with a positional weld (**Figure 10**). As the range of both robots is limited, the side surface of the mining machine working unit is placed on a rotating positioner table with the vertical axis PEV-1-2500 (by ZAP Robotyka).

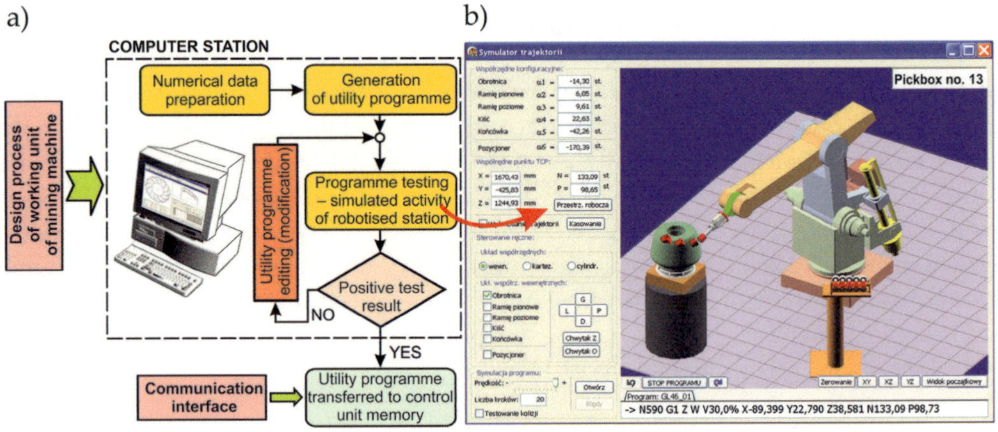

Figure 9. Development of a utility programme for a robotised station for mounting pickboxes to the side surface of the working unit of a mining machine: (a) procedure algorithm [18], (b) simulated work of utility programme [19].

The first phase of generating utility programmes for the positioning and welding robot is performed in the *KREON* environment. It is based on the data set (stereometric parameters) obtained when designing a system of picks of the working unit of a mining machine. A string of instructions controlling the work of robots is generated based on such data in the form of scripts in Python language (an interpreter of this language was implemented in *KUKA.SimPro* software).

For example, a utility programme for the positioning robot, KR 16-2, comprises instructions executing successive operations for a positioning sequence of a single pickbox, namely [14]:

- pickbox is collected,
- a request is sent to a positioner to position the side surface of the working unit of a mining machine in the set position (rotation angle of the positioner disc is an argument of this instruction);
- a given pickbox is brought to a given position on the side surface of the working unit;
- waiting until a positional weld is executed by the KR 5arc-welding robot and
- a gripping device is released and withdrawn to the home position.

Positioning instructions (movement instructions) are the most essential element of a programme controlling the work of a robot distributing pickboxes on the working unit side surface. A set of values is created in *KREON* software for each pickbox for parameters describing the position and spatial orientation of the robot gripping device (being the arguments of robot tool positioning instructions). The parameters' values are determined based on the values of stereometric parameters assigned to individual pickboxes. This is executed according to homogeneous transformations discussed in the work [14]. The scripts, generated as text files, are then read into a script editor implemented in *KUKA.SimPro* environment (**Figure 10**). The Python language interpreter translates the successive utility programme instructions as a code in the form of a string of pictograms symbolising particular instructions. The pictograms are displayed in Teach tab of *KUKA.SimPro* (they are surrounded with an ellipsis in **Figure 10**).

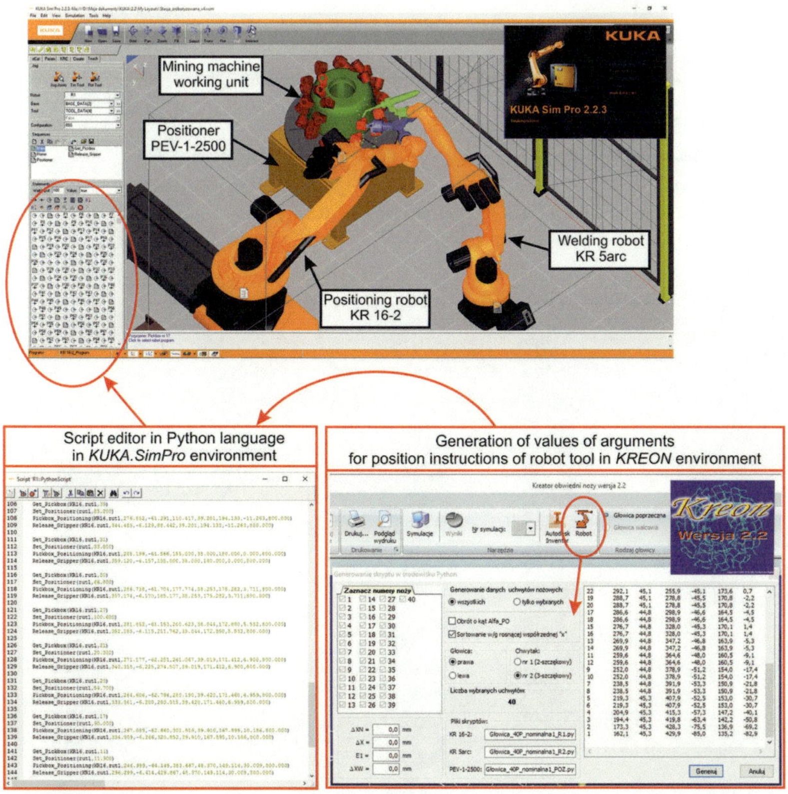

Figure 10. Virtual assembly station and progress of the utility programme generation process for robotised station for mounting pickboxes to the side surface of the working unit of a mining machine with *KREON* and *KUKA.SimPro* software.

Collision analysis is carried out when the generated utility programmes are tested in *KUKA.SimPro* environment. When robot movements are simulated on a virtual stage, the software analyses the distance between the elements indicated by the programmer. The elements for analysis are selected and the minimum permitted distance between them is established in the Collision Detector Editor dialogue window (**Figure 11**). If any collision is detected, the programme executes an action chosen by the programmer (collision occurrence is indicated, the tested utility programme is deactivated) [20]. A utility programme in such case is manually modified to eliminate the risk of collision.

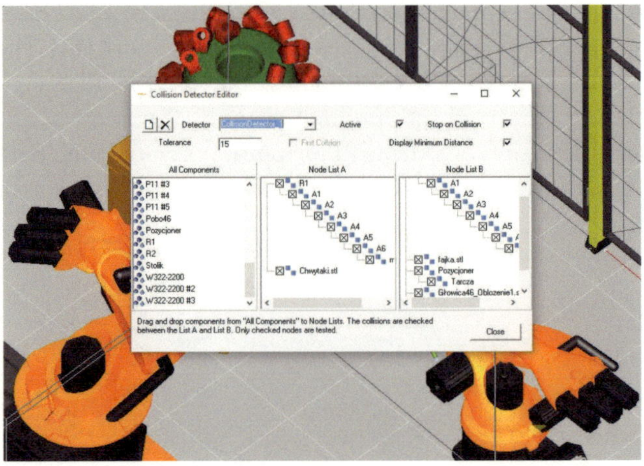

Figure 11. Collision detection module in *KUKA.SimPro* environment.

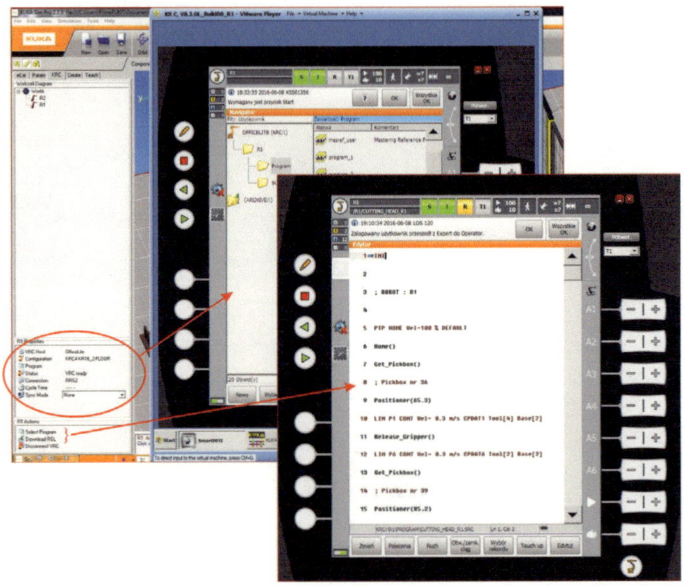

Figure 12. 'Cutting_head_R1' utility programme for the robot positioning the pickboxes generated in *KUKA.SimPro* environment transferred to the virtual operating system of *KUKA.OfficeLite* robot.

A positive result of robotised station software test enables to transfer real robots into the operating system via a communication interface. For KUKA robots, this is done via a virtual-operating system, *KUKA.OfficeLite*. It is an image of the actual KUKA robot operating system, installed in *VMware Player* virtual machine [21]. A virtual operating system can communicate with any virtual robot model in *KUKA. SimPro* environment (Connect feature). The connection status is highlighted in Properties → Status (**Figure 12**—rounded with an ellipsis). Such communication enables to transfer utility programmes between *KUKA. SimPro* and *KUKA.OfficeLite* virtual-operating system. When communication is initiated in KRC tab of *KUKA.SimPro* software with a virtual operating system of the robot ('Status: VRC ready') and when Download RSL function is called, the utility programme is transferred and translated into KRL (Kuka Robot Language) language supported by KUKA robots operating system. The utility programme can then be transferred into the actual robot control system with portable USB disc storage.

4. Automation of production quality control

Production quality control is critical for product acceptance and for putting the product into use. Due to the complicated stereometry of the working units considered in this work, this issue can be effectively solved by applying reverse engineering with three-dimensional (3D) scanning. Due to a complex shape of the working units of cutting machines, manual scanning methods already at the stage of measuring data acquisition are not effective and very working intensive. Robotic techniques are useful here again such as automatic scanning using robotised-measuring stations. A utility programme for a robot must be prepared for an automatic scanning process, which can be created using offline programming. The geometric characteristics of a working unit can be identified, in accordance with the way of recording the dimensioning of a pick system in technical documentation, by parsing out information from the data acquired by scanning, based on which a measurement model is built. The process of processing measurement data (scans) to parameter values characterising the arrangement and setting of individual pickboxes is performed with advanced computer techniques—software for processing and analysing 3D mesh. An important aspect for this type of measurement tasks is a possibility of measurement data automatisation to shorten, as much as possible, the time for producing measurement results.

The stereometry of working units in mining machines is measured in two stages. In the first stage, measurement itself is performed with a 3D scanner mounted to a robot arm. The next positions of the scanner—in relation to the scanned object—are set by an industrial robot manipulator executing successive positioning instructions. Measuring data is also initially prepared at this stage for further processing in scanner software. Another stage of measurement is performed with computer software for processing meshes representing the scanned object surface. *GOM Inspect* is an example of such software.

A robotised-measuring station was constructed for the stereometry measurement of mining machines working units in a laboratory of the Institute of Mining Mechanisation, Faculty of Mining and Geology, Silesian University of Technology. It incorporates the KUKA KR 16-2 robot with smartSCAN 3D-HE scanner (by Breuckmann Aicon 3D Systems) attached to its arm and PEV-1-2500 positioner. **Figure 13** shows a virtual 3D model of a robotised-measuring station created in *KUKA.SimPro* software. The measuring station is controlled with a utility programme created for this purpose. Two layers can be distinguished in the software hierarchy. A subordinate layer with a subprogramme is executing the entire scanning sequence for the given setting of the scanned object on the positioner disc (**Figure 14**). It comprises a number of successive instructions for robot arm positioning. A scanning procedure is called after each of them during which the control process scanning system (*Optocat* programme in this case) acquires measuring data. The robot control system communicates with *Optocat* software via a TCP/IP link in client (robot controller)—server (*Optocat* software) architecture using XIRP protocol [22]. A loop is executed in the control programme master layer of the robotised-measuring station, in which the positioner disc setting is changed (its rotation angle ϕ_T) between zero and 360°, with the defined step $\Delta\phi_T$ [1].

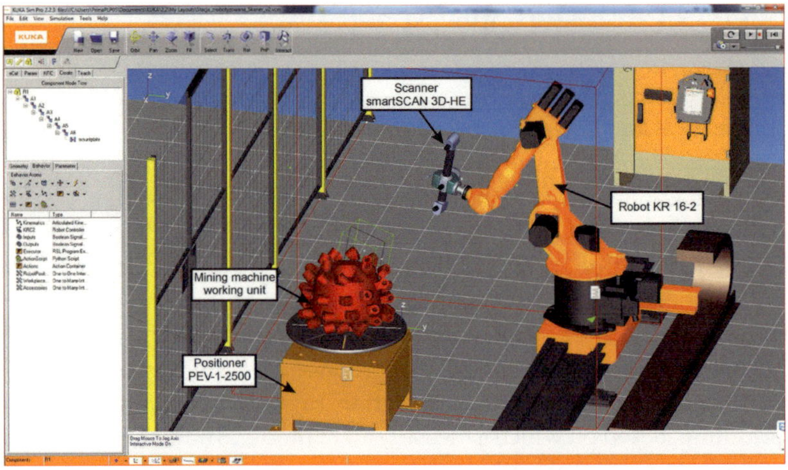

Figure 13. Virtual model of a robotised-measuring station in *KUKA.SimPro* environment.

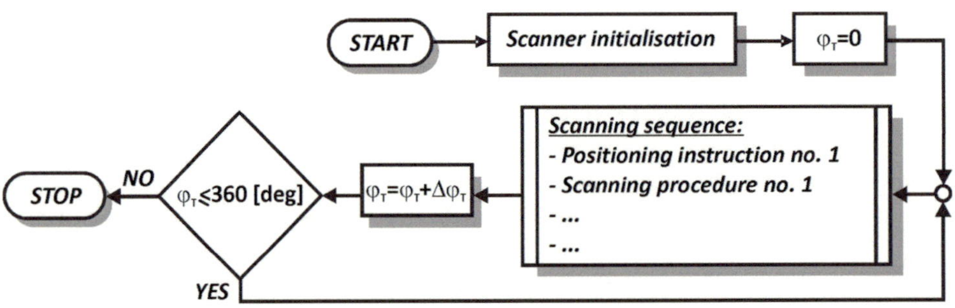

Figure 14. The algorithm of procedure of automated measurement of stereometry of mining machines working units by means of a structured light scanner mounted to the robot arm.

A control programme scanning sequence is generated in *KUKA.SimPro* software. The particular positions of the scanner are set manually, after which they are memorised as positioning instructions. Due to the complicated shape of the mining machine working unit surface, a large number of scanner positions have to be programmed to execute the measuring task considered here. This results from a generally high density of pickboxes. For example, even 68-scanner positions had to be programmed to measure the cutting heads of a boom-type roadheader with the diameter of ~750 mm and the length of ~500 mm. This is derived from the fact that the scanned surface had many areas with hard access by the scanner; however, with fewer scans, the mesh representing the scanned surface had many discontinuities (holes). By assuming the positioner disc rotation step of $\Delta\phi_T = 10°$, the number of scans used to build the model of a cutting head surface was more than 2400. Such massive amounts of data require high computational capacity of a computer used for processing and analysing measurement results.

In order to position the scanner correctly in relation to the scanned object, a scanner measuring field position is displayed on a virtual stage of the measuring station with the corresponding aperture value (**Figure 13**—green cuboid).

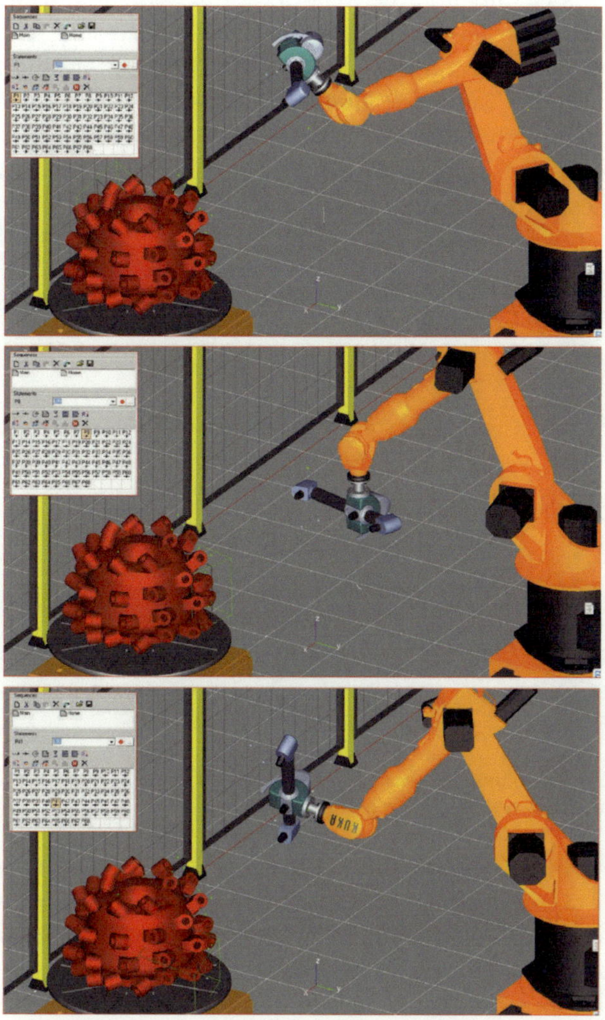

Figure 15. Simulation of the scanning process of boom-type roadheader cutting heads in *KUKA.SimPro* environment.

Three selected scanner positions are shown in **Figure 15**, resulting from the execution of the positioning instructions P1, P8 and P41. The whole sequence of the programmed instructions for positioning the successive scanner positions relative to the cutting head is shown in the left top corner, for which measurement is executed (the pictograms of the shown examples of positioning instructions are marked orange). After testing the created utility programme, it is converted into KRL language during transmission into a virtual control system of *KUKA. OfficeLite* environment (this is discussed in item 3 of this work). Using a virtual robot programming panel, scanning procedure calls are added after each positioning sequence to a subprogramme executing the scanning sequence. It is then transferred to a memory of the actual robot's control system using portable USB disc storage.

In the second stage of the stereometry measurement of the working units of mining machines in line with the discussed method, the measuring data obtained as a result of automatic scanning are processed in order to produce a measurement result. It is done using special computer tools—metrological programmes for, among others, analysing meshes representing the scanned object surface. The *GOM* environment of GOM mbH is an example of such software. It is worth noting that the basic version of the software is free. It also features a full metrological functionality. Scripts in Python language can be created in a paid version (Professional) and measuring procedure automation is available.

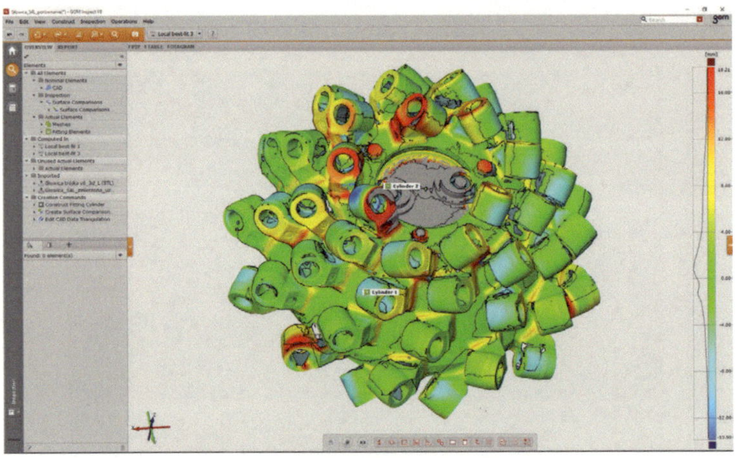

Figure 16. Analysis of measurement results of roadheader cutting head stereometry in *GOM Inspect* environment—distribution map of deviations of an actual surface from the nominal surface.

The software used for measuring data analysis allows to follow two measurement strategies of the working units of mining machines [1]. The shape of the scanned surface is compared with the nominal surface (CAD model) in the first of them. It is possible to make a quick inspection this way, the result of which is the determination of dimensional deviations in the actual surface area from the reference surface area. The measurement result in this case has the form of a colourful map with a distribution chart of values of such deviations (**Figure 16**). It is also possible to analyse deviations in the shape of section lines in the needed cross sections of the scanned object and to determine the values of deviations in the defined control points [23]. A mathematical measurement model has to be built in the second measurement strategy for each pickbox. The values of parameters describing the arrangement and spatial positioning of particular pickboxes and related picks are established on the basis of such a model according to characteristic geometrical features measured in a metrological programme. The consistency of the so-established measured values is determined in relation to the nominal values provided in technical documentation in order to assess whether or not the mining machine working unit has been executed correctly in this case. In particular, the work [1] describes the construction of a stereometry measurement model of the working units of mining machines.

In the example shown in **Figure 16**, the actual arrangement of some of the pickboxes clearly differs from that set in the design of the cutting head. In the map generated in *GOM Inspect* program, the areas of the minimal deviations of the actual surface from the nominal surface are marked green. The more red or blue the area is, the greater are the deviations (with respect to the absolute value). The degree of variation of the surface adaption of the individual pickboxes varies. The greatest deviations of the actual surface from the nominal surface were reported in case of the pickboxes arranged the closest to the face surface of the cutting head (in the upper part of the model). The surfaces of these pickboxes are marked red (the corresponding deviations are even greater than +18 mm). This proves that the arrangement of the pickboxes does not comply with the technical documentation. A similar effect is visible also in case of some of the pickboxes arranged near the base of the cutting head (in the lower part of the model). The production errors, which occurred at the stage of manufacturing of the measured head, result largely from the fact that the installation (attaching) of pickboxes to its side surface has been carried out at a manual assembly station. In such case, the quality of workmanship depends largely on the skills and conscientiousness of the operator.

5. Conclusion

This work discusses comprehensively the issue of manufacturing the working units of mining machines and the potential use of computer aid in particular phases of executing this process. Considering the efficient and effective work of mining machines, it is fundamental to optimise the construction of this type of working units, especially with regard to the way of arranging working tools and compliance of the final product with technical documentation. This is confirmed by practical experience and scientific investigations. They indicate that working units designed improperly for service conditions or constructed not in accordance with documentation may cause low-working capacity, considerable dynamic overloads of working machine's drives and its load-bearing system. This results in low-operating efficiency and low durability and reliability of such machines, especially when operated in difficult mining and geological conditions. This risk can be mitigated by using modern manufacturing techniques of the working units of mining machines based on computer-aided design and optimisation, computer-aided design of their manufacturing technology and production quality monitoring. A broad array of computer tools should be utilised in the successive steps of such a design, namely, standard CAD programmes, dedicated software aiding the design of mining machines working units and a computer simulation of the working process they execute, tool software for aiding the technology design and for simulating the manufacturing process, or metrological software allowing fast, automated inspection for quality control at the key stages of such units' production. The way how this issue can be solved practically has been presented with the example of boom-type roadheader working units. The usefulness of the computer tools presented in this work has been confirmed practically. Software for the aided design of pick systems is widely used by the manufacturers of mining machines for designing and selecting working units for particular service conditions. The capabilities of offline programming of robotised stations for the assembly of pickboxes and for measuring the stereometry of roadheader cutting heads were tested at a semi-industrial scale on a robotised assembly station and a robotised-measuring station created in the laboratory of the Institute of Mining Mechanisation, Faculty of Mining and Geology, Silesian University of Technology.

The use of computer aid is contributing to a significantly improved manufacturing quality of such important elements—considering the efficient operation of cutting machines—whilst reducing the time and work input of their production. Different configurations of picks are achievable by optimising the construction of working units and by applying robotised manufacturing technologies and this contributes to their enhanced service life. This, in turn, leads to the improved utilisation of technical potential of working machines, having a beneficial effect on the economical aspects of mining works carried out with such machines. A necessary condition critical to pursue this direction effectively is to minimise the design implementation time—starting with the formulation of technical assumptions to producing a final product. Such requirements can be successfully satisfied by using computer tools at each stage of such a process.

Author details

Piotr Cheluszka

Address all correspondence to: Piotr.Cheluszka@polsl.pl

Institute of Mining Mechanisation, Faculty of Mining and Geology, Silesian University of Technology, Gliwice, Poland

References

[1] Cheluszka P, Nocoń M. Robotised digitalisation technology of roadheader working units for the purpose of manufacturing quality control. Surface Mining. 2015;56(6):11–23 (in Polish).

[2] Bharath V G, Pati R. Virtual Manufacturing: A Review. In: NCERAME–2015 Conference Proceedings; 27 March 2015; Bangalore, India. International Journal of Engineering Research & Technology (IJERT):2015. p. 355–364.

[3] Marinov V. On Some Aspects of the Virtual Manufacturing Concept. In: Third International Conference on Metal Cutting and High Speed Machining; 27–29 June, 2001; Metz, France. p. 27–29.

[4] Słota A, Krupa K. Virtual manufacturing with the use of Delmia system. Logistyka. 2014;6:9675–9684 (in Polish).

[5] Depince Ph, Chablat D, Woelk P.-O. Virtual Manufacturing: Tools for improving Design and Production. In: CIRP International Design Seminar; Cairo, Egypt. p. 1–12, 2004

[6] Famur S.A. FR 160 – Roadheaders – Gallery Systems – Products and Services – Famur [Internet]. Available from: https://www.famur.com/en/products-and-services/gallery-systems/roadheaders/fr-160-1045.html [Accessed: 06.06.2016].

[7] Westland J. The Project Management Lifecycle. 1st ed. London, UK: Kogan Page Limited; 2006. pp. 256.

[8] Lester A. Project Management, Planning and Control: Managing Engineering, Construction and Manufacturing Projects to PMI, APM and BSI Standards. 5th ed. Oxford, UK: Butterworth–Heinemann, Jordan Hill; 2007. pp. 435.

[9] Archibald R D. Managing High–Technology Programs and Projects. 3rd ed. Hoboken, NJ, USA: Wiley & Sons; 2003. pp. 396.

[10] Dolipski M, Jaszczuk M, Cheluszka P, Sobota P. Designing of New Energy-Saving Cutting Drums of Longwall Shearers. Proceedings of the 12th International Symposium on Mine Planning & Equipment Selection. Kalgoorlie, Western Australia, 23–25.4.2003, p. 331–340.

[11] Hurt K G, Morris C J. Computer designed cutting heads improve roadheader performance. Tunnel & Tunnelling 1985, No. 3, p. 37–38.

[12] Rostami J, Ozdemir L, Neil D. M. Roadheaders performance optimization for mining and civil construction. 13th Annual Technical Conference. Las Vegas; 1994.

[13] Tiryaki B, Ayhan M, Hekimoglu O Z. A New computer program for cutting head design of roadheaders and drum shearers. 17th International Mining Congress and Exhibition of Turkey – IMCET 2001, p. 655–662.

[14] Cheluszka P. Computer–aided design of robotised technology for manufacturing working units of mining machines. International Journal of Mining, Reclamation and Environment. 2015;29(1):62–81. DOI: 10.1080/17480930.2014.955959.

[15] Dolipski M, Cheluszka P, Sobota P. Criteria of designing of cutting heads for roadheaders. In: Proceedings of the 4th International Conference on Theoretical and Experimental Problems of Materials Engineering. Puchov, Slovakia; 9–11 September, 1999. p. 1–8.

[16] Dolipski M, Cheluszka P, Sobota P. Criterions of cutting heads selection for energy–saving heading machines. Polish Mining Review. 2007;63(7–8):64–70 (in Polish).

[17] GLScene for Delphi and C++ Builder [Internet]. Available from: http://glscene.sourceforge.net/wikka/HomePage [Accessed: 08.06.2016].

[18] Cheluszka P. Application of an industrial robot for setting of holders of cutting tools on a side surface of a roadheader's cutting head. In: Proceedings of the VI International Conference Mining Techniques TUR 2009; September 15–18 2009; Krakow–Krynica, Poland. Krakow: University of Science and Technology AGH; 2009. p. 215–226 (in Polish).

[19] Dolipski M, Cheluszka P, Remiorz E, Sobota P, Osadnik J. The manufacturing processes of mining machines working units using robotised technologies. In: Mikołajczyk T, editor. Computer-aided science and technology CAX'2010. Bydgoszcz, Poland: UTP University of Science and Technology; 2011. p. 85–90 (in Polish).

[20] KUKA.SimPro 2.2 – User manual. KUKA Robotem GmbH. Augsburg, 2010.

[21] KUKA.OfficeLite 8.2 – User manual. KUKA Robotem GmbH. Augsburg, 2011.

[22] 3D Measurements with Robots: OptocatRobot XML – User manuals. Breuckmann GmbH, 2011.

[23] GOM Inspect [Internet]. Available from: http://www.gom.com/3d-software/gom-inspect-professional.html [Accessed: 10.06.2016].

Chapter 3

Joining in Nonrigid Variation Simulation

Kristina Wärmefjord, Rikard Söderberg,
Björn Lindau, Lars Lindkvist and Samuel Lorin

Additional information is available at the end of the chapter

http://dx.doi.org/10.5772/65851

Abstract

Geometrical variation is closely related to fulfillment of both functional and esthetical requirements on the final product. To investigate the fulfillment of those requirements, Monte Carlo (MC)-based variation simulations can be executed in order to predict the levels of geometrical variation on subassembly and/or product level. If the variation simulations are accurate enough, physical tests and try-outs can be replaced, which reduce cost and lead-time. To ensure high accuracy, the joining process is important to include in the variation simulation. In this chapter, an overview of nonrigid variation simulation is given and aspects such as the type and number of joining points, the joining sequence and joining forces are discussed.

Keywords: variation simulation, joining, spot welding, clip fastener, welding, sequence, holding forces, assembly forces

1. Introduction

Computer-aided tolerancing (CAT) is a research area within computer-aided technologies. Tolerances are a way to describe the allowed variation in a specific dimension or feature. Variation on part level will, together with a number of other influencing factors, control the variation on product level of an assembled product. To fulfill assembly requirements as well as functional and esthetical requirements of the final product, the allowed tolerances play an important role. **Figure 1** illustrates a product not fulfilling the esthetical requirement of parallelism of a split line. These kinds of problems can be caused by geometrical variation. However, tight tolerances are costly and tolerancing is therefore a balancing between cost and quality [1]. There are also other methods, such as stability analysis [2], to decrease the sensitivity to geometrical variation on part level. In that way, the geometrical quality of the assembly can be improved without tightening tolerances with increased cost as a consequence.

Generally, methods to minimize the effects of geometrical variation are gathered under the term "geometry assurance" [3].

Within CAT, variation simulation is used to support the choice of design concepts and tolerances. Variation simulation is used to predict the geometrical result of a final assembly, given part variation as inspection data or tolerances and information about the joining and assembly process. By the use of variation simulation, different design concepts can be compared early on in the product development cycle and the predicted variation on assembly level can be compared to geometrical assembly requirements. In this way, the product development time and cost can be reduced and the geometrical quality of the final assembly or product can be increased. There are several different software tools for variation simulation, such as 3DCS [4], VSA [5] and RD&T [6].

In this chapter, both the terms variation and deviation are used. On individual basis, a part or an assembly can deviate from their nominal value in a critical dimension. The reason for this

Figure 1. A nonparallel split line, caused by variation due to the stamping, joining and assembly processes.

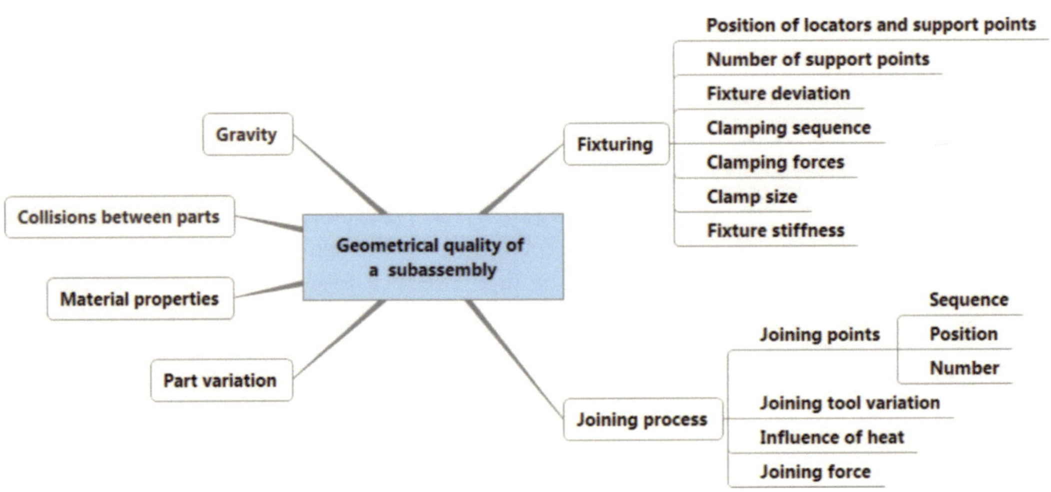

Figure 2. Factors affecting geometrical deviations of a subassembly.

is usually a large number of underlying factors. The effects from these factors can lead to a mean shift, where all individual parts in a population deviate from nominal values in a similar way, or to a variation affecting the deviations of the individual parts in a population independently. Usually, a deviation is caused by a combination of the two phenomena. If a sample of parts or subassemblies is considered, there will be a mean shift and a variation within the sample.

The accuracy of the simulations is a critical issue—if the simulations shall be trustworthy and simulation results shall replace physical tests and prototypes, the difference between simulated result and real result must be minimized. To reach a good agreement, it is important to include in the simulation as many as possible factors that influence the result in reality. In **Figure 2**, different factors affecting the geometrical result of an automated joining process in the body shop are outlined.

The main factors affecting the geometrical variation and mean shift of a subassembly are:

- **Part variation**, i.e., how a sample of parts differs from nominal geometry. This variation is due to variation in material properties and variation in previous manufacturing processes. A good estimate of part variation is necessary to include in the variation simulation. This can be done by using part tolerances or inspection data. How to include inspection data in the simulation is treated in [7, 8].

- **Fixturing**, i.e., how the parts are positioned in the assembly fixtures during joining. This is usually referred to as the locating scheme [9, 10]. The positions of locating points (also referred to as locators) and additional clamps are important since they control the robustness (i.e., sensitivity to part variation). A rigid part has six degrees of freedom which are locked by the master locating points, while a nonrigid part can be overconstrained and additional clamps are added to the master locating points.

Also deviations in the fixture caused by lack of repeatability [11, 12] and the clamping sequence [13] affect the result. The forces applied in the clamps constitute another important factor. A too low clamping force can result in a locator not be able to force the part to nominal position and a too high clamping force may lead to unwanted steering due to high friction between the part and the clamp. Friction and steering directions are also related to the size and shape of the clamp [14]. Fixtures are compared to the parts to be joined very stiff and are therefore modeled as rigid bodies in this chapter.

- **The joining process**, including the number, position and sequence of joining points. For some joining processes, such as spot welding, the result might also be influenced by variations in the welding gun, leading to that the welding gun forces the assembly to a non-nominal position. Furthermore, the heat generated by the spot welding process can lead to local deformations, usually considered to be of minor importance [15]. If there is a large gap between the parts to be joined, due to part or fixture variation, and the force applied by the joining tool is too low to close the gap, this will lead to failing joints, which of course affect the geometrical outcome and also the strength of the assembly. Spot welding is a frequently used joining method in automotive industry, but also methods such as riveting, clinching, clip fastening and adhesive joining occur.

- **Gravity** can affect part positions and lead to parts being assembled in erroneous positions.
- **Material properties** such as stiffness and density. The part deviations are usually assumed to be small compared to the part dimensions in order to speed up the calculations in nonrigid variation simulation. The material models are linear, and it is assumed that the changes in the stiffness matrix due to part and positioning variation can be neglected. Only elastic behavior is taken into consideration.
- **Collisions** between parts lead to forces making the parts deform. In the simulation model this can be taken care of using contact modeling [16, 17].

In this chapter, the main focus is on the joining process and on how to include that in variation simulation. The joining methods considered are mainly spot welding, riveting, bolts, clip fasteners and continuous welding. Some attention is also paid to how to minimize the geometrical variation caused by the joining process, especially by finding good joining sequences.

2. Nonrigid variation simulation

In nonrigid variation simulation, the parts are allowed to bend, i.e., there is no assumption that the parts are rigid. To perform a nonrigid simulation, finite element analysis (FEA) is integrated in the simulation. The benefits of nonrigid variation simulation, compared to the rigid one, are in many cases an increased accuracy and also the ability to overconstrain parts and assemblies, calculate forces and how the parts are bent, to see the effects from gravity, include effects from heat, etc.

FEA in nonrigid modeling is used to discretize the geometry using a set of finite elements gathered in a mesh. All the elements in the mesh are joined by shared nodes. In nonrigid analysis, the displacements in the nodes are studied. The magnitudes of the displacements depend on what forces that are applied to the geometry. The forces can be caused by, for example, variation in single parts, assembly fixtures and the joining process.

To calculate the forces, the stiffness of the material must be known. The stiffness information is gathered in the so-called stiffness matrix and describes how resistant each node is to deflection when exposed to an applied force.

The sum of the forces must be in balance and FEA is used to solve the equilibrium equations describing this. Assembly deviations can be predicted through the use of this method.

The direct Monte Carlo (MC) simulation, combined with FEA, is a standard technique for the variation simulation of nonrigid parts. However, since a large number of runs are required to achieve satisfactory accuracy in a direct Monte Carlo simulation, the simulation time will be very long since a new FEA calculation must be executed in each run. Liu and Hu [18] presented a technique called method of influence coefficients (MICs) to solve this problem. The main idea of the proposed method is to find linear relationships between part deviations and assembly spring-back deviations. A set of sensitivity matrices, constructed using FEA, describes that linear relationship. These sensitivity matrices can then be used in the simulations, and in this way the number of FEA calculations can be reduced. Camelio et al. [19] applied the method to a multistation system. Dahlström and Lindkvist [20] combined MIC with contact modeling. Contact modeling is a method to avoid that parts virtually penetrate each other during assembly. Contact modeling was also treated in [16, 17].

2.1. Simulation methodology

To include joining sequence in a nonrigid variation simulation methodology, the steps described below are generally necessary to include in the calculations to be able to predict variation and mean shift in critical dimensions of a subassembly:

Step 1: The parts are positioned in their assembly fixtures, and overconstrained locating systems (i.e., clamps) are applied. To clamp non-nominal parts, forces are applied.

Step 2: The parts are joined together according to a defined joining sequence. The gaps in the joining points are closed one by one using the defined sequence.

Step 3: When the last joint is set, the assembly is released from the clamps and is allowed to springback.

These steps can be included in a Monte Carlo (MC)-based variation simulation [17]. The assembly forces and the geometrical variation of the final assembly are calculated in each MC replication. For a node-node based balanced joining method, such as spot welding using a balanced gun, an overview of the modeling of Steps 1–3 is given below.

Modeling of step 1: Positioning/clamping the parts in the assembly fixture.

The parts *a* and *b* are positioned in their assembly fixtures. Overconstrained locating systems, i.e., clamps are applied. The magnitude of the gaps to be closed in the clamping points are collected in the vectors $\left\{\mathbf{u}_{\mathrm{p}}^{\mathrm{a}}\right\}$ and $\left\{\mathbf{u}_{\mathrm{p}}^{\mathrm{b}}\right\}$, respectively. The gaps are closed by applying the forces $\left\{\mathbf{F}_{\mathrm{p}}^{\mathrm{a}}\right\}$ and $\left\{\mathbf{F}_{\mathrm{p}}^{\mathrm{b}}\right\}$, respectively. The part stiffness matrices are represented by $\left[K_{\mathrm{p}}^{\mathrm{a}}\right]$ and $\left[K_{\mathrm{p}}^{\mathrm{b}}\right]$. The relations between the required forces and the gaps are described in Eqs. (1) and (2):

$$\left\{\mathbf{F}_{\mathrm{p}}^{\mathrm{a}}\right\} = \left[K_{\mathrm{p}}^{\mathrm{a}}\right]\left\{\mathbf{u}_{\mathrm{p}}^{\mathrm{a}}\right\} \tag{1}$$

$$\left\{\mathbf{F}_{\mathrm{p}}^{\mathrm{b}}\right\} = \left[K_{\mathrm{p}}^{\mathrm{b}}\right]\left\{\mathbf{u}_{\mathrm{p}}^{\mathrm{b}}\right\} \tag{2}$$

Modeling of step 2: Welding the parts, weld point (wp) $i = 1, \ldots, N$

To close the gap in weld point (wp) *i*, a force $\{\mathbf{F}_{\mathrm{A}}^{\mathrm{i}}\}$, where the index *A* stands for assembly, is applied and the relation becomes:

$$\{\mathbf{F}_{\mathrm{A}}^{\mathrm{i}}\} = \left[K_{\mathrm{A}}^{\mathrm{i}-1}\right]\{\mathbf{u}_{\mathrm{A}}^{\mathrm{i}-1}\} \tag{3}$$

After setting wp *i*, the assembly is released from its fixture and will then springback (the release step is executed since it gives clearer and easier calculations compared to accumulating the resulting forces for each wp). To calculate the springback, the stiffness matrix $[K_A^i]$, is used. This matrix describes the stiffness of the assembly after wp *i* is set and is determined using Eq. (4).

After the springback calculation, the assembly is brought back to its clamped position again, and the forces $\{F_A^i\}$ required to do this are registered. Both clamping forces and forces due to contact modeling are taken into consideration.

The stiffness matrix K_A^i is updated for every new wp by adding a matrix $\left[K_{wp(ia,ib)}^i\right]$ to the stiffness matrix from the previous step. The added matrix describes how the new wp locks three translations and three rotations. This is described in Eq. (4):

$$[\mathbf{K_A}^{\mathbf{i}}] = [\mathbf{K_A}^{\mathbf{i-1}}] + [\mathbf{K_{wp(ia,ib)}}] \tag{4}$$

For the very first wp, the matrix $[\mathbf{K}_A^0]$ refers to the original part stiffness matrices, i.e., one for each part. The deviation used for the first welding point, $\{\mathbf{u}_A^0\}$, corresponds to the part deviations.

Modeling of step 3: Final springback

When all welding points are set and the assembly is unclamped it will springback due to previously applied forces. To simulate this springback, a force$\{\mathbf{F_a}\}$ corresponding to the force $\{\mathbf{F}_A^N\}$, but in the opposite direction, is applied. Using the relation

$$\{\mathbf{F_a}\} = [\mathbf{K}_a^N]\{\mathbf{u_a}\} \tag{5}$$

the final assembly deviation $\{\mathbf{u_a}\}$ can be calculated:

$$\{\mathbf{u_a}\} = [\mathbf{K}_a^N]^{-1}\{\mathbf{F_a}\} \tag{6}$$

The above description was intentionally kept simple in order to provide a first rough picture of the modeling. It is in fact much more complicated. Still much simplified, the following summarizes what information that needs to be calculated in order to predict the final springback of an assembly.

Step 1: The parts are positioned/clamped in their fixtures. Forces are applied to clamp the non-nominal parts. Overconstrained locating systems are often applied, locking the part in more than six degrees of freedom. Simplified, the following are established in this first step:

a) Position and orientation of the parts (or subassemblies) to be assembled, by locking each part in six degrees of freedom.

b) Deformation of the parts due to possible overconstrained clamping of the parts to be assembled.

c) The resulting penetrations or gaps arising between the mating surfaces. In the following this is referred to as the penetration state.

Step 2: The parts are welded together in a predefined welding sequence. The gaps in the weld points are closed one by one. The force needed to close a gap interplay with the forces arising in the mating surfaces, which in turn affects the penetration state. Solving the resulting force pairs can be done using contact modeling, using iterative [17] or more advanced optimization methods, e.g., quadratic programming [16]. The following is calculated for each welding point in this step:

a) Force pair needed to close the gap in the welding point and the resulting force pairs necessary to hinder penetration of the parts.

b) The resulting deformation of the parts due to introduced weld and contact forces.

c) The resulting changes of clamping forces.

Step 3: After the spot welds are set, the assembly is unclamped and is allowed to springback. The following is then calculated, constraining the assembly in only six degrees of freedom:

a) Changes in stiffness of the parts due to the added welds.

b) Changes of the part geometries and the springback of the assembly, due to the release of contact and clamp forces.

Step 1b, Step 1c, Step 2 and Step 3 are iterated until all the spot welds are set.

Step 4: After the last spot weld is set, the assembly is unclamped and is allowed to springback. The resulting springback is established positioning the assembly in a targeting fixture. This fixture can be either constrained to evaluate the total springback or overconstrained to match the locating system used in the tolerancing of the assembly. A bit simplified, the following steps are repeated taking into account the new locating system:

a) Step 1, to calculate the final penetration state.

b) Steps 2a and 2b, to calculate the final shape of the assembly.

As previously mentioned, the above steps can be included in a Monte Carlo (MC)-based variation simulation [21]. The joining forces and the geometrical deviation of the final assembly are calculated in each MC replication. The method described in this section is implemented in the variation simulation tool RD&T [6], which is used for the case studies presented in this chapter.

For large assemblies with dense meshes and many weld points, the model size and the simulation time has been an issue, although the MIC is used. However, there has recently been some work done in this area to reduce the simulation models by Lindau et al. [22].

2.2. Case study

In **Figure 3**, a case study of an A-pillar can be seen. This assembly consists of two parts which are joined with nine spot welds. The joining sequence used in industrial production is seen in the figure. For this case study, there exist inspection data for both part A and part B. This data can, together with information about the locating schemes, be used as input to a variation simulation. The result from the simulation, based on the method described above, is then

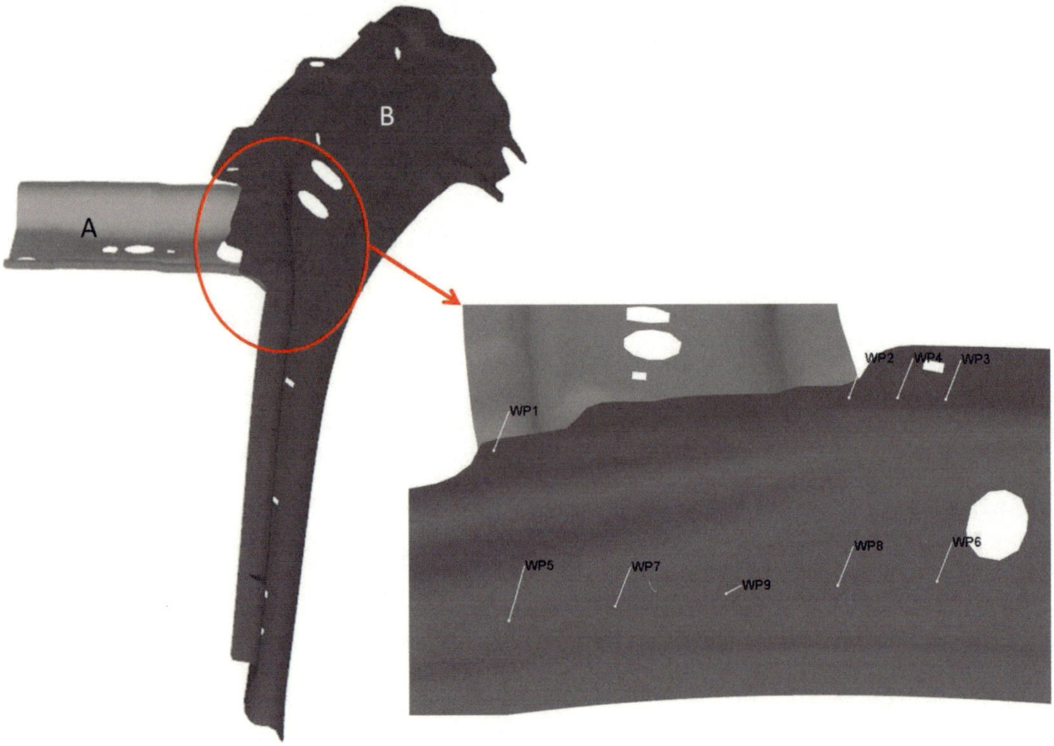

Figure 3. An A-pillar assembly. The two parts are joined by nine spot welds.

compared to inspection data on assembly level in a number of inspection points, see **Figure 4**. The data is originating from industrial settings, but it should be pointed out that this subassembly was chosen for analysis since there have been a lot of difficulties associated with it. The level of variation in the subassembly has been unacceptably high and the behavior of particularly part A has been hard to predict.

The case study is used to illustrate the difference between rigid and nonrigid modeling and also how the inclusion of contact modeling and joining sequence can affect the simulation result.

The inspection data on assembly level is blue in **Figure 4**. As can be seen, the rigid prediction (black line) is quite far from the inspection data. Nonrigid modeling but without contact modeling (pink line) gives approximately the same result as the rigid modeling. When adding contact modeling (red line) a much better agreement with inspection data is achieved and when also welding sequence is added to the simulation model (green line), additional improvements can be reached.

The inspection points 51–59 are all positioned on part A. This part is 0.97 mm thick compared to 1.6 mm for part B. During inspection, the locating scheme from part B is used. These

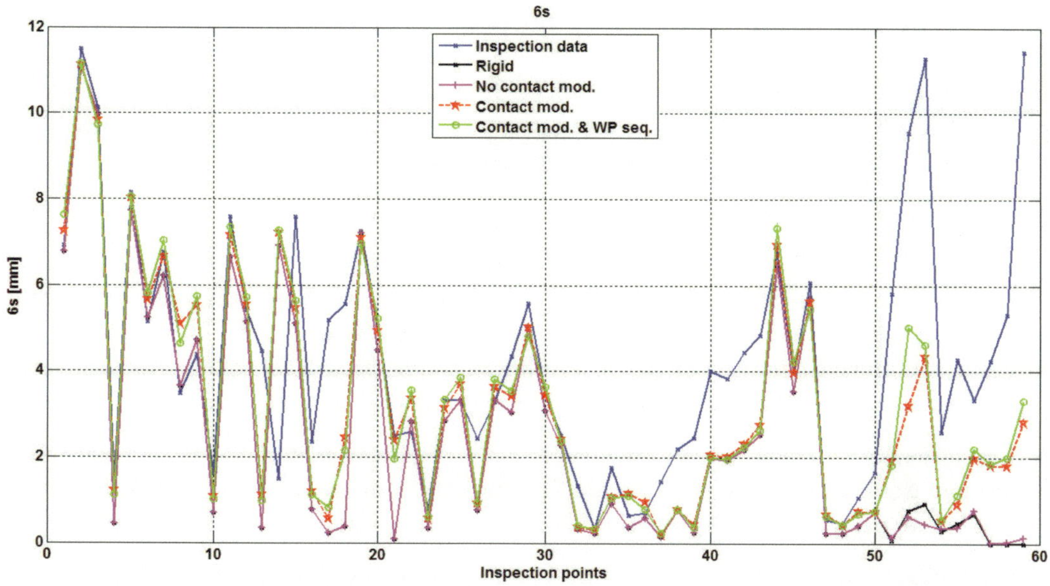

Figure 4. A comparison between simulated data and inspection data.

Model	Rigid	No contact	Contact	Contact and wp seq.
Correlation	0.26	0.02	0.87	0.87

Table 1. Correlation between simulated data and inspection data for different modeling alternatives.

factors simply that it is more difficult to predict the springback for part B than for part A, and from **Figure 4** it can be seen that there is a bigger difference between the different simulation results for the points on part A. Correlation values, which measure the linear relationship between simulated data and inspection data, for inspection points on part A can be seen in **Table 1**. As can be seen, the correlation increases when more influencing factors are taken into account in the simulation model. However, for this case study there is no difference between the correlation values with and without welding sequence. The deviations between simulated and inspected values are though slightly less for the model where welding sequence is included.

For the full simulation model the correlation is 0.87 which is a very high value. This indicates that the trends are captured very well by the simulation model. However, there is still a gap between simulated and real values for some of the inspection points. This needs to be closed by refinement of the simulation methodology and/or better input data. The input data for this case study consist of inspection data on part level. The parts should ideally be measured unclamped, i.e., not forced to a specific shape. In this case, additional clamps were applied, leading to an overconstrained condition and information loss on the actual springback shapes of the parts [23].

3. The type and number of joining points

In this section, different joining methods will be discussed as well as how to choose geometry points. Geometry points are the set of joining points that are assumed to lock the geometry of a subassembly. These points are set first in a joining sequence.

There are many different joining methods and as mentioned in the Introduction, the ones considered here are joining by:

- Bolts, rivets, clinches and spot welds: These are treated together, since they all are assumed to lock two parts together in all degrees of freedom. Therefore, they can be modeled in the same way. The heat induced by the spot welding, and possible local deformation caused by this, is not considered here. Neither are local deformations caused by clinching.
- Clip fasteners: clip fasteners are often used to join dissimilar material, such as plastic parts to more rigid, structural parts. The clip fasteners can lock the parts in varying degrees of freedom depending on their configuration. Clip fasteners are discussed in Section 6.
- Continuous welding: continuous welding is used to join two structural parts. The main challenge in modeling continuous welding with respect to geometrical deviation is that the heat generated by the welding process leads to deformations of the parts. Continuous welding is discussed in Section 7.

In FEA-based variation simulation the joining is modeled by constraining the allowed displacement of one or several nodes from one part to corresponding nodes on the other part. These corresponding nodes are in previous work [16, 17] referred to as node-pairs. The constraints set on the nodes in a node-pair depend on the type of joint to be modeled. Depending on the type, the relative displacement of the corresponding nodes are locked in one to six degrees of freedom (dof), where three dofs prevent possible translation in orthogonal directions and three dofs prevent the rotations.

3.1. Geometry points

The geometrical outcome of the assembly is of course affected by the number and position of the joining points. Generally, the choice of joining points is based on requirements of strength of the assembly and also the accessibility for the joining tools.

The geometry of an assembly is mostly affected by the first joining points when the joining is done in a sequence. To set all joining points might be a time-consuming task, and for spot welding in automotive industry, the set of spot welds is often divided into two. The first set of points, the geometry points, is supposed to lock the geometry of the assembly. After the geometry points are welded, the assembly can be released from its fixtures and the remaining points, the respot points, or simply the respots, can be welded in any of the following stations with minimal effects on the geometry. Which respot that should be set in which station is a question about balancing the capacity between stations and robots to minimize cycle time [24]. By this procedure the cycle time can be kept down and the welding sequence for the respots is chosen mainly with respect to cycle time. To maintain a high geometrical quality and a low

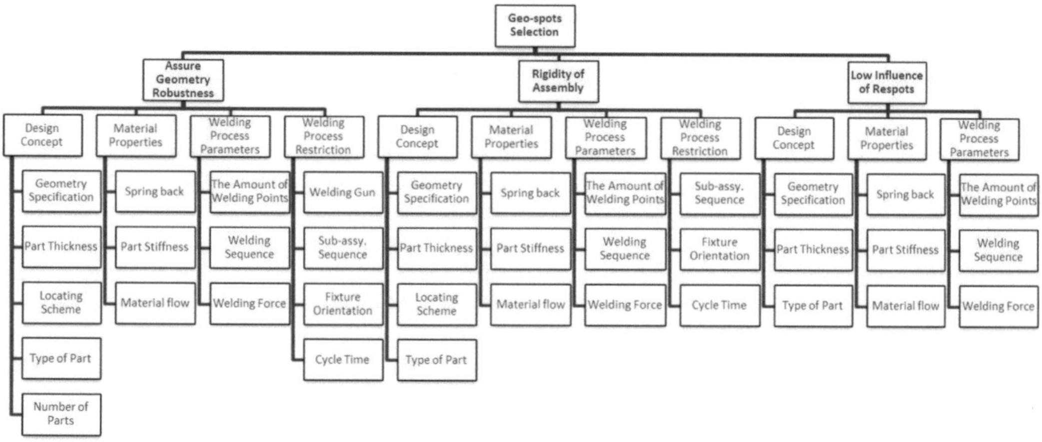

Figure 5. Factors affecting the choice of geometry points. The results are based on interviews with engineers in automotive industry.

cycle time, the division of a set of welding points into geometry points and respots is an important task. Generally, the three criteria below should be taken into consideration when choosing the set of geometry points.

Criterion 1: assure geometry robustness and product functions. The assembly should be geometrically robust, i.e., insensitive to variation, and the key features of the product should be assured. This criterion is evaluated after all joining points are set, but since the joining sequence affects the outcome, this is necessary to keep in mind when choosing the geometry points.

Criterion 2: assure rigidity of parts to withstand forces. The assembly should, after setting the geometry points, be stiff enough to withstand the applied forces from the subsequent processes, such as forces from the robot's gripper, welding guns and handling operations between stations.

Criterion 3: minimizing the influence of respots. A minimal influence from the respots on the geometry of the assembly is sought.

In industry, the choice of geometry points is often based on experience. A small interview study, based on 14 engineers from two different companies in the automotive industry, has been performed in a master thesis [25]. The study focused on spot welding and shows that choosing geometry points is a complex task and a lot of different considerations need to be taken. In **Figure 5**, an overview of factors affecting the choice is given. The factors are categorized using the criteria 1–3. As can be seen, factors such as design concept, locating schemes and material properties affect the choice.

Based on the interviews, some best practice guidelines to select a set of geometry points were established:

- Choose geometry points close to the locators and clamps.

- Spread the geometry points over the surfaces to be joined.
- Make sure that there are geometry points to lock the main axis of the assembly, i.e., choose geometry points on surfaces with different normal directions.

This complex process of choosing geometry points can be supported by the use of variation simulation. Different sets of geometry points can be compared and for each set, the criteria listed above can be evaluated in software for variation simulation.

A case study, consisting of five parts, is used to illustrate the idea, see **Figure 6**. Here, a color coding of the difference between geometrical deviations from nominal values before and after the respots are set is shown for four different sets of geometry points. Blue colors correspond to a very small difference and red values indicate bigger values. Therefore, from this aspect, the second set of geometry points is preferable.

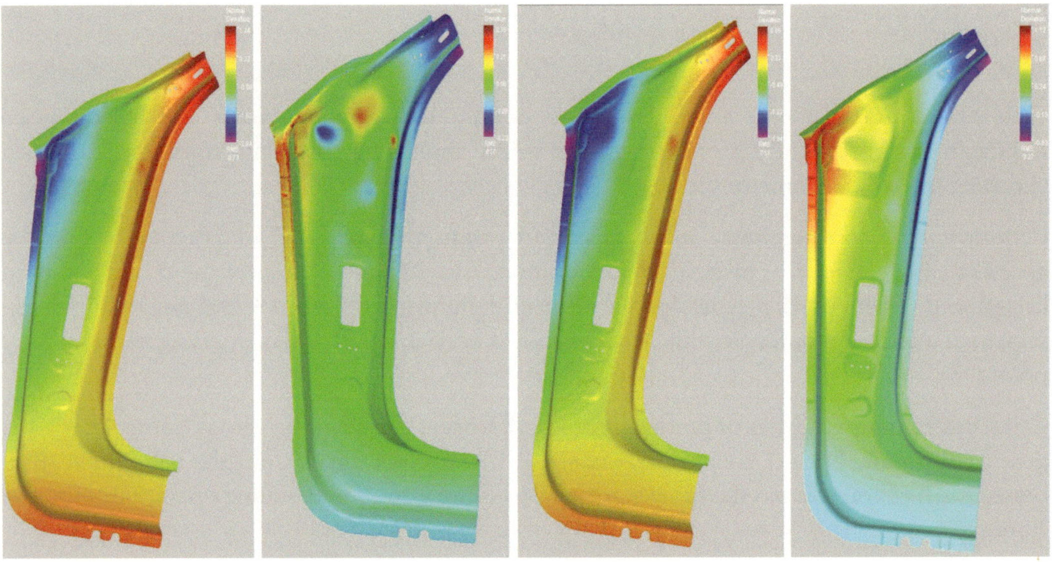

Figure 6. The differences between geometrical deviation before and after the respots are set for four different sets of geometry points.

4. Joining sequences in variation simulation

The joining sequence is well known to affect the geometrical outcome of an assembly. In **Figure 7**, a subassembly of a reinforcement and a torsional stiffness bracket is shown. The upper part and the lower part are joined using seven spot welds, seen in the left part of the figure. The result is evaluated using the locating scheme for the lower part, why most of the variation in the assembly is seen on the upper part. Red color indicates high level of variation and blue colors indicate no, or low, variation.

http://dx.doi.org/10.5772/65851

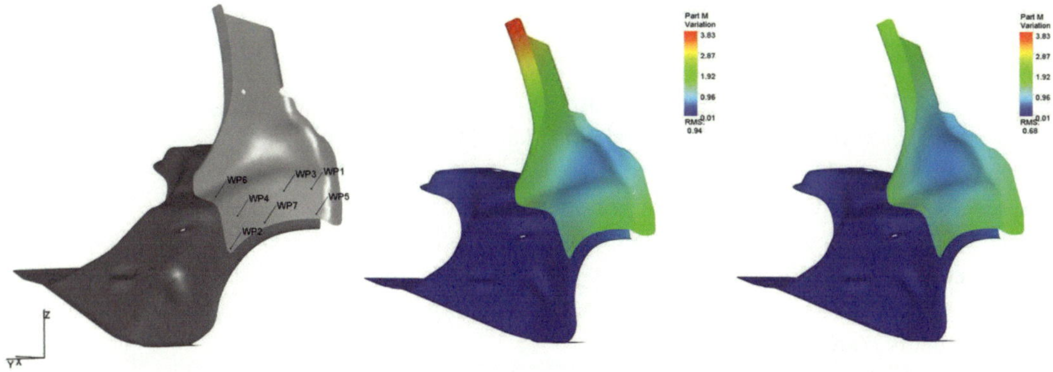

Figure 7. The importance of joining sequence for geometrical variation in an assembly. Left: the different spot welds. Middle: geometrical variation in the assembly for a bad joining sequence. Right: geometrical variation in the assembly for a good joining sequence.

The color-coded pictures in the middle and to the right show the simulated result for two different spot welding sequences. The major difference between the two different sequences is that the good sequence (picture to the right) starts with the spot weld set in z-direction (wp 6 in the figure), while that spot weld is set last in the picture in the middle.

This example shows the importance of choosing a good joining sequence. The joining sequence is usually set early on in the product development phase and by finding a good sequence the geometrical variation can be reduced without additional costs.

The sequence should be chosen in such a way that requirements on both geometrical quality and cycle time can be fulfilled. As mentioned in the previous section, the sequence of the geometry points is often chosen with respect to geometrical quality and the sequence of the respots with respect to cycle time.

The joining sequence is often discussed in terms of spot welding sequence, but the problem of finding a suitable joining sequence is of course not less important for joining with rivets, bolts or clip fasteners.

There are two main problems with finding a suitable joining sequence. The first is that this is a fast growing problem. The number of possible sequences for n joining points is $n!$ If there are, for example, 10 different joining points the number of possible joining sequences is 3,628,800. Even with a fast simulation tool where each sequence can be evaluated in minutes it will take many years to test all sequences. The second problem is that in most cases there is no analytical function relating the sequence to the geometrical variation of the assembly. The relation between input and output is also highly nonlinear since for some input, the parts collide with each other and the assembly is deformed.

There is some research done on optimization of spot welding sequences. Shiu et al. [26] investigate the relationship between stress build-up due to different spot welding sequences and the resulting dimensional variation. General guidelines for welding sequences are also established. A method for quality and throughput optimization based on a systematic search algorithm was suggested in [27].

Liu and Hu [28] present two principles for minimizing the dimensional variance, namely to weld from weak to strong and to weld simultaneously if possible. This work was used as a starting point in [29] where different general strategies for finding optimal spot welding sequences were evaluated on eight different industrial case studies. The most promising strategy was to investigate how a disturbance in each weld point w_i affects the gap in the unwelded joining points and in each step choose the welding points w_i that affected the other points the most. The strategy worked out quite well for the case studies, but the results were not completely convincing.

The major part of the work done in joining sequence optimization has however been based on genetic algorithms. Liao [30] is using genetic algorithms to find the optimal number and position of spot welds. The objective function to be minimized is the weighted sum of the deviations and/or variations in a number of predefined inspection points. Xie and Hsieh [31] minimize the deformation in a number of user-defined points by using genetic algorithms. They also take cycle time into consideration. The developed algorithm is implemented in the software EAVS (elastic assembly variation simulation). Only deformation, no variation, is considered in their work. Genetic algorithms are also used by Segeborn et al. [32, 33] to minimize geometrical variation and cycle time.

A drawback of GA is that even though not all possible sequences need to be tested, there is still a need to run a non-negligible portion of all sequences, which might be time consuming. Furthermore, it is difficult to interpret the result and understand the reasons for a certain sequence being the best one.

An interview study, presented below, has been made to clarify how experienced engineers in industry find good spot welding sequences. Even though the choice of sequence is highly case-dependent and based on craftsmanship, some guidelines have been reached.

4.1. Geometry-dependent guidelines for choosing spot welding sequence

This study is a continuation of the study described in Section 3 about how to choose geometry points. According to the engineers participating in the study, the task of choosing geometry points and finding a suitable sequence can be done independently and the set of geometry points should of course be established before the sequence is set. This reduces the problem of finding good sequences significantly.

Two special cases where the welding sequence has a significant influence on the geometrical quality of the subassembly were pointed out. These are illustrated using basic sketches in **Figure 8**.

The first case is described in **Figure 8(a)**, where one thinner and one thicker part is joined with weld points in different directions.

By looking at the requirements and shape of the assembly, it can be realized that an important requirement is that the bottom surfaces meet. Thus, the best option is to start with wp1 and close the biggest gap to secure this requirement. Since the inner flanges are thinner than the

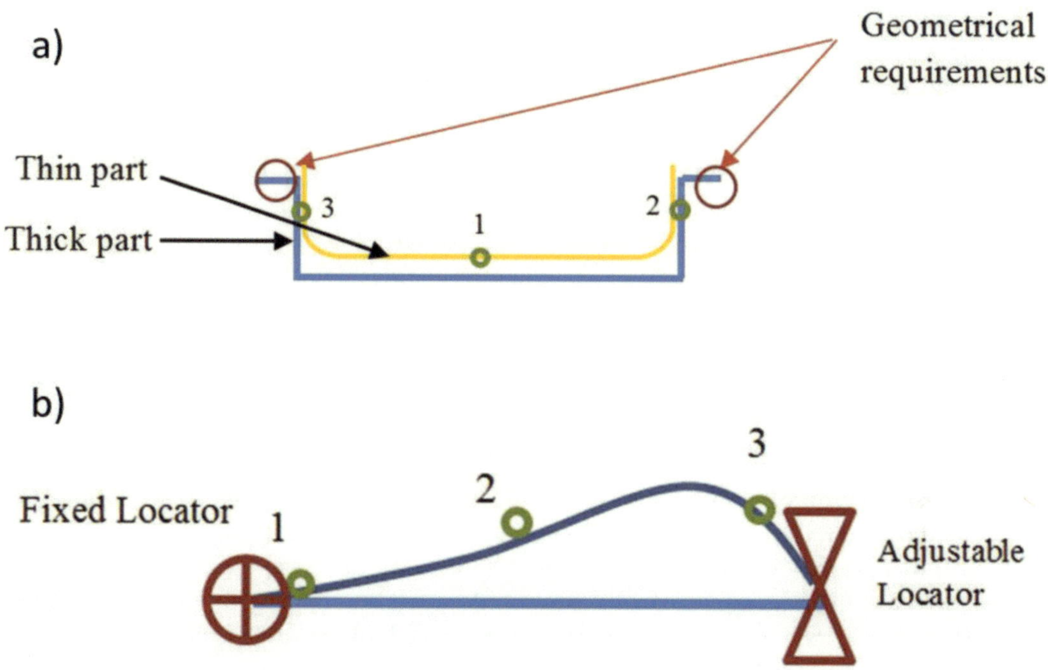

Figure 8. Two typical cases when a spot welding sequence should be chosen. The green circles with numbers indicate different welding points.

outer ones, they will have the ability to bend after welding the middle point. If wp2 and wp3 should have been set first, this would result in a stiffer assembly and forcing the parts together in wp1 would then probably have caused a distortion of the assembly. By closing the gap in wp1 first, no new gaps in wp2 or wp3 will be introduced and thereby no distortion will be added when welding these points.

In **Figure 8(b)**, part variation leads to a gap between the parts to be joined. Here, the welding sequence should be chosen in such a way that the material flow is controlled. The adjustable locator is assumed to only steer in the normal direction of the surface, i.e., the material is allowed to glide under the locator when a force is applied by the welding gun. The preferred sequence here is to first set wp2, since it has the biggest effect on material flow. To start with the weld point that affects the material flow the most might seem as an easy task when looking at the sketch in **Figure 8**. However, **Figure 8** illustrates only two of many possible situations and only two dimensions. For three dimensions, this is more complex and simulation software can be a good support.

5. Simulation of distribution of joining forces

When joining two parts, a force must be applied to press the parts to be joined against each other before the actual joining takes place. In resistance spot welding, the parts must be pressed against each other in order to allow the current to pass through both parts and melt them together. If a clip joint is used, a force is needed to apply the clip fastener, and so on. The quality and strength of the achieved joint are usually affected by the magnitude of the applied force.

Part variation and variation in assembly fixtures may lead to gaps between the parts in the locations of the joining points. These gaps need to be closed, and some of the predefined joining forces are then consumed for closing the gaps. Therefore, the variation in initial gaps needs to be taken into consideration when defining suitable joining forces. This variation can be predicted using the methods described in the earlier sections. The term joining force refers to the total force applied to join the parts and the term assembly force is used for the force needed to close the initial gap. The assembly force is by that a subset of the total welding force. The total joining force is usually constant, and therefore it is important to minimize the variation in assembly forces in order to achieve joints of good quality.

A too low force will obviously lead to a joint of low quality, and also a too high force might lead to a joint that will decrease in strength. For spot welding, a too high electrode force will increase the welding contact zone and thereby decrease the electric resistance, leading to a too small nugget size. In this work the variation in assembly forces is considered. This should generally be more interesting than looking at the mean value of the forces, since the total force applied from the welding gun can be adjusted to fit a certain level of assembly forces. A large variation in the assembly forces is more difficult to compensate.

Murakawa and Ueda [34] investigated the force needed to close an initial gap by applying parametric curves and approximation curves to two simple structures. Due to the variation in magnitude of the initial gap, the force required to close it will of course also vary.

Wärmefjord et al. [35] described a method for predicting variation in assembly forces due to part variation. In [36] the effect of variation in spot weld position on assembly forces was investigated.

To calculate the distribution of assembly forces, Eq. (3) is used. This is done for a case study shown in the left part of **Figure 9**. This is a D-pillar consisting of two parts joined by four spot welds. The four spot welds lead to 4! = 24 different possible spot welding sequences. The predicted values of the level of variation for the different spot welding sequences are illustrated together with the predicted maximum assembly force in any of the four spot welds. The maximum force equals the range in this case, since the minimum force is 0 N for every sequence.

The bars represent a value of the geometrical variation given by $6s_{RMS}$. The total root mean square (RMS) value for standard deviation is a general measure of the variation in all nodes of the assembly. For each node j, $j = 1, \ldots, k$, the magnitude of the variation in x-, y- and z-direction is calculated as the sum of the variations in the three directions:

$$s_j^2 = s_{jx}^2 + s_{jy}^2 + s_{jz}^2 \tag{7}$$

The RMS value is then calculated:

http://dx.doi.org/10.5772/65851

$$s_{RMS} = \sqrt{\frac{s_1^2 + \ldots + s_k^2}{k}} \tag{8}$$

The worst value (sequence 21) is 35% larger than the best value (sequence 3).

The maximum assembly force needed to close the gap, i.e.,

$$F_A^{max} = \max_i \{\mathbf{F_A^i}\}, \qquad i = 1, \ldots, 4 \tag{9}$$

for the four different spot welds in every sequence is illustrated by the black line in **Figure 9**. The maximum assembly force for welding sequence 23 is 0.46 kN. This is a value similar to the sequence demanding the least assembly force, sequence number 9. It can be noted that these two sequences have similar levels of geometrical variation. Therefore, by choosing sequence 9 instead of sequence 23, the range of the assembly forces can be reduced without changing any tolerances or affecting the level of geometrical variation.

The maximum assembly force for a certain sequence does not, of course, occur in every Monte Carlo replication. The joining process should, however, be designed with those extreme values taken into consideration.

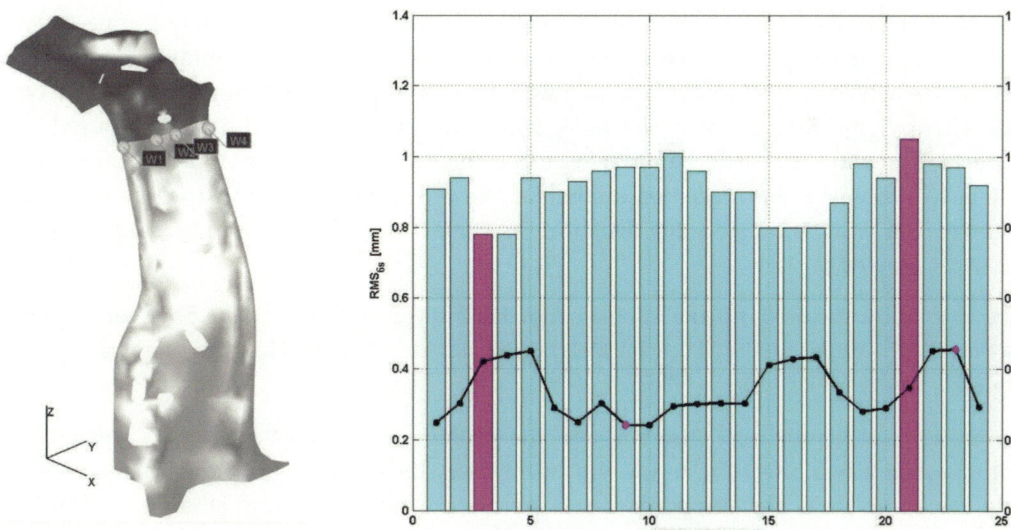

Figure 9. Simulation results for a D-pillar assembly.

6. Clip fasteners

Another kind of joining method is the use of clip fasteners. Clip fasteners are often used to join parts of dissimilar materials, such as plastic parts and more rigid, structural parts. From a modeling perspective, the major differences between clip fasteners and spot welds are that:

1) Spot welds are usually assumed to lock all degrees of freedom of a node. A clip fastener is often allowed to slide in one or two directions.

2) Spot welds are modeled using a node-node contact. Clip fastener is usually covering an area, see **Figure 10**. Therefore, for non-nominal parts, levering effects affecting the whole subassembly will rise and this must of course be included in the model.

For clip fasteners, an area for the clip should be defined and also what degrees of freedom that are locked by the clip. Also play should be possible to model. Both those issues are, in the approach presented here, solved using contact modeling. This is included in the theory described in Section 2.

Normally, the purpose of a contact pair is to draw two parts apart to avoid penetration. The same method can however be used to push two nodes together in a certain direction. By defining double contact pairs with opposite directions, the parts are joined together, but still no penetration is allowed. Assuming a rectangular clip fastener, as the gray rectangle in **Figure 11**, a double contact pair is defined in each corner (red circles in **Figure 11**). In this way the area of a clip fastener can be taken into account. Circular contact areas between the fastener and the part can be modeled by using additional contact points. Using the contact modeling approach, contact pairs can be defined for several directions, so the clip fastener can be modeled to lock movement in *X*, *Y* and/or *Z* direction in the coordinate system.

It is however quite common that a clip fastener is locking a part completely in one or two direction and that a play is allowed in one direction. In this section, a case study consisting of a wheel arch extension joined to a rear fender with five clip fasteners, see **Figure 12**. For the case study, circular clip fasteners in a slot hole, with 5 mm play in one direction are used, see **Figure 13**. The play can easily be modeled using the contact modeling approach. Instead of pushing two contact points together, a nominal allowed distance is defined where the points can move. If a point is outside this distance, the contact modeling is used to push the point back to an allowed position.

In the case study, the fender is made of sheet metal and the extension of the polymer acrylonitrile butadiene styrene (ABS). The clip fastener encircled in **Figure 12** is investigated more in detail.

Both the level of geometrical variation and the joining forces are of interest to predict. The joining sequence will affect the result, but in the case study here, a simplified model is used where all clip fasteners are assumed to be set simultaneously. Then the joining force equals the

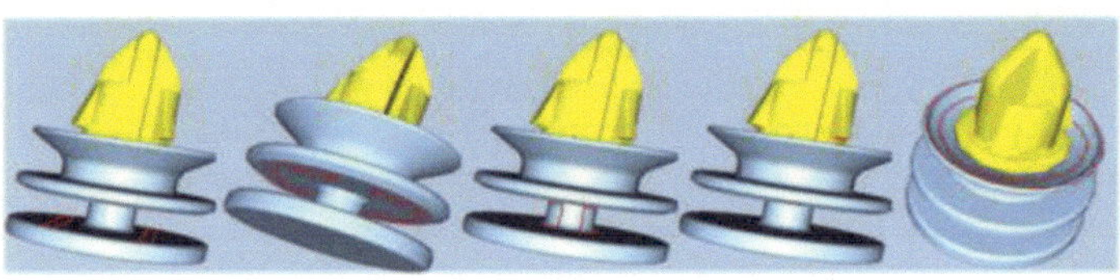

Figure 10. Illustration of clip fasteners.

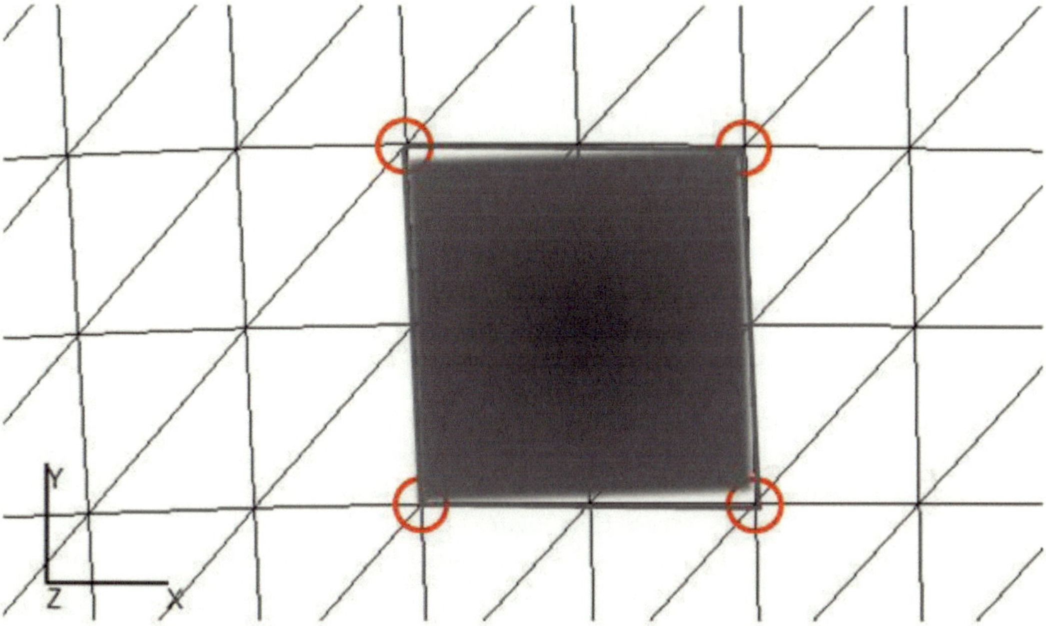

Figure 11. The clip fastener modeling approach.

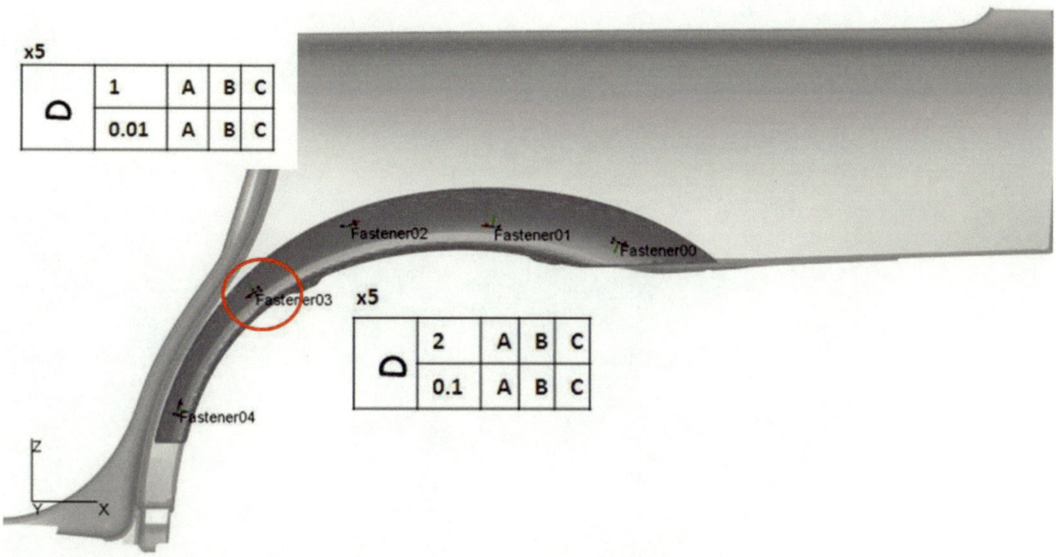

Figure 12. A wheel arch extension joined to a rear fender using five clip fasteners.

holding force, which is the force the clip fastener must withstand after the parts are joined. There exist a number of different clip fastener alternatives and the expected holding forces affect the choice of fastener.

Since the two parts are of different material, they will respond differently to changes in temperature. The effect from this on the holding forces will be investigated in future work.

The bars in **Figure 13** show how the result for holding forces and the RMS value of geometrical variation (see Eq. (8)) differs depending on modeling strategy. Two different modeling alternatives are compared:

- A node/node based approach where two nodes, one from each part, are locked together. This is the traditional modeling approach for clip fasteners.
- A new modeling approach, as suggested in this section, where the area of the clip fastener is taken into account. This modeling alternative is more realistic compared to the node/node based alternative.

For each model, a scenario with and without play is tested. 3000 Monte Carlo iterations are run and the results are illustrated in **Figure 14**. The results presented in the upper part of **Figure 14** are the maximum value of the holding forces (see Eq. (9)), taken over all iterations, in the clip fastener encircled in **Figure 12**. As seen from **Figure 12**, the node-node based joint with no area is differing from the other values. This is due to the lack of levering effects and this shows the

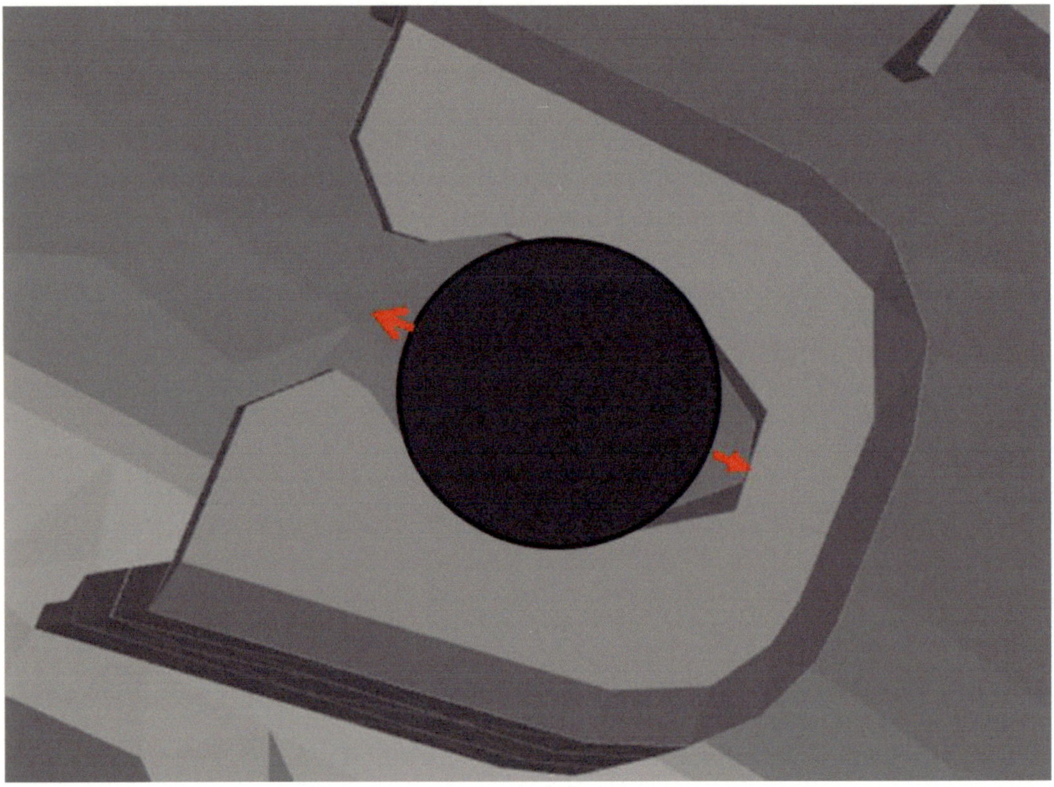

Figure 13. A clip fastener where play is allowed in one direction (indicated by red lines).

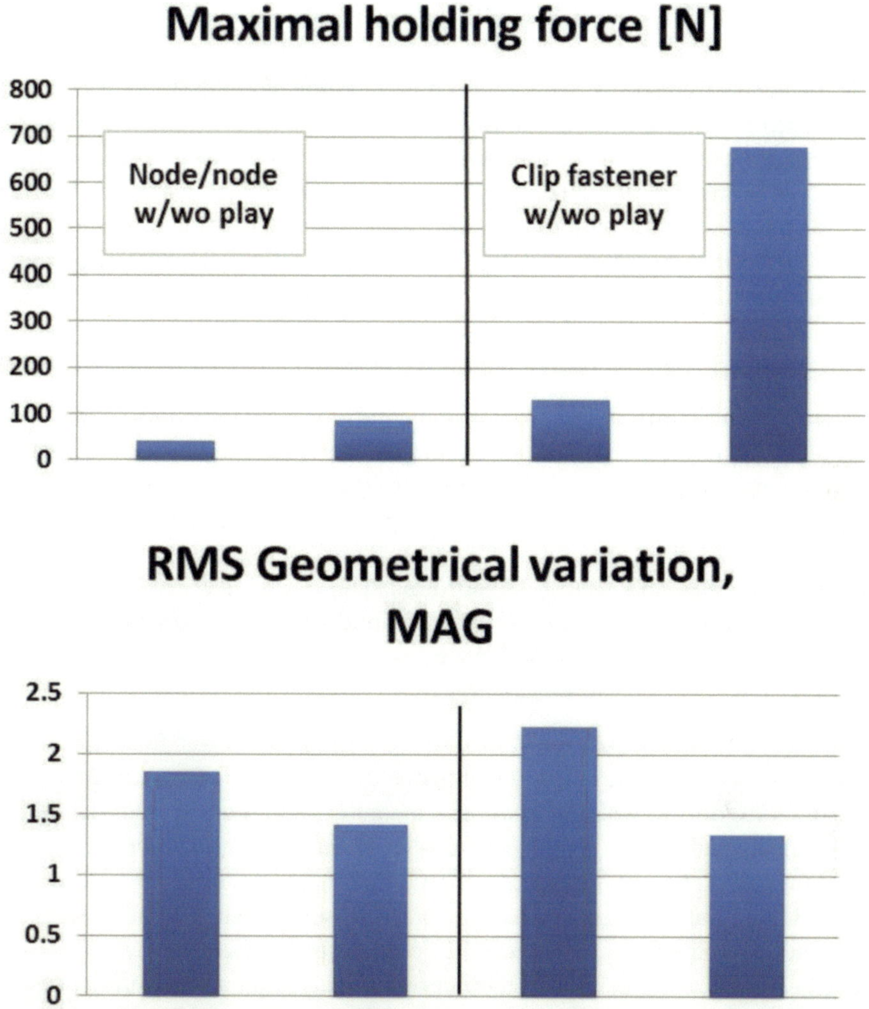

Figure 14. Forces and geometrical variation for the different modeling alternatives.

importance of inclusion of the joint area. For both modeling alternatives, the versions without play result in higher forces. This is expected due to the extra constraints.

In the lower part of **Figure 14**, the RMS value, measuring geometrical variation on assembly level, is shown. The variation is reduced with more constraints, i.e., without play. Variation is not as sensitive as holding forces to changes in the area of the clip fastener and the difference between the node-node based model and the clip fastener model is not as large as when the holding forces were predicted. However, there is still a difference and to improve the accuracy of the variation simulation it can be concluded that the area of clip fasteners should be included in the simulation model, and this is extra important when simulating holding forces. It is also necessary to be able to include plays in the modeling.

7. Continuous welding and the effect from heat

To include the effects from continuous welding in variation simulation is a difficult challenge. The heat induced by the welding gives rise to deformations of the parts and also changes the material properties. Welding simulations are today done on nominal parts and each simulation is very time consuming. Simulation times of many hours are not uncommon. To include this in a Monte Carlo based variation simulation where thousands of iterations are run is not possible. However, it has been shown that the distortion introduced by welding is dependent on part variation and assembly fixture variation [37, 38], so in order to obtain an accurate result, a new welding simulation need to be run for each Monte Carlo iteration, i.e., there is a need for methods for predicting the effects of non-nominal welding.

Also for welding simulation based on nominal conditions the long simulation time and the large memory consumption has been a problem. Therefore methods have been proposed aiming at reducing computation time and memory consumption. These methods are usually based on the assumption that the main driving force causing distortion in the welding process is the shrinkage of the material that has been melted by the weld gun, and then cooled down to solidify and recover its stiffness. These methods are based on applying a strain to the structure, see for example [39] for inherent strain, [40] for models based on different strains in the longitudinal and the transverse direction and [41, 42] for volumetric shrinkage.

Test has been done to use the methods based on volumetric shrinkage for approximating non-nominal welding, see [43]. This method comprises three steps: the first step involves calculating the temperature during welding to approximate the section of the material that is melted. This can be done by simulating the heat transfer as the weld gun traverses the weld joint. However, although the heat transfer simulation is generally faster than the mechanical part of welding simulation, this is generally too slow. Instead, since the temperature surrounding the weld gun during welding in many cases can be considered to be constant it is possible to use a steady state heat calculation using an Eulerian frame. This requires the simulation of only one time step. The second step involves the approximation of the melted section of the structure. Using the result from the steady state heat simulation from step one, where the weld gun is positioned somewhere along the weld joint with the temperature distribution applied to the mesh, a surface is traveling through the weld path. This surface has a local coordinate system with the origin at the weld joint for a discrete set of succeeding points; it has further one axis pointing at the direction of the tangent of the weld path which is also the normal to this surface, and another axis pointing in the surface of the welded pieces. The third axis is pointing in the outward normal direction to this surface. As this surface is traveling through the weld path, it records the position, in this plane, for all nodes above the melting temperature. Hence, a 2-dimensional projection of the melted volume surrounding the weld gun is achieved. The smallest 2-dimensional convex hull is calculated from these projections.

In the third and final step, we are again traveling through the weld path with this surface. This time all nodes that are encapsulated in the tube that is the result of the 2-dimensional convex hull moving through the weld path are collected.

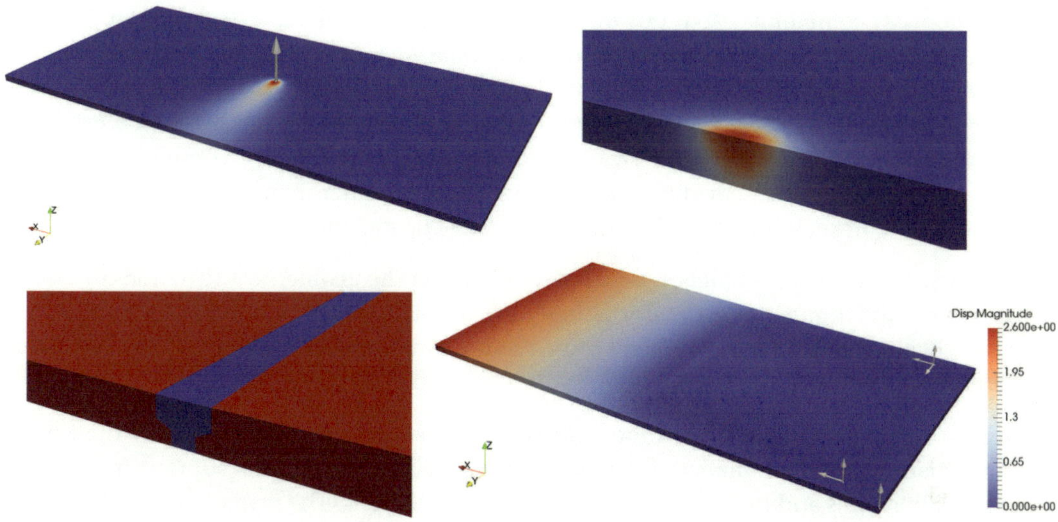

Figure 15. The steps in the SCV method.

These nodes are assigned a temperature that corresponds to the temperature difference between melting temperature and room temperature. An elastic structural calculation gives us the final distortion after welding. An illustration of the different steps is given in **Figure 15**.

The method explained above only involved one thermal FEA and one elastic structural FEA. Therefore, it is much less time consuming compared to transient welding simulation. Therefore, it can be used for iterative use in, for example, variation simulation or optimization. However, since it is an approximate method it is suggested that transient welding simulation is used in later development stages to ensure that right design decisions have been made.

The method described above is called the steady-state, convex hull, volumetric-shrinkage method, or the SCV-method. The method was first proposed in [43] where it was compared to transient simulation, and developed to account for variation of the convex hull along the weld joint in [44] and the use of a temperature distribution in the melted zone for better approximation of the shrinkage in [45].

8. Summary and outlook

In this chapter nonrigid variation simulation has been described. This method is used to predict geometrical variation and mean shifts in critical dimensions of a subassembly or a final assembled product. For nonrigid parts, the inclusion of their nonrigid behavior is necessary in order to achieve good accuracy in the simulations. Moreover, a number of other factors affecting the geometrical outcome of an assembly need to be taken into account. In this chapter, how to model different joining processes in nonrigid variation simulation has been in focus. Among the joining processes that can be modeled are point-based methods locking two parts together in all degrees of freedom in a node-pair. In this class of joining, spot welding is one of the most commonly used, but there are also clinching, riveting and bolting. How to model clips fastener has also been discussed. The clip fasteners are often used to join dissimilar materials, such as plastic and more structural parts. They often lock the part in less than six degrees of freedom and they also often cover an area, which can lead to levering effects and this must of course be included in the variation simulation. Furthermore, continuous welding has been discussed. The major difference compared to the other joining methods is that the geometrical distortion induced by the heat source must be included.

Topics such as the joining sequence, which strongly affect the geometrical variation on assembly level, and the number of geometry points have also been discussed. It is shown that how inclusion of the joining sequence leads to increased correlation between simulated and real result for an industrial case study.

Nonrigid variation simulation is for most cases where the parts are not completely rigid more accurate than the rigid simulation. Drawbacks can be lack of input data, support from variation simulation tools and more computer expensive calculations. The method described here is implemented in a commercial tool for variation simulation and there is ongoing work to reduce simulation time and model sizes. However, this is a critical issue for nonrigid variation simulation and there is still work need to be done in this area. Furthermore, the simulation tools need to be refined even more to be able to handle, for example, different materials and their material models and large deformations (outside the linear regime).

Moreover, with an increased access to inspection data in the footsteps of Industry 4.0, fast algorithms for quick adjustments of the assembly process with respect to, for example, joining sequences and position of locators, based on individual part deviations need to be developed.

Acknowledgements

This work was carried out at the Wingquist Laboratory VINN Excellence Centre within the Area of Advance—Production at Chalmers, supported by the Swedish Governmental Agency for Innovation Systems (VINNOVA). The support is gratefully acknowledged.

Author details

Kristina Wärmefjord[1*], Rikard Söderberg[1], Björn Lindau[2], Lars Lindkvist[1] and Samuel Lorin[3]

*Address all correspondence to: Kristina.warmefjord@chalmers.se

1 Department of Product and Production Development, Chalmers University of Technology, Gothenburg, Sweden

2 Volvo Car Corporation, Torslanda, Sweden

3 Fraunhofer Chalmers Research Centre, Gothenburg, Sweden

http://dx.doi.org/10.5772/65851

References

[1] Lööf J, Hermansson T, Söderberg R. An efficient solution to the discrete least-cost tolerance allocation problem with general loss functions. Models for computer aided tolerancing in design and manufacturing. Springer; Dordrecht, The Netherlands, 2007. p. 115–24.

[2] Söderberg R, Lindkvist L. Computer aided assembly robustness evaluation. Journal of Engineering Design. 1999;10:165–81.

[3] Söderberg R, Lindkvist L, Wärmefjord K, Carlson JS. Virtual geometry assurance process and toolbox. Procedia CIRP. 2016;43:3–12.

[4] DCS webpage. Available from http://www.3dcs.com/ [Accessed 2015-07-10]

[5] VSA webpage. Available from http://www.plm.automation.siemens.com/en_us/products/tecnomatix/quality_mgmt/variation_analyst/ [Accessed 2015-07-10]

[6] RD&T Technology. RD&T webpage. Available from www.rdnt.se. [Accessed 2016-07-10]

[7] Lindau B, Lindkvist L, Andersson A, Söderberg R. Statistical shape modeling in virtual assembly using PCA-technique. Journal of Manufacturing Systems. 2013. p. 456–463.

[8] Schleich B, Anwer N, Mathieu L, Wartzack S. Skin model shapes: a new paradigm shift for geometric variations modelling in mechanical engineering. Computer-Aided Design. 2014;50:1–15.

[9] Söderberg R, Lindkvist L, Carlson JS. Managing physical dependencies through location system design. Journal of Engineering Design. 2006;17:325–46.

[10] Cai W, Hu SJ, Yuan J. Deformable sheet metal fixturing: principles, algorithms, and simulations. Journal of Mechanical Design. 1996;118:318–24.

[11] Wärmefjord K, Carlson JS, Söderberg R. Controlling geometrical variation caused by assembly fixtures. Journal of Computing and Information Science in Engineering. 2016;16:011007.

[12] Wärmefjord K, Söderberg R, Carlson JS. Including assembly fixture repeatability in rigid and non-rigid variation simulation. In: Proceedings of ASME 2010 International Mechanical Engineering Congress and Exposition. 2010. p. 355–61.

[13] Liu SC, Hu SJ, Woo TC. Tolerance analysis for sheet metal assemblies. Journal of Mechanical Design. 1996;118:62–7.

[14] Lindau B, Wärmefjord K, Lindkvist L, Söderberg R. Aspects of fixture clamp modeling in non-rigid variation simulation of sheet metal assemblies. In: ASME 2013 International Mechanical Engineering Congress and Exposition. 2013. p. V02BTA040–V02BT02A.

[15] Cai W, Wang PC, Yang W. Assembly dimensional prediction for self-piercing riveted aluminum panels. International Journal of Machine tools and Manufacuture. 2005;45:695–704.

[16] Lindau B, Lorin S, Lindkvist L, Söderberg R. Efficient contact modeling in nonrigid variation simulation. Journal of Computing and Information Science in Engineering. 2016;16:011002.

[17] Wärmefjord K, Söderberg R, Lindkvist L. Tolerance simulation of compliant sheet metal assemblies using automatic node-based contact detection. In: Proceedings of ASME IMECE, 2008. Boston, USA.

[18] Liu SC, Hu SJ. Variation simulation for deformable sheet metal assemblies using finite element methods. Journal of Manufacturing Science and Engineering. 1997;119:368–74.

[19] Camelio JA, Hu SJ, Ceglarek D. Modeling variation propagation of multi-station assembly systems with compliant parts. Journal of Mechanical Design. 2003;125:673–81.

[20] Dahlström S, Lindkvist L. Variation simulation of sheet metal assemblies using the method of influence coefficients with contact modeling. In: Proceedings of ASME International Mechanical Engineering Congress and Exposition. 2004. Anaheim, California, USA.

[21] Wärmefjord K, Söderberg R, Lindkvist L. Variation simulation of spot welding sequence for sheet metal assemblies. In: Proceedings of NordDesign2010 International Conference on Methods and Tools for Product and Production Development. 2010, Gothenburg, Sweden.

[22] Lindau B, Wärmefjord K, Lindkvist L, Söderberg R. Method for handling model growth in nonrigid variation simulation of sheet metal assemblies. Journal of Computing and Information Science in Engineering. 2014;14:031004.

[23] Lindau B, Andersson A, Lindkvist L, Söderberg R. Body in white geometry measurements of non-rigid components: a virtual perspective. ASME 2012 International Design Engineering Technical Conferences and Computers and Information in Engineering Conference: American Society of Mechanical Engineers; 2012. p. 497–505.

[24] Segeborn J, Segerdahl D, Ekstedt F, Carlson JS, Andersson M, Carlsson A, et al. An industrially validated method for weld load balancing in multi station sheet metal assembly lines. Journal of Manufacturing Science and Engineering. 2014;136:011002.

[25] Shao J, Tabar RS. Non-rigid sheet metal assembly simulation and selection of the geospots for further optimization. Master thesis, Chalmers University of Technology, Gothenburg, Sweden.

[26] Shiu BW, Shi J, Tse KH. The dimensional quality of sheet metal assembly with welding-induced internal stress. Proceedings of the I MECH E Part D Journal of Automobile Engineering. 2000;214:693-704.

[27] Carlson JS, Spensieri D, Wärmefjord K, Segeborn J, Söderberg R. Minimizing dimensional variation and robot traveling time in welding stations. Procedia CIRP. 2014;23:77–82.

[28] Liu SC, Hu SJ. Spot weld sequence in sheet metal assembly: its analysis and synthesis. ASME IMECE Proceeding, Manufacturing Science and Engineering. 1995;2:21995.

[29] Wärmefjord K, Söderberg R, Lindkvist L. Strategies for optimization of spot welding sequence with respect to geometrical variation in sheet metal assemblies. Proceedings of ASME International Mechanical Engineering Congress & Exposition. 2010. Vancouver, Canada.

[30] Liao YG. Optimal design of weld patterns in sheet metal assembly based on a genetic algorithm. International Journal of Manufacturing Technology. 2005;26:512–6.

[31] Xie LS, Hsieh C. Clamping and welding sequence optimization for minimizing cycle time and assembly deformation. International Journal of Materials & Product Technology. 2002;17. p. 389–399.

[32] Segeborn J, Carlson JS, Wärmefjord K, Söderberg R. Evaluating genetic algorithms on welding sequence optimization with respect to dimensional variation and cycle time. Proc of ASME IDETC 2011. 2011. Washington.

[33] Segeborn J, Torstensson J, Carlson JS, Söderberg R. Evaluating genetic algorithms that optimize welding sequence with respect to geometrical assembly variation. Proceedings of the NordDesign 2010 Conference, August 25–27. Gothenburg, Sweden, 2010.

[34] Murakawa H, Ueda Y. Mechanical study on the effect of the initial gap upon the weldability of spot weld joint. Trans of JWRI1989. p. 51–8.

[35] Wärmefjord K, Söderberg R, Lindkvist L. Simulation of the effect of geometrical variation on assembly and holding forces. International Journal of Product Development. 2013;18:88–108.

[36] Wärmefjord K, Söderberg R, Lindkvist L. Simulation of variation in assembly forces due to variation in spot weld position. smart product engineering, Proceedings of the 23rd CIRP Design Conference. 2013.

[37] Pahkamaa A, Wärmefjord K, Karlsson L, Söderberg R, Goldak J. Combining variation simulation with welding simulation for prediction of deformation and variation of a final assembly. Journal of Computing and Information Science in Engineering. 2012;12:021 002–7.

[38] Wärmefjord K, Söderberg R, Ericsson M, Appelgren A, Lundbäck A, Lööf J, et al. Welding of non-nominal geometries—physical tests. Procedia CIRP. 2016;43:136–41.

[39] Ueda Y, Kim YC, Yuan MG. A predicting method of welding residual stress using source of residual stress (report I): characteristics of inherent strain (source of residual stress) (mechanics, strength & structural design). Transactions of JWRI. 1989;18:135–41.

[40] Camilleri D, Comlekci T, Gray TF. Computational prediction of out-of-plane welding distortion and experimental investigation. The Journal of Strain Analysis for Engineering Design. 2005;40:161–76.

[41] Bachorski A, Painter M, Smailes A, Wahab MA. Finite-element prediction of distortion during gas metal arc welding using the shrinkage volume approach. Journal of Materials Processing Technology. 1999;92:405–9.

[42] Sulaiman MS, Manurung YH, Haruman E, Rahim MRA, Redza MR, Lidam RNA, et al. Simulation and experimental study on distortion of butt and T-joints using WELD PLANNER. Journal of Mechanical Science and Technology. 2011;25:2641–6.

[43] Lorin SC, Cromvik C, Edelvik F, Lindkvist L, Söderberg R. Variation simulation of welded assemblies using a thermo-elastic finite element model. Proc of ASME IMECE 2013. 2013. San Diego, CA, USA.

[44] Lorin S, Cromvik C, Edelvik F, Lindkvist L, Söderberg R, Wärmefjord K. Simulation of non-nominal welds by resolving the melted zone and its implication to variation simulation. ASME 2014 International Design Engineering Technical Conferences and Computers and Information in Engineering Conference: American Society of Mechanical Engineers; 2014. p. V004T06A18–VT06A18.

[45] Lorin S, Cromvik C, Edelvik F, Lindkvist L, Söderberg R. On the robustness of the volumetric shrinkage method in the context of variation simulation. ASME 2014 International Mechanical Engineering Congress and Exposition: American Society of Mechanical Engineers; 2014. p. V02ATA053-V02AT02A.

Chapter 4

Computer-Aided Techniques for Geometry Assurance

Andrea Corrado and Wilma Polini

Additional information is available at the end of the chapter

http://dx.doi.org/10.5772/65474

Abstract

Geometry assurance can be described as a number of activities, all contributing to minimize the effect of geometrical variation in a final product. This work aims to introduce a new type of comparison between a computer-aided technique for geometry assurance and some models proposed by the literature. In particular, the aim of this work is to solve, through a computer-aided technique, some case studies that were already solved by different methods of the literature. The different case studies that have been introduced and solved in this paper aim to highlight the potentialities and the limits in using a computer-aided technique for geometry assurance. Because this type of comparison is not present in the literature yet, this work wants to place the emphasis on the fact that till now there is not a unique approach to solve problems of geometry assurance and no approach can be defined as better than another, in terms of results.

Keywords: geometry assurance, tolerance analysis, computer-aided tolerancing, assembly, Monte Carlo simulation

1. Introduction

Manufacturing often involves geometrical variation that propagates and accumulates in assembly processes, thus giving products that do not satisfy functional, esthetical or assembly conditions. Quality problems due to the geometrical variation are often discovered late, thus involving huge cost for changes and delays in delivery time. To simulate the geometry problems allows to discover them early and, therefore, to optimize the applied tolerances and the assembly sequence.

Geometry assurance consists of all the activities that minimize the effect of geometrical variation in the final product [1]. Activities are in all the different steps of the product development.

In the concept phase, the effect of manufacturing variation is tested virtually by means of the available production data in order to analyze different alternative concepts. The robustness of the product concept and the appearance of the product are optimized, and then, they are verified by means of statistical tolerance analysis assuming a given production system. The product tolerances are allocated down to the components of the product. In the verification phase, the product and the production system are physically tested and verified. Adjustments are made to both product and production system to correct errors and prepare full production. In this phase, computer-aided inspection planning of coordinate measurement machines and scanning equipment takes place to decide inspection strategies and sensor path. In the production step, all needed adjustments are carried out on production processes. Inspection data are collected to control the production. Ebro et al. [2] states that unclear concepts or tolerances typically cause 60% of all late changes in the development of a new product. Late changes involve high costs for a company; therefore, it has a great potential to anticipate the changes in order to prevent failure, by using more robust concepts.

In this context, tolerance analysis is a key tool for product and process developers to predict the effects of inevitable part deviations on functional key characteristics (KCs) of mechanical assemblies and to assess the consequences of variation on product quality [3, 4]. Tolerance analysis is widely used in engineering design to verify the functionality, the manufacturability, and the perceived quality of a product. Assembly requirements depend on individual geometric tolerances, and it means that assembly requirements and performance vary with the constituent tolerances. The individual tolerances have their own distributions for mass production; their random assembly gives the distribution of the assembly requirement. Tolerance analysis aims to estimate the resultant variation of the assembly requirement, once defined the tolerances of the individual parts and the functional relationship between the individual tolerances and the assembly requirement [5]. If the range of the assembly requirement is set, the fraction of random assemblies that falls inside the limits refer to the total number of sampled assemblies may be estimated as a necessary step in any design evaluation. When working with tolerance analysis, the main aim is to find out the functional relationship between independent and dependent variables:

$$y = f\left(x_1, x_2, \ldots, x_n\right) \tag{1}$$

where y is the dependent variable aimed to evaluate, while x_i with $i = 1,\ldots, n$ is the list of assigned deviations (independent variables). Function f takes into account all phenomena, which may occur during the assembly process, such as assembly constraints, assembly sequence, flexibility of parts being assembled, variability of fixturing and tooling systems, and nonlinear stack-up conditions.

In the literature, various approaches for computer-aided tolerance analysis were proposed with specific advantages and disadvantages. Most of these approaches are not completely conformed to international standards for the geometric product specification (GPS) and verification, as deeply discussed in the following.

This contribution presents the quantitative assessment of a computer-aided tolerance analysis tool in comparison with established tolerance analysis methods, where the focus is laid upon rigid mechanical assemblies. This comparison is performed employing some tolerance analysis case studies of the literature.

2. State of the art

Tolerancing limits geometric deviations of parts, which inevitably are due to the manufacturing [6], to ensure the product to assemble and to function rightly [3, 7]. Tolerance analysis predicts the effects of geometric part deviations on assembly requirements, that is, "the objective of tolerance analysis is to check the extent and the nature of the variation of an analyzed dimension or geometric feature of interest for a given Geometric Dimensioning and Tolerancing (GD&T) scheme" [8] (see **Figure 1**).

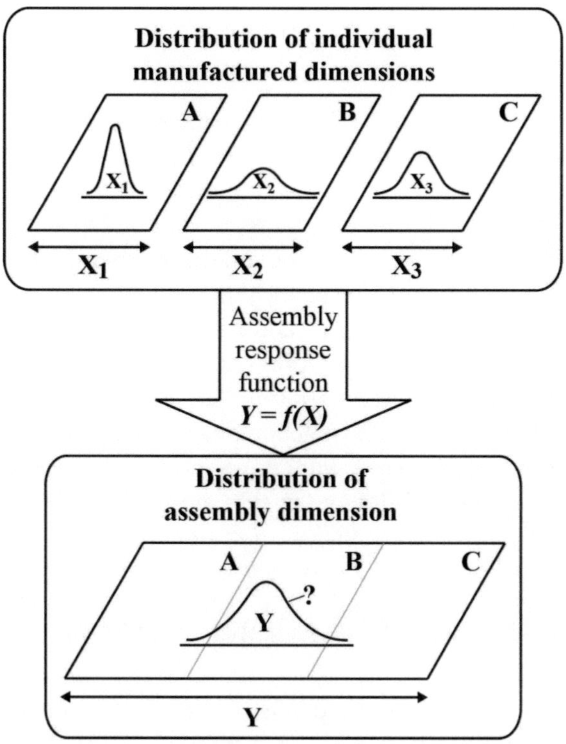

Figure 1. Scheme of tolerance analysis for mechanical assemblies.

In the literature, the three main issues on tolerance analysis are to represent geometric deviations, geometric specifications, and geometric requirements by means of mathematical relationships, to model the effects of these geometric deviations on the assembly and the product working, and to solve these models by means of worst-case or statistical techniques

[9]. The worst-case model was first introduced by Fortini [10]. It considers all tolerances of the chain to assume simultaneously the extreme values, and therefore, it describes the worst assembly. The worst-case model has a mathematical nature, so it may be applied for low production volume and for short tolerance chain. Fortini [10] also introduced statistical models to perform tolerance stack-up functions. The most simple of the statistical models is the root sum square (RSS): it is a linear variation approach and it assumes Gaussian probability density function for each tolerance of the assembly. The RSS model is very optimistic: it is applied to high volume production and to long tolerance chains. Another statistical model is the Monte Carlo simulation: it is a nonlinear variation approach that was applied to tolerance analysis for the first time by Knappe [11]. Shan et al. [12] use a Monte Carlo approach to perform 3D statistical tolerance analysis. In the last decades, various models have been proposed for tolerance analysis, which can be divided into deviation accumulation methods that express the functional requirements in terms of geometric part deviations, and tolerance accumulation approaches that express the tolerance zones to analyze as subsets of multidimensional spaces [3]. For these two categories, several models exist in the literature: parametric tolerance analysis [13], simple tolerance stacks [8], solid offsets [14], vector loops [15], direct linearization method [16], small displacement torsor [17, 18], tolerance-maps® [19], deviation domains [20], and polytopes [21].

Furthermore, a considerable number of review papers highlighting the similarities and differences of the aforementioned approaches exist, such as [8, 13, 19, 22–25]. Most of the proposed tolerance analysis methods of the literature are not completely conformed to geometric product specification (GPS) standards and are not able to take into account the combination of 3D tolerance zones, the envelope and the independence principles, the material condition modifiers, and the datum precedence. Moreover, these methods are not able to handle point cloud representation of the variant parts. Computer-aided technologies (CAT) for tolerance analysis based on point cloud representation is highly desirable, since assembly and measurement tasks give point clouds as output. Therefore, to deal with point clouds allows to connect design, manufacturing, and inspection in a unique way. Recently, a new model for tolerance analysis, based on the representation of nonideal workpieces employing point clouds, has been presented, which is known as skin model [26, 27].

3. Computer-aided techniques for geometry assurance

Many are the computer-aided techniques (CATs) for tolerance analysis that allows to assure the geometry of the assembly product by analyzing the geometrical interferences. These tolerance analysis software packages are based on the approaches cited in the previous paragraph [8, 28], such as MECAMaster®, which is based on the SDT, 3DCS®, VSA®, and CeTol®, which use parametric approaches (CeTol® used vector loops in former versions), and PolitoCAT®, which employs polytopes. They efficiently deal with simple geometrical feature of mechanical assemblies, such as plane and hole-pin, while they hardly treat of sculptured surfaces to connect. Moreover, they are not completely true to the GPS standards. To use these tools, the user should understand the packages' theoretical base of modeling to build a valid model and to have accurate results.

Requirements	Computer-aided techniques for tolerance analysis		
	CeTol®	VSA®	3DCS®
Tolerancing scheme			
Dimensional tolerances	Yes	Yes	Yes
Geometric product specification (GPS)	Yes	Yes	Yes
Automatic utilization of CAD model, once defined GPS data	No	No	No
Tolerance analysis			
Worst-case approach	Yes	Yes	Yes
Statistical approach	Yes	Yes	Yes
Sensitivity analysis	Yes	Yes	Yes
Uncertainty qualification methods			
Monte Carlo	Yes	Yes	Yes
Simplifying assumptions			
Rigid body	Yes	Yes	Partial
Limit on variation size	No	No	No
Further considerations			
Compatible CAD tools	SolidWorks, Pro/E	CATIA, NX I-deas, Pro/E, NX	CATIA, Unigraphics, STEP, IGES
Distributed/parallel computing	No	No	No
Integration with external CAE modeling tools	No	No	No
Accommodation of assembly loads	No	No	Limited

Table 1. Comparison among computer-aided techniques for tolerance analysis.

A number of comparative review and survey works of computer-aided techniques for tolerance analysis were presented in the literature. Initial works focused on the limitations of the two-dimensional geometry capabilities of the contemporary systems [29]. Other review works focused on CATs for tolerance analysis developed from a research perspective [23]. A number of recent reviews offer a more detailed overview of the nature of contemporary commercial CATs for tolerance analysis [13, 28]. A particularly comprehensive review of some of the most popular CATs for tolerance analysis has noted a number of common capabilities as well as shortcomings [28]. Additional investigation carried out in association with this dissertation has identified changes in the CAT capabilities, since the previously published reviews. Furthermore, current limits associated with uncertainty quantification method capabilities and accommodations of assemblies under loading have been identified. **Table 1** summarizes the results of three CATs for tolerance analysis. **Table 1** shows how the CATs for tolerance analysis may adopt a "tolerance scheme" that models only dimensional tolerances, GPS, but they do not automatically extract tolerance information by model, even if it has been specified in Computer Aided Design (CAD) environment. Moreover, CATs for tolerance analysis may use different approaches for "tolerance analysis": worst-case and/or statistical one. They may carry out a sensitivity analysis to identify the tolerances mainly affecting assembly requirements. They may use Monte Carlo simulation, they are based on rigid body assumption, and they do not have any limits about size variation.

Despite the extensive capabilities of commercial CATs for tolerance analysis, some notable limits remain (see the last three lines of **Table 1**):

1. GPS data defined in the CAD model may not be automatically imported into the CAT due to the limits of the CAD geometry translator standards, such as Standard for The Exchange of Product model data (STEP) or Initial Graphics Exchange Specification (IGES);

2. none of the currently available tools offer distributed/parallel computing capabilities, which can offer reduced analysis times by distributing simulations over multiple computers;

3. lack of ability to accommodate general tolerance analysis and synthesis problems involving assemblies under loading. CAT tools have been identified that accommodate a limited subset of physical phenomena, such as deformation of sheet assemblies. However, in general, the abstracted geometric model employed in current CAT systems becomes incompatible when dealing with tolerance analysis and synthesis involving a general class of problem requiring the numeric simulation of assemblies under loading conducted on Computer Aided Engineering (CAE) models (such as FEA, CFD, or multi-body dynamics simulations).

This paper considers a typical CAT for tolerance analysis, called VSA® of Siemens; it involves a set of nine steps (see **Figure 2**):

1. Define CAD models for each part of the product assembly.

2. Import CAD model into CAT environment and interactively create tolerance modeling geometry superimposed on the original CAD data.

3. Specify tolerance types for features of interest on each part in the assembly.

4. Define part relationships that constitute the assembly, such as assembly sequence and mating conditions.

5. Specify Key Product Characteristics (KPC), e.g., assembly clearances, which must be satisfied in order to fulfill design requirements.

6. Simulate the effect of part tolerances on Key Product Characteristics using a stochastic or worst-case tolerance analysis approach.

7. Record outcomes such as yield and associated tolerance cost.

8. Possible sensitivity analysis to determine the most influential part tolerances contributing to variation in assembly Key Product Characteristic.

9. Subsequently, based on analysis outcomes and CAT tool capabilities, reallocate part feature tolerances to target the total allowable variation in Key Product Characteristics. The allocation may be achieved manually, or automated through tolerance synthesis aimed at maximizing yield and/or minimizing tolerance cost.

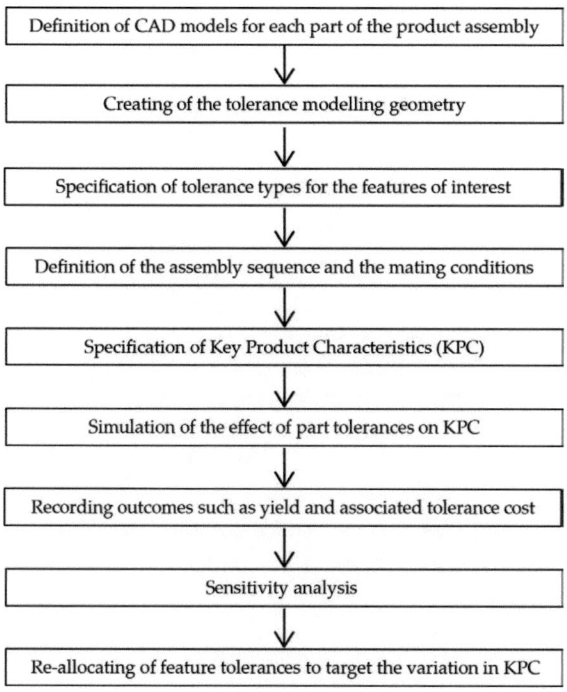

Figure 2. Flow chart of a computer-aided technique for tolerance analysis.

The present work gives the application of the VSA® software to four case studies from the literature. The four case studies have been chosen since they were used in the literature to apply five important approaches for tolerance analysis: the tolerance charting, the Jacobian model, the vector loop model, the proprietary software, and the skin model. The results due to the application of the VSA® software have been compared with those of the literature for each case study, as deeply described in the following.

4. Case study 1: R-A assembly

The first case study is the R-A assembly (see **Figure 3**); it consists of two nominally parallel shafts (Item 3) mounted into a housing (Item 1). During assembly, the bushings (Item 2) have a slight interference fit with the holes of the housing and a small amount of clearance with the shafts in order to allow the shafts to rotate. Retaining rings (Item 4) do not slide the shaft out of the housing along the axial direction. This assembly is simple, but it represents many common products in industry, such as blowers, gear boxes, and pumps.

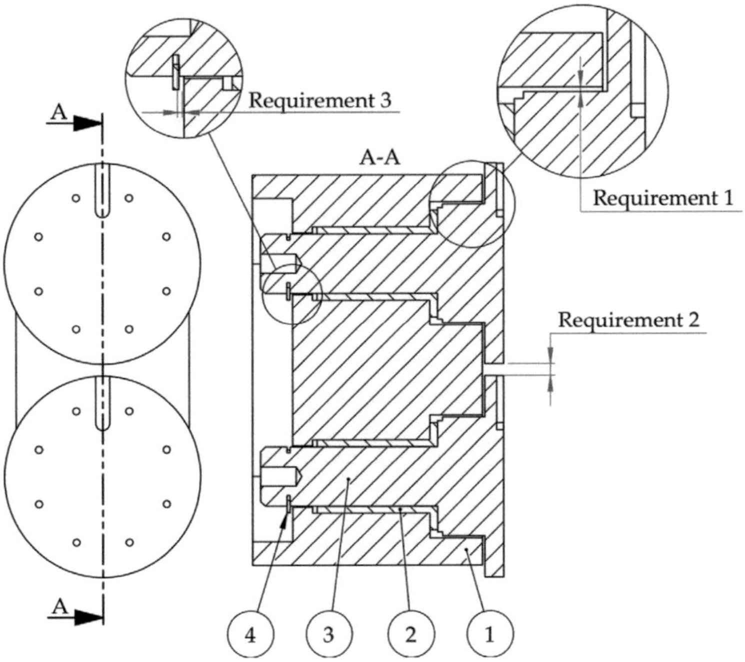

Figure 3. First case study: R-A assembly.

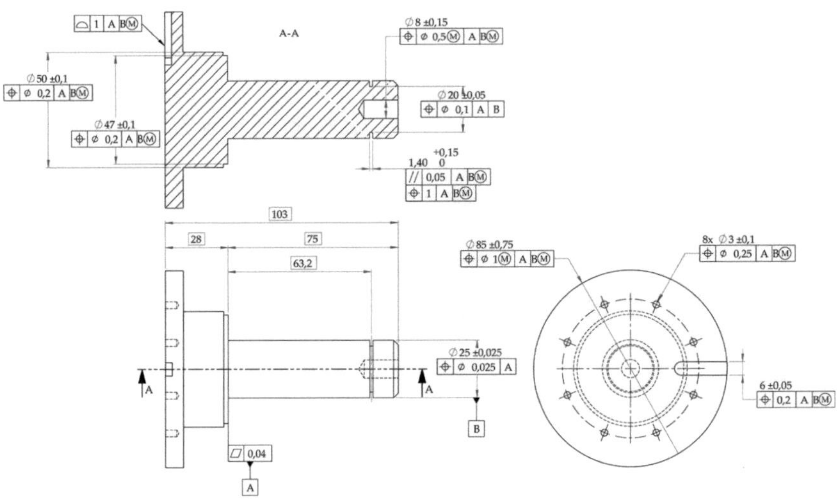

Figure 4. R-A assembly: shaft drawing.

http://dx.doi.org/10.5772/65474

Drawings for the shaft, bushing, and housing are shown in **Figures 4–6**. These parts are dimensioned and toleranced using GPS, and the GPS scheme reflects the functional requirements of the parts and the assembly. Three tolerance stack-ups are included in the following material: two radial tolerance stack-ups and one axial tolerance stack-up.

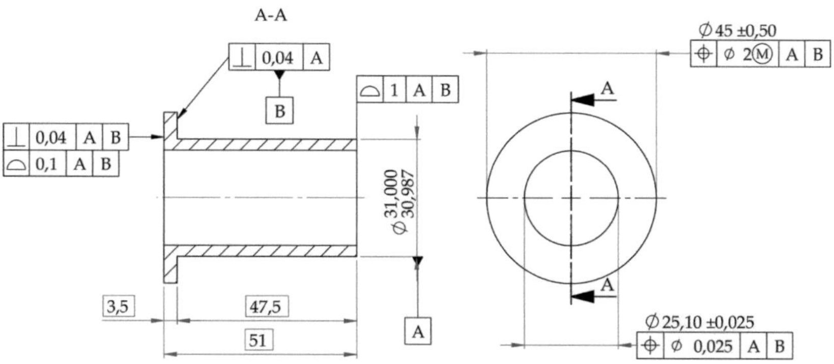

Figure 5. R-A assembly: bushing drawing.

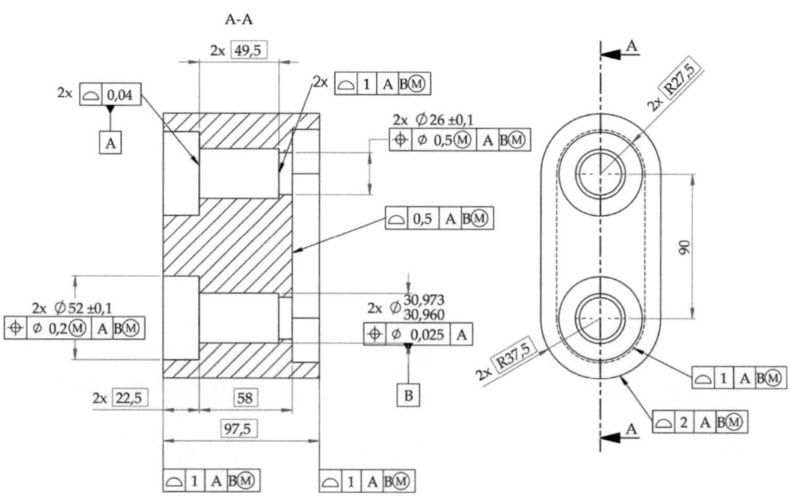

Figure 6. R-A assembly: housing drawing.

It is assumed that the inside diameter (ID) of the bushing does not deform when its outside diameter (OD) is pressed into the housing. The ID of the bushings continues to satisfy the dimension and the tolerance specifications shown in **Figure 5**. This is possible by machining the ID of the bushings to their stated diameter and tolerance after installation. The functional requirements to check are shown in **Figure 3**.

The tolerance charting approach has been applied to this case study in Ref. [30] by using a root sum squared method without or with a multiplier factor. The VSA® software of Siemens has been used in this work. The results are shown in **Table 2**. It can be observed that the results due to VSA software stay always between those due to the two tolerance charting methods.

Approach		[mm]	Requirement 1	Requirement 2	Requirement 3
Tolerance charting [30]	RSS	μ	1.00	5.00	0.96
		σ	0.07	0.30	0.19
	RSSx multiplier	μ	1.00	5.00	0.96
		σ	0.10	0.45	0.28
VSA® software		μ	1.01	5.02	1.09
		σ	0.07	0.41	0.23
Differences	(VSA®-tolerance charting)/tolerance charting	$\Delta\mu$	+1.14%	+0.41%	+13.72%
		$\Delta\sigma$	+7.64 ÷ −28.25%	+37.90 ÷ −8.07%	+18.82 ÷ −20.78%

Table 2. Results of the first case study.

5. Case study 2: an assembly of three blocks

The second case study is an assembly that contains three parts. The functional requirement is the gap shown on the leftmost side of the assembly (see **Figure 7**). Two analytical approaches that are the Jacobian and the vector loop have been applied to this case study in Ref. [31], and the obtained results are given in the first two lines of **Table 3**.

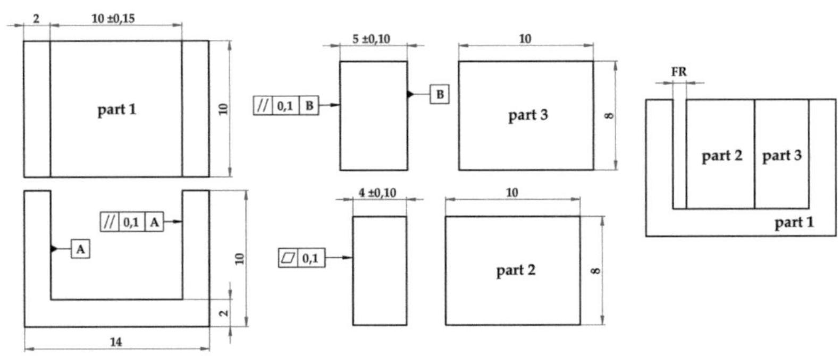

Figure 7. Second case study.

The application of the VSA® software to the case study is required to calculate five measurement operations, as shown in **Figure 8**, to obtain the functional requirement that is the distance between Blocks 1 and 2, once assembled. The results about the mean and the standard deviation of the five measurements are shown in **Table 4**; then, the mean values of the means and the standard deviations have been calculated and reported in the last line of **Table 4** and in the third line of **Table 3**. It can be observed that the values due to VSA® software are lower than those due to the two analytical models. However, some interesting considerations may be made by comparing the values due to the dimensional tolerances only with those due to the dimensional and the geometrical tolerances together. The two analytical approaches give a value of the standard deviation that increases when the geometrical tolerances are applied together with the dimensional ones, whereas it should decrease, since some further constraints are added to the part. This is probably due to the fact that the two analytical approaches add the contribution of geometrical tolerances to that of dimensional tolerances. VSA® software instead gives the same result with and without the geometrical tolerance, and this is probably due to the fact that it is not able to deal with the form tolerances applied to the planes of the components.

Approaches	[mm]	Dimensional tolerances	Dimensional and geometric tolerances
Jacobian [31]	μ	1	1
	σ	0.069	0.073
Vector loop [31]	μ	1	1
	σ	0.069	0.075
VSA® software	μ	0.891	0.956
	σ	0.066	0.060
(VSA®-Jacobian)/Jacobian	$\Delta\mu$	−10.85%	−4.45%
	$\Delta\sigma$	−4.13%	−16.83%
(VSA®-vector loop)/vector loop	$\Delta\mu$	−10.85%	−4.45%
	$\Delta\sigma$	−4.13%	−18.94%

Table 3. Results of the second case study.

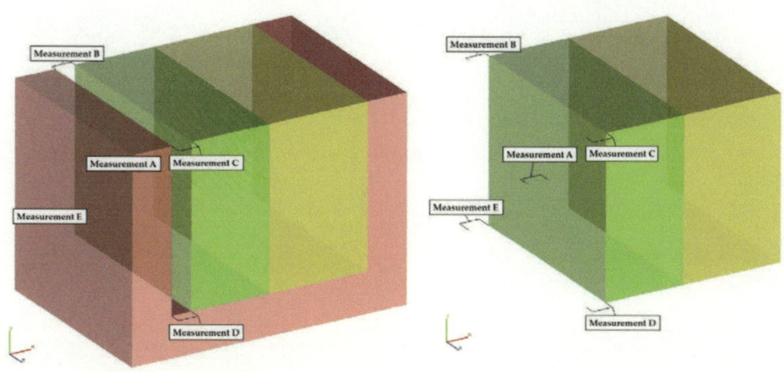

Figure 8. Measurements required by VSA® software.

Measurements	Dimensional tolerances		Dimensional and geometric tolerances	
	μ [mm]	σ [mm]	μ [mm]	σ [mm]
A	0.891	0.050	0.956	0.053
B	0.886	0.066	0.953	0.061
C	0.898	0.073	0.958	0.064
D	0.898	0.074	0.958	0.064
E	0.885	0.067	0.953	0.062
Mean value	0.891	0.066	0.956	0.060

Table 4. Results of measurements of VSA software.

6. Case study 3: three-part assembly

The third case study is a three-part assembly, as shown in **Figures 9** and **10**. The aim is to analyze the minimum distance "D_f" and the angle "A_f", between the pin of the part C and the hole of the part A. Mate conditions have been established between part A and part B ("mate1," "mate2," and "mate3"). The pin/hole joint has been modeled through a contact constraint ("contact1")—no penetration allowed. Moreover, a "minimum distance" contact constraint ("contact2") has also been defined to assure part C and part B was close as much as possible to each other. Tolerances were defined for each part according to **Figure 9**. Each tolerance has been modeled with a statistical normal distribution (natural tolerance range = 6). Monte Carlo method has been used to generate random variational features (number of simulation = 1000). The following assembly sequence has been assigned: mate1 + mate2 + mate3 + mate4 + contact1 + contact2. The Monte Carlo simulation has been carried out by means of a proprietary

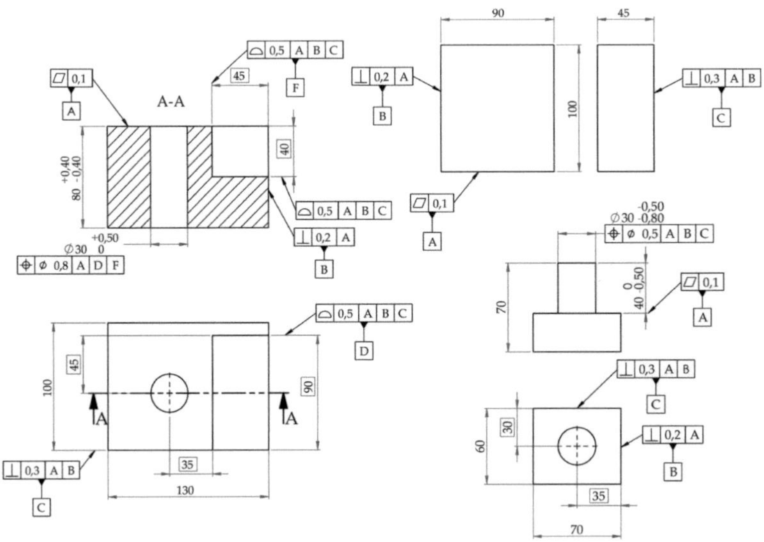

Figure 9. Tolerance specification of the third case study.

software presented in Ref. [32] in the literature, and the obtained results are reported in the first two lines of **Table 5**, respectively, for the two functional requirements. As expected, the minimum value of the functional requirement is right zero (see **Table 5**), since assembly features cannot penetrate each other. Moreover, the maximum value is about 0.7 mm, which is lower than the maximum radial gap (1.3 mm) between pin and hole features.

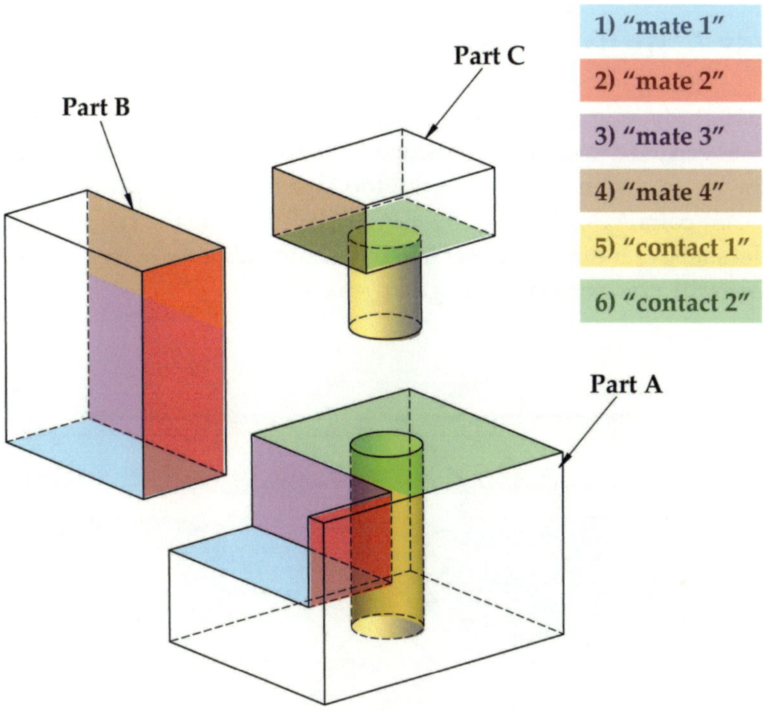

Figure 10. Assembly features of the components belonging to the third case study.

Approaches	Values	A_f [°]	D_f [mm]
Proprietary software [32]	μ	179.36	0.35
	σ	0.41	0.16
	Max	179.99	0.77
	Min	177.91	0.00
VSA® software	μ	179.99	0.41
	σ	0.32	0.13
	Max	180.94	1.06
	Min	179.04	0.06
(VSA®-proprietary software)/proprietary software	$\Delta\mu$	+0.35%	+17.14%
	$\Delta\sigma$	−21.95%	−18.75%

Table 5. Results of the third case study.

The VSA® software has been applied to the case study by using the same assembly sequence and the same normal distribution of the applied tolerances. The obtained results are shown in the last two lines of **Table 5**. The proprietary and the commercial software packages give different results for the two functional requirements. This is probably due to the different ways the two software packages simulate the assembly constraints.

7. Case study 4: two flat plates and a cube

The fourth case study is an assembly comprising two flat plates and a cube, as shown in **Figure 11**. It has been used to illustrate the skin model shapes approach in Ref. [27]. It is needed to evaluate the seven distances between the top and the bottom plates and the tilt angles between the point pairs AC-A′C′ (α) and AE-A′E′ (β). These are the key characteristics (KCs). The skin model shape of the cube is generated by a Gaussian probability density function with $\mu = 0.00$ mm, $\sigma = 0.01$ mm, correlation length: $\rho = 5.00$ mm.

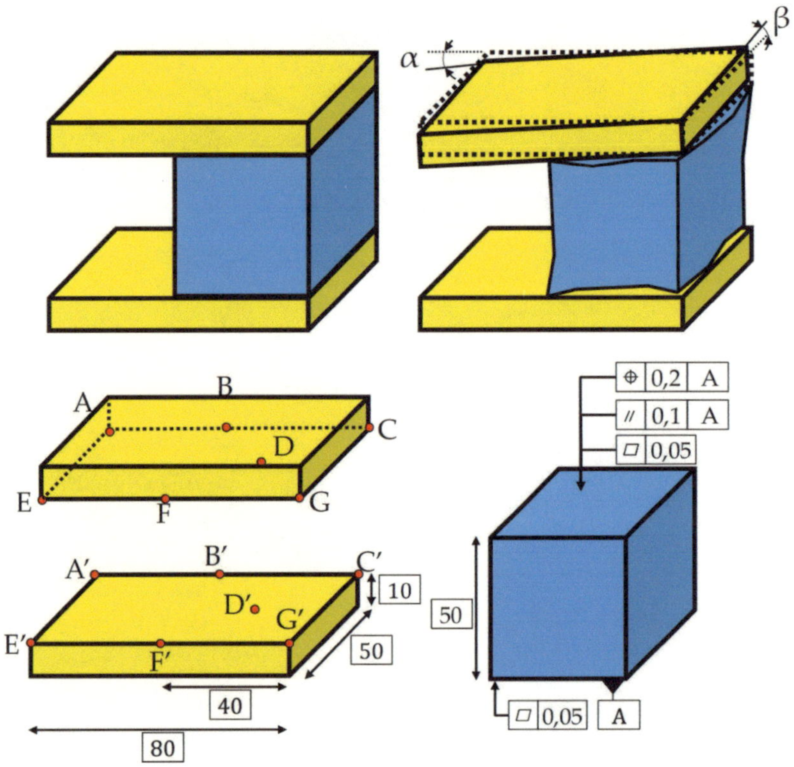

Figure 11. Fourth case study.

The KCs results of the example for 1000 skin model shapes are given in the first two lines of **Table 6**.

Approach	[mm]	AA′	BB′	CC′	GG′	FF′	EE′	DD′	α	β
Skin model [27]	μ	0.21	0.13	0.15	0.10	0.21	0.14	0.15	2.4	1.7
	σ	0.046	0.032	0.035	0.030	0.048	0.033	0.035	0.60	0.40
VSA® software	μ	0.25	0.19	0.18	0.19	0.18	0.23	0.16	3.5	2.9
	σ	0.041	0.031	0.030	0.032	0.030	0.039	0.027	0.50	0.40
(VSA®-skin model)/skin model	$\Delta\mu$	+17%	+42%	+19%	+90%	−13%	+67%	+9%	+45%	+68%
	$\Delta\sigma$	−11%	-4%	−15%	+5%	-37%	+18%	−22%	-23%	+9%

Table 6. Results of the fourth case study.

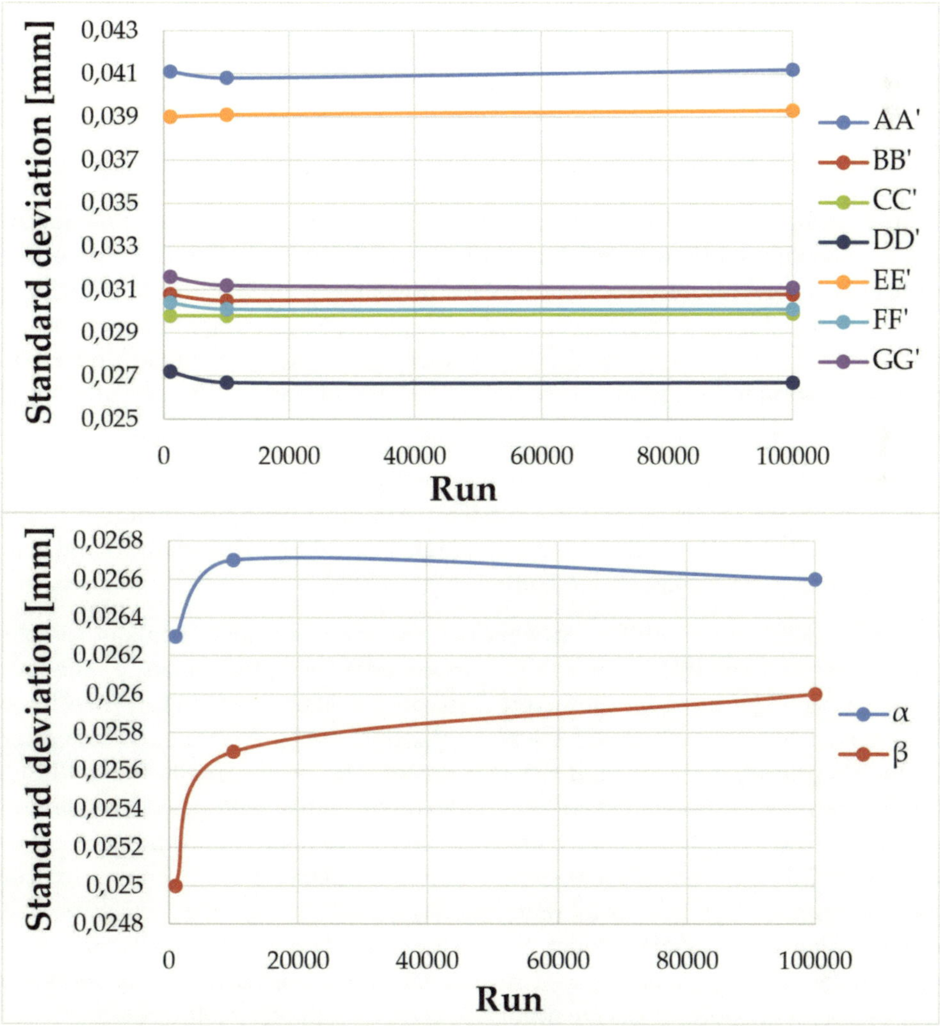

Figure 12. Deviation standard of the KPC refers to the number of simulation runs.

The case study has been solved by the VSA® software of Siemens, and the results obtained by a Monte Carlo simulation with 1000 runs are reported in the second two lines of **Table 6**. To evaluate the stability of the results further Monte Carlo simulations have been performed by varying the number of runs up to 100,000 runs, and the results are shown in **Figure 12**. It is evident that the standard deviation remains the same with the increase in the number of the simulation runs.

The results due to VSA® software are very different from those due to the skin model. The difference between the two approaches is the largest among all the four case studies. This difference is due to the simulation of the form tolerances. VSA® considers only the roto-translation of the nominal feature to which a form tolerance is applied, while the skin model considers each feature as a set of control points whose movement depends on the applied form tolerance. Moreover, the point of a plane is considered geometrically correlated. It is evident that the skin model represents the form deviations in agreement with reality.

8. Results discussion and conclusions

Many are the computer-aided techniques for tolerance analysis. These software packages allow to assure the geometry of the assembly product by analyzing the geometrical interferences. They efficiently deal with simple geometrical feature of mechanical assemblies, such as plane and hole-pin, while they hardly treat of sculptured surfaces to connect. Moreover, they are not completely true to the GPS standards. To use these tools, the user should understand the packages' theoretical base of modeling to build a valid model and to have accurate results.

This work underlines that GPS data, defined in the CAD model, may not be automatically imported into the CATs due to the limits of the CAD geometry translator standards, such as STEP or IGES. None of the currently available CATs offer distributed/parallel computing capabilities, and they lack of ability to accommodate general tolerance analysis and synthesis problems involving assemblies under loading.

The present work shows the application of one of these computer-aided technique for tolerance analysis, knows as VSA® by Siemens, to four case studies from the literature. The four case studies have been chosen since they were used in the literature to apply five important approaches for tolerance analysis: the tolerance charting, the Jacobian model, the vector loop model, the proprietary software, and the skin model. The results due to the application of the VSA® software are different from those due to all of the five methods of the literature for many reasons. The CATs for tolerance analysis have a 3D nature, and they are not able to consider 1D or 2D case studies. They are not able to simulate a form tolerance according to international standard for GPS, or more tolerances applied to the same surface, or assembly constraints refer to actual assembly operations. This paper demonstrates how computer-aided technologies for tolerance analysis need further knowledge of the assembly problems and further development. More efforts are needed to clarify the limits and the potentialities of the computer-aided technologies for tolerance analysis in order to better define their domain of applicability.

Acknowledgements

This research received no specific grant from any funding agency.

Author details

Andrea Corrado* and Wilma Polini

*Address all correspondence to: a.corrado@unicas.it

Department of Civil and Mechanical Engineering, University of Cassino and Southern Lazio, Cassino, Italy

References

[1] Söderberg R, Lindkvist L, Wärmefjord K, Carlson JS. Virtual geometry assurance process and toolbox. Procedia CIRP. 2016;*43*:3–12. doi:10.1016/j.procir.2016.02.043

[2] Ebro M, Olesen J, Howard TJ. Robust Design Impact Metrics: measuring the effect of implementing and using Robust Design. In: Proceedings of the 1st International Symposium on Robust Design (ISoRD14); 14–15 August 2014; Copenhagen. Denmark. 2014. p. 1–9.

[3] Dantan JY, Qureshi AJ. Worst-case and statistical tolerance analysis based on quantified constraint satisfaction problems and Monte Carlo simulatio. Comput-Aided Des. 2009;*41*(1):1–12. doi:10.1016/j.cad.2008.11.003

[4] Söderberg R, Lindkvist L, Dahlström S. Computer-aided robustness analysis for compliant assemblies. J Eng Des. 2006;*17*(5):411–428. doi:10.1080/09544820500275800

[5] Bjorke O, editor. Computer aided tolerancing. 2nd ed. New York, NY: ASME Press; 1989. p. 216

[6] Srinivasan V. Computational metrology for the design and manufacture of product geometry: a classification and synthesis. J Comput Inf Sci Eng. 2006;*7*(1):3–9. doi: 10.1115/1.2424246

[7] Weill R, Clément A, Hocken R, Farmer L, Gladman C, Wirtz A, et al. Tolerancing for function. CIRP Ann. 1988;*37*(2):603–610. doi:10.1016/S0007-8506(07)60757-4

[8] Shen Z, Ameta G, Shah JJ, Davidson JK. A comparative study of tolerance analysis methods. J Comput Inf Sci Eng. 2005;*5*(3):247–256. doi:10.1115/1.1979509

[9] Dantan JY, Gayton N, Dumas A, Etienne A, Qureshi AJ. Mathematical issues in mechanical tolerance analysis. In: Proceedings of the 13th Colloque National AIP PRIMECA; 2012.

[10] Fortini E.. Dimensioning for Interchangeable Manufacture. New York: Industrial Press; 1967. 276 p

[11] Knappe L.F.. A technique for analyzing mechanism tolerances. Mach Des. 1963;25:155–157.

[12] Shan A, Roth NR, Wilson JR. A new approach to statistical geometrical tolerance analysis. Int J Adv Manuf Tech. 1999;*15*:222–230. doi:10.1007/s001700050060

[13] Shah JJ, Ameta G, Shen Z, Davidson J. Navigating the tolerance analysis maze. Comput-Aided Des Appl. 2007;*4*(5):705–718. doi:10.1080/16864360.2007.10738504

[14] Requicha AAG. Toward a theory of geometric tolerancing. Int J Robot Res. 1983;*2*(4): 45–60. doi:10.1177/027836498300200403

[15] Gao J, Chase KW, Magleby SP. Generaized 3-D tolerance analysis of mechanical assemblies with small kinematic adjustments. IIE Trans. 1998;*30*(4):367–377. doi: 10.1023/A:1007451225222

[16] Wittwer JW, Chase KW, Howell LL. The direct linearization method applied to position error in kinematic linkage. Mech Mach Theory. 2004;*39*(7):681–693. doi:10.1016/ j.mechmachtheory.2004.01.001

[17] Bourdet P, Mathieu L, Lartigue C, Ballu A. The concept of the small displacement torsor in metrology. Ser Adv Math Appl Sci. 1996;40:110–122.

[18] Li H, Zhu H, Li P, He F. Tolerance analysis of mechanical assemblies based on small displacement torsor and deviation propagation theories. Int J Adv Manuf Technol. 2014;*72*(1–4):89–99. doi:10.1007/s00170-014-5630-0

[19] Ameta G, Serge S, Giordano M. Comparison of spatial math models for tolerance analysis: tolerance maps, deviation domain and TTRS. J Comput Inf Sci Eng. 2011;*11*(2): 021004. doi:10.1115/1.3593413

[20] Giordano M, Samper S, Petit J. Tolerance analysis and synthesis by means of deviation domains, axi-symmetric cases. In: Davidson J, editor. Models for Computer Aided Tolerancing in Design and Manufacturing. Netherlands: Springer; 2007. p. 85–94

[21] Homri L, Teissandier D, Ballu A. Tolerance analysis by polytopes: taking into account degrees of freedom with cap half-spaces. Comput-Aided Des. 2015;*62*:112–130. doi: 10.1016/j.cad.2014.11.005

[22] Farmer L, Gladman C. Tolerance technology—computer-based analysis. CIRP Ann. 1986;*35*(1):7–10. doi:10.1016/S0007-8506(07)61827-7

[23] Chase K, Parkison A. A survey of research in the application of tolerance analysis to the design of mechanical assemblies. Res Eng Des. 1991;*3*(1):23–37. doi:10.1007/BF01580066

[24] Nigam SD, Turner JU. Review of statistical approaches to tolerance analysis. Comput-Aided Des. 1995;*27*(1):6–15. doi: 10.1016/0010-4485(95)90748-5

[25] Polini W. Taxonomy of models for tolerance analysis in assembling. Int J Prod Res. 2012;*50*(7):2014–2029. doi:10.1080/00207543.2011.576275

[26] Schleich B, Anwer N, Mathieu L, Wartzack S. Skin model shapes: a new paradigm shift for geometric variations modelling in mechanical engineering. Comput-Aided Des. 2014;*50*:1–15. doi:10.1016/j.cad.2014.01.001

[27] Anwer N, Schleich B, Mathieu L, Wartzack S. From solid modelling to skin model shapes: shifting paradigms in computer-aided tolerancing. CIRP Ann. 2014;*63*(1):137–140. doi:10.1016/j.cirp.2014.03.103

[28] Prisco U, Giorleo G. Overview of current cat systems. Integr Comput-Aid Eng. 2002;*9*:373–387.

[29] Turner JU, Gangoiti A. Tolerance analysis approaches in commercial software. Concurr Eng. 1991;*1*:11–23.

[30] Fischer B.R.. Mechanical tolerance stackup and analysis. 2nd ed. Boca Raton: CRC Press; 2011. 508 p.

[31] Bo C, Yang Z, Wang L, Chen H. A comparison of tolerance analysis models for assembly. Int J Adv Manuf Technol. 2013;*68*:739–754. doi:10.1007/s00170-013-4795-2

[32] Franciosa P, Gerbino S, Patalano S. A sequential constraint solver to simulate assembling operations for tolerance analysis. Procedia CIRP. 2013;*10*:169–177. doi:10.1016/j.procir.2013.08.028

Section 3

Computer-Aided Technologies in Medicine

Chapter 5

Computer-Aided Clinical Decision Support Systems for Atrial Fibrillation

Prasanth Ganesan, Mark Sterling,
Steven Ladavich and Behnaz Ghoraani

Additional information is available at the end of the chapter

http://dx.doi.org/10.5772/65620

Abstract

Clinical decision support systems (clinical DSSs) are widely used today for various clinical applications such as diagnosis, treatment, and recovery. Clinical DSS aims to enhance the end-to-end therapy management for the doctors, and also helps to provide improved experience for patients during each phase of the therapy. The goal of this chapter is to provide an insight into the clinical DSS associated with the highly prevalent heart rhythm disorder, atrial fibrillation (AF). The use of clinical DSS in AF management is ubiquitous, starting from detection of AF through sophisticated electrophysiology treatment procedures, all the way to monitoring the patient's health during follow-ups. Most of the software associated with AF DSS are developed based on signal processing, image processing, and artificial intelligence techniques. The chapter begins with a brief description of DSS in general and then introduces DSS that are used for various clinical applications. The chapter continues with a background on AF and some relevant mechanisms. Finally, a couple of clinical DSS used today in regard with AF are discussed, along with some proposed methods for potential implementation of clinical DSS for detection of AF, prediction of an AF treatment outcome, and localization of AF targets during a treatment procedure.

Keywords: clinical decision support systems, atrial fibrillation, cardiac signal processing, machine learning, Bayesian filtering

1. Introduction

Decision support systems (DSSs) are computer systems that assist in making logically and strategically appropriate decisions for complex tasks [1]. DSSs are used in a variety of applications such as making a financial decision, an administrative decision, a scientific, or even in making engineering-based decisions (e.g., process control in manufacturing and clinical diagnosis) [2–6]. Highly sophisticated DSSs that are being built today not only play the role of offering opinions to the users for them to make a decision, but they also learn from previous instances and from manually corrected mistakes aiming to offer better decisions in future. Research on DSS today is focused on improving their reliability so that they can perform major decision making without a human in the loop. Although DSS can solve very elementary problems, they are specifically used to solve complex semistructured and unstructured problems in a fully automated or a semiautomated fashion [7, 8].

Studies on the development of DSS gained attention in the 1960s and the first experimental study was reported by Ferguson and Jones in 1969 [7, 9]. There were many simultaneous advancements in the field of engineering, data analytics, and artificial intelligence (AI), which supported the enhancement of DSS. Several applications of DSS were developed during that period. A DSS was designed for business intelligence that used a business analytic model to provide advice to administrative authorities on critical planning decisions for the company [10]. A DSS was built for implementing a digital library to automatically search and fetch books and documents electronically from the library database based on manually entered query tags [11]. An engineering-based DSS would be any expert system used for solving complex mathematical problems, for example, symbolic automatic integrator commonly called SAINT was such an expert system that was developed in the beginning of the era of practical AIs. It was used to perform symbolic mathematical integrations using heuristic methods [12]. A DSS called Brandaid was developed in 1975 to solve problems in the field of marketing, which includes decisions on advertising and promotion [13]. Later, different innovative methodologies were put to use to develop the DSS; this led to different categories of them based on the methods/tasks that the DSS performs [14].

The modern-day DSS employ complex algorithms with highly interactive graphical user interfaces, thus increasing the flexibility of use. Today, for major industrial applications, a combination of all the types of DSS is also incorporated. The technology to help improve DSS is highly evolving, such as better communication protocols, wireless and mobile devices, improved operating systems for smart phones that supports powerful software applications, efficient and fast signal and image processing algorithms, improved machine learning, and artificial intelligence techniques. More improvements are underway in the future with more reliable algorithms in order to increase the robustness of the DSS with the aim of getting their abilities as close to human-made decisions [15].

1.1. Clinical decision support systems

A DSS that supports decision-making tasks related to medical and healthcare benefits is a clinical decision support system (clinical DSS) [16–18]. A considerable part of clinical DSS is a knowledge-driven DSS [8] that has the ability to understand clinical problems and provide reliable suggestions and directions to physicians and patients. The medical tasks requiring the assistance of a clinical DSS can be a simple patient database management using a data-driven DSS [8], to as complex as, making real-time decisions while performing a surgery using a knowledge-driven DSS. Clinical DSS is primarily employed only to enhance decision

http://dx.doi.org/10.5772/65620

making in the clinical routine, and not to give the machine the authority of a clinician. A common clinical DSS widely used today is a computer-aided diagnosis system, which assists the doctors in making the diagnosis for a patient [19, 20]. Physicians and other medical practitioners make critical decisions generally based on their knowledge and medical expertise, but with the implementation of clinical DSS they get suggestions that are more logical, which can thus be considered as an additional opinion to their personal ones. Some important advantages of clinical DSS are that it provides increase in quality of service to the patients, it helps in avoiding human errors during the process of diagnosis or treatment, and it improves efficacy of treatment procedures. It is believed that clinical DSS has the potential to improve health care although evaluation of clinical DSS has shown only equivocal results. A review of the clinical DSS in the context of evaluation can be found in the article by Kaplan and group [21].

A well-known project of clinical DSS was developed in the early 1970s at Stanford University called the MYCIN [4]. It was an expert system developed mainly to support the treatment of blood diseases and bacterial infections. It is a rule-based AI meaning that it was designed to work based on a set of rules that is defined in a grammar, and there is an action output defined for every input in the grammar. This way the system outputs the diagnosis of an infection, based on the given input set of patient symptoms. It also tries to perform additional diagnosis by suggesting relevant laboratory tests before arriving at a conclusion on the treatment procedure. In addition to diagnosis, MYCIN was designed to provide recommendations of antibiotics and other medications with the right dosage suitable for the patient. This clinical DSS used about 500 rules in order to process its decision, which is said to be most of the times acceptable compared to the decisions made by medical experts.

A number of clinical DSSs exist in the field of medical imaging [22, 23]. Medical imaging is a key tool to diagnosis of most of the diseases today. The method of imaging may be of a wide variety, such as magnetic resonance imaging (MRI), computerized axial tomography (CAT), and ultrasound imaging. Each of these image output has distinct characteristics, and hence its respective purpose of diagnosis. For example, the characteristic of a CAT technique is that it enhances the soft tissues and is hence used to examine diseases related to soft organs such as a liver tumor. Most of the imaging tools and concomitant software available fall under computer-aided diagnosis. A computer-aided diagnosis system can still be considered as a clinical DSS since they assist in decision making for the radiologists and other clinicians. A fully automated computer-aided diagnosis can be created but cannot be completely relied upon unless they have high accuracy (i.e., high sensitivity and specificity). The computer systems used in acquisition of these images itself are a component of a clinical DSS. An image diagnosis system that performs automatic analysis of a medical image or a series of images to detect abnormalities specific to a disease through image processing techniques is an automated computer-aided diagnosis; developing algorithms for this operation is a critical area of research. There are several systems today for automatic detection of lesion sites in a CAT image for mammary cancer and lung cancer [24]. Apart from the above-mentioned systems, there are various clinical DSS algorithms that are being developed today for different purposes and applications [24–27].

This chapter is devoted to introducing clinical DSS specific to the systems used in the field of cardiac electrophysiology (EP) to treat a condition called atrial fibrillation (AF). AF is a highly prevalent heart rhythm disorder affecting over 2.7 million people in USA annually [28] and over 30 million people worldwide [29]. It also increases the risk of stroke [28], and hence is a serious health concern leading to frequent hospitalizations and deaths. AF is basically caused due to disorganization of the electrical signals in the atria. There are several mechanisms associated with AF, and based on one or more of these mechanisms there are various treatment methods to control AF. Some of these treatment methods are discussed later in this chapter.

Intelligent computer systems are used throughout the process of assisting AF patients. In general, there are three major tasks involved in AF therapy: diagnosis of AF, treatment of AF, and monitoring/follow-up. Each of these tasks is assisted by sophisticated clinical DSS in order to ease the respective process and also to prevent overlooking of any important issues. Most of the algorithms used for EP procedures are mostly signal processing based, i.e., the electrical signals from the heart (see Section 2.1) are analyzed to extract information and derive inferences. These algorithms are designed to address the challenges in the management of AF therapy such as detection of AF episodes, prediction of a treatment outcome, and localization of AF targets during catheter ablation procedure. This chapter hence focuses on the clinical decision support technologies that are available today for AF management and some proposed algorithms for potential clinical DSS implementations. A background on atrial fibrillation and some relevant concepts are discussed in Section 2, followed by a discussion of some of the developed algorithms.

2. Background

The heart forms the major part of the circulatory system in the human body. It is essentially a blood pump that regulates oxygenated and deoxygenated blood. The upper chambers of the heart, the atria, and the lower chambers, the ventricles, both contract following a particular rhythm of synchrony. Such a healthy contraction rhythm is called a normal sinus rhythm (NSR). Any anomaly in this rhythm leads to a cardiac arrhythmia and AF is one of the common types. This section presents an introduction to the mechanisms behind the heart's function, an introduction to cardiac arrhythmia and AF, and finally some treatment options available for AF.

2.1. Electrical system of the heart

The contraction of the heart chambers are essentially triggered by electrical signals propagating along the myocardium [30]. As shown in **Figure 1**, a location called the sinoatrial node (SA node) is present in the right atrium and it produces the necessary stimulus for the cardiac cells to get activated. The cardiac cells possess the characteristic of producing action potentials (APs, special type of voltage signals) due to ion exchange mechanisms, when sufficient external stimulus is applied to it. A phase of this AP where the transmembrane potential (TMP) reaches its peak due to intracellular mechanisms in turn causes the cell to contract; this produces the myocardial contraction. The signals from the SA node propagate following the distinct NSR pathway to create the rhythmic contraction synchrony between the atria and the ventricles. The signals from the right atrium propagate to left atrium (LA) through intraatrial pathways called Bachmann's bundle. The signals exiting the atria are then delayed by the atrioventricular node (AV node) before passing into the ventricles. AV node is the only electrical junction of the atria and ventricles. The signals are then distributed across the ventricles through the Purkinje fibers. Hence, during an NSR, the signals take this specific pathway in an organized fashion, indicating a healthy cardiac rhythm. The TMP in a part of tissue collectively results in an electrogram (EGM) signal when measured using a voltage sensing electrode. The effect of the TMPs when measured using electrodes placed on the chest surface as opposed to those on the tissue itself produces surface electrocardiogram (ECG). More about these signals are discussed further.

2.1.1. Characteristics of ECG

A human ECG signal has a unique characteristic of what is called as PQRST complex that refers to the morphology of any ECG. The activations during NSR phase creates the PQRST complex shown in **Figure 2**. P, Q, R, S, T, are the labels given to specific activation peaks in ECG which are the P-wave, QRS complex, T-wave, and the less common U-wave [31]. The P-wave corresponds to the depolarization of the cells in the atria. The next part is the QRS complex and it represents the activations that cause the ventricles to contract. This is the most important part of the PQRST complex since it corresponds to systolic interval and is used for determining heart rate. Finally, the T-wave is said to occur due to the repolarization of the ventricles. Some theories suggest that the U-wave could also be due to repolarization of the

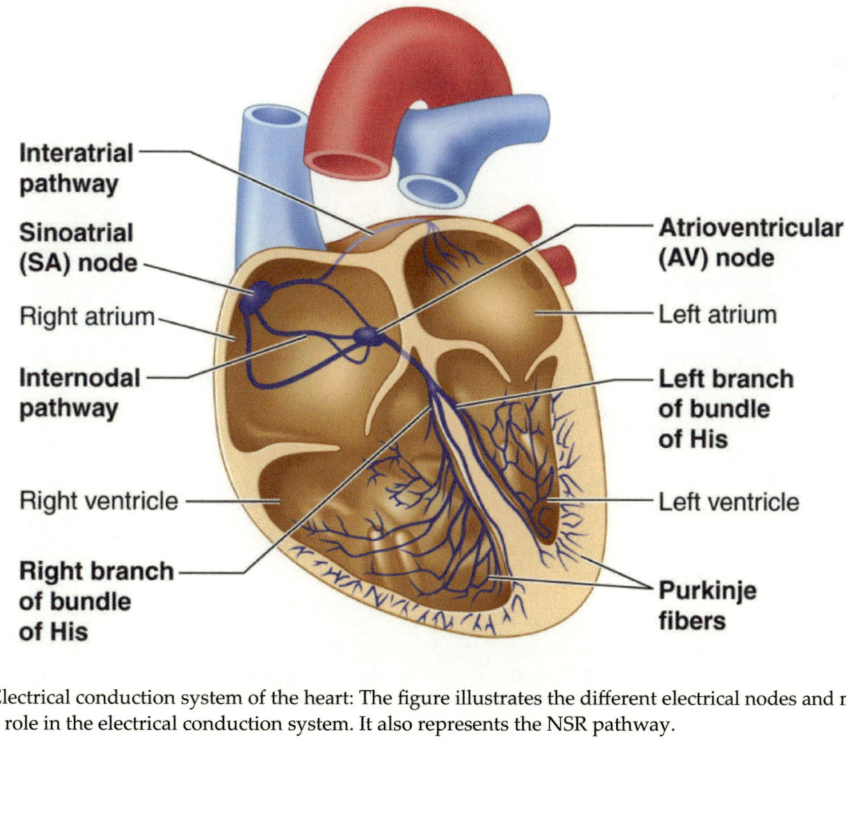

Figure 1. Electrical conduction system of the heart: The figure illustrates the different electrical nodes and muscle fibers that play a role in the electrical conduction system. It also represents the NSR pathway.

ventricles [32]. During NSR, the deflections of each wave starting from P-wave all the way to T-wave occur with the exact same signal polarities. As seen from **Figure 2**, the QRS complex has larger amplitude of deflection from the isoelectric line because of the larger mass of the ventricle cells that is getting depolarized.

Professionals trained in ECG interpretation would be able to detect even minor variations in the ECG signals. The idea of a clinical DSS here would be to assist such professionals by automatically interpreting the ECG. Any abnormality such as an arrhythmia or coronary heart disease can be detected using the ECG morphology. In case of AF, then the ECG demonstrates high heart rate along with absence of P-waves.

2.1.2. Intracardiac electrograms

Intracardiac electrograms (EGMs) are the signal obtained from locations of the myocardium. In general, they are recorded from the following regions using cardiac catheters: the high right atrium, coronary sinus, bundle of His, and the apex. The leads are placed at these locations and the outputs are arranged in such a way that a sequential activation is seen during NSR. This way the clinicians could easily confirm the pathway starting from SA node all the way to apex. EGMs, just like the ECGs, have its characteristic properties and can be used to determine abnormalities.

In general, there are two measurement configurations by which the EGMs can be represented, namely, the unipolar and the bipolar (refer **Figure 3**) [33]. Unipolar EGMs are those that are recorded using a single electrode catheter or the EGMs obtained from each electrode separately

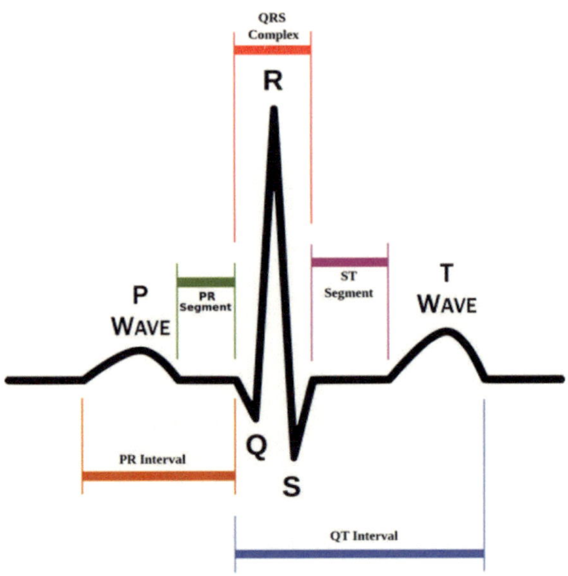

Figure 2. PQRST complex of surface ECG: This figure shows the general representation of the different complexes in a surface ECG. P-wave is due to atrial depolarization, QRS is due to ventricle depolarization and T-wave is associated with ventricular repolarization [34].

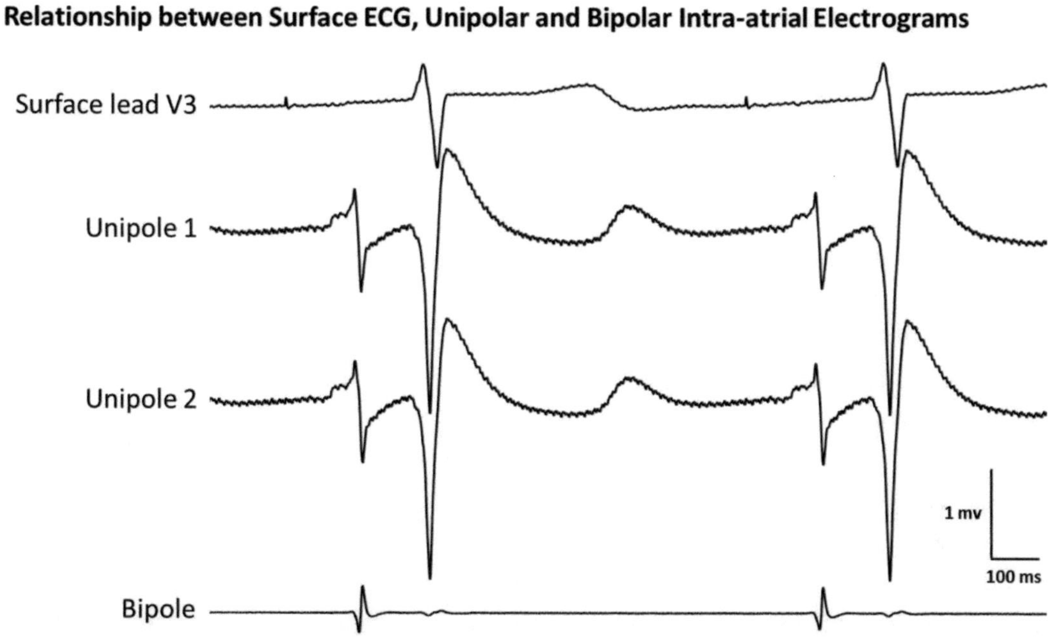

Figure 3. Relationship between different types of electrograms: The top-most plot is the surface lead which illustrates the QRS complex. The next two signals are two closely spaced unipoles; the far-field ventricular activations can be clearly seen in them. The last signal is the resultant bipole of the two unipoles in the figure. It can be clearly seen that the ventricular activations gets canceled giving rise to atrial activations alone. Also, the baseline noise present in unipoles is removed in the bipole signal.

from a multipole catheter. Bipolar EGMs are those that are obtained with respect to a nearby reference. The two types of EGMs have its own benefits and limitations [30]. Unipolar EGMs are very helpful in determining the wave direction using Einthoven's convention of positive and negative deflections [35], since it preserves the properties of the raw activation signals. It is also useful in determining conduction velocity and the signal amplitude. Bipolar EGMs do not preserve any of the information such as the wave direction because it is calculated with a reference and hence the signals might cancel out giving rise to a peak at an activation time different from unipolar and also might result in different deflection polarities. However, bipolar EGMs are an excellent means of removing noise and far-field effects which, in often case, are the most challenging criteria that hides the local activations present in an EGM. For example, the bipoles calculated in the LA will cancel out any activation that has occurred due to ventricular depolarization resulting in successful capture of the local atrial activations in the LA.

2.2. Cardiac arrhythmia and introduction to AF

Cardiac arrhythmia is a condition occurring when there is a perturbation in the NSR activity. The NSR pathway could go wrong in several ways resulting in several types of arrhythmias that are defined based on the abnormality mechanism [36]. Broadly speaking, the general types of arrhythmias are tachycardia and bradycardia. Tachycardia is the condition where the heart rate is higher than the normal, and bradycardia is its counterpart (lower heart rate).

Atrial tachycardia is a common arrhythmia which is caused by a rapidly periodically firing focus that could be located anywhere in the atrial myocardium. It is mostly treated by catheter ablation (see Section 2.3.4) and has a relatively high success rate of 90% after repeated procedures [37]. Another well-known atrial tachyarrhythmia and that that is also closely related to AF, is atrial flutter. Similar to AF, it results in a rapidly beating atria but it has its own mechanism causing it. The mechanism is said to be a single reentrant circuit mostly originating in the right atrium. With respect to the atrial arrhythmias, AF could be grouped as a tachyarrhythmia but the difference between AF and atrial tachycardia is that the rapid beating is not as regular as the tachycardia, in fact there is no beating at all–the atria during AF simply randomly quivers due to chaotic signals as shown in **Figure 4**.

Symptoms of AF include palpitations, unconformable flip-flopping in the chest, physical weakness, dizziness, shortness of breath, chest pain, and syncope. Some risks involved in AF in addition to stroke are, heart failure, high blood pressure, and lung disease. There are different types of AF categorized based on the duration of AF episodes. From a clinical standpoint, according to the established consensus [37], some of the types of AF are paroxysmal, persistent, and permanent AF. Paroxysmal AF is defined as recurrent AF (≥two episodes) that involves spontaneous termination within 7 days. Persistent AF is defined as continuously occurring episode that is sustained for more than 7 days. Finally, permanent AF, which is a rare condition, is when the physician and the patient together take the decision of not undergoing any procedures to control the AF, and so the patient permanently stays in AF.

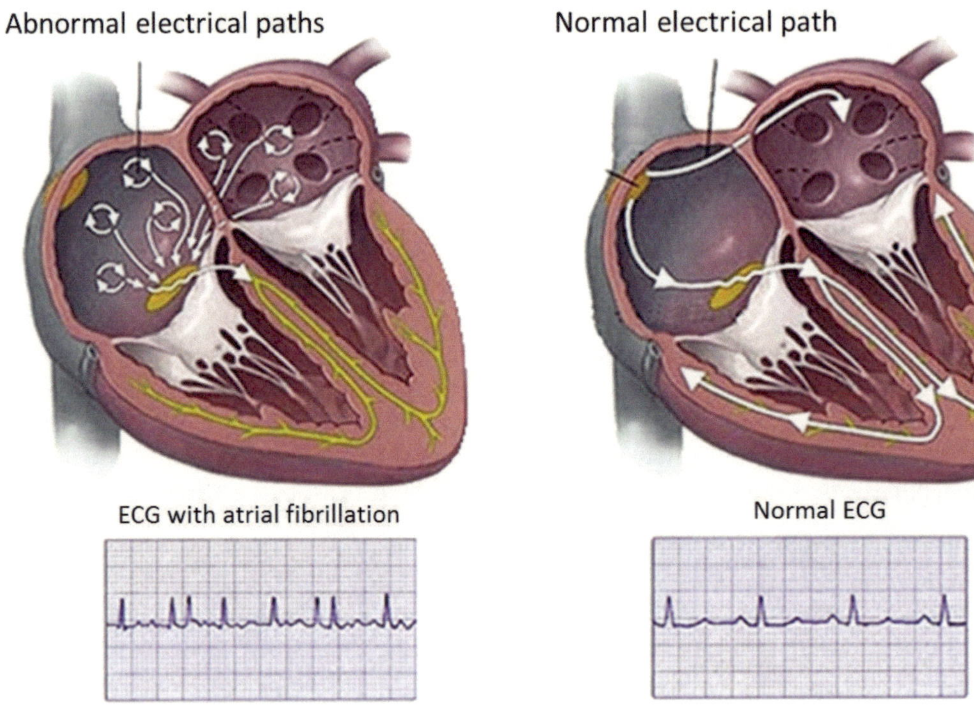

Figure 4. Atrial fibrillation vs normal sinus rhythm: The figure illustrates the disorganization of the signals in atria during AF (shown on the left), in contrast to the regular path of the signal during NSR (shown on the right).

http://dx.doi.org/10.5772/65620

2.3. Methods of AF treatment

The results of several scientific and clinical studies on AF have led to the development of many mechanistic and nonmechanistic approaches for treating AF. Every treatment procedure has its own benefits and limitations. So, the treatment method that gives the maximum patient outcome is what is followed widely. Each treatment also has its specific endpoint, however, the ultimate goal of any treatment is to successfully terminate AF and restore sinus rhythm. Some common treatment methods are discussed below.

2.3.1. *Pharmocological therapy*

The studies on different ionic mechanisms of the cardiac cells and how they are related to the arrhythmia (e.g., formation of AP alternans), have led to the development and synthesis of various rate-control and rhythm-control drugs. They directly interact with the ion channels, and control and regulate the exchanges in order to maintain a normal AP thus maintaining NSR. The antiarrhythmic drugs are categorized into various classes based on the behavior of the drug on different ion channels. Class-I drugs are related to sodium channels, e.g., quinidine. Class-II are effective beta blockers, e.g., propranolol. Class-III type interacts with potassium channels and prolongs the action potentials, e.g., sotalol, and Class-IV helps in regulating the calcium channels, e.g., diltiazem. Class-III is a commonly prescribed antiarrhythmic for the fact that it prolongs the AP, increases the refractory period, and so the AP cannot be fired instantly, thus preventing reentries. Some popular Class-III drugs are amiodarone and dofetilide. Unfortunately, the drugs may not be much effective as a standalone AF treatment especially for patients showing poor response [38], and it might also produce some side effects for the patients.

2.3.2. *Direct current electrical cardioversion*

Direct current electrical (DCE) cardioversion or simply cardioversion, is the procedure by which an electric voltage is applied to the chest at particular instants of the heart beat in order to reset the rhythm back to NSR [39]. The electric shock at a specific power is applied to the chest using electrode patches to the patient under anesthesia. The power is decided according to the intensity of AF. The shock is provided in such a way that it synchronizes with the R-wave of the PQRS complex, mainly because the atria would have passed the refractory period during R-wave, and the application of the current will excite the cells and start a fresh cardiac cycle. This treatment, most of the time terminates AF immediately, however, some patients experience AF episodes return after cardioversion. Hence, it is important for the clinician to make a reliable decision on whether or not the patient would benefit from DCE cardioversion therapy.

2.3.3. *Open-heart maze procedure*

The maze procedure is a surgical treatment by which lesions are created using incisions to various regions of the myocardium after opening up the chest. The treatment technique was introduced by James Cox in 1991 [40]. The lesion set resembles the structure of a maze, which gives it the name. The lesions basically are designed in such a way that the signals in the atrium do not form a reentry. The maze procedure has proved to be effective in terminating

AF; however, it is highly invasive and is normally provided for patients who undergo an open-heart surgery as part of their treatment for other types of heart complications.

2.3.4. *Catheter ablation therapy*

Catheter ablation therapy is a method by which ablation lesions are formed using radio frequency (RF) energy delivered via a catheter. The conventional catheter ablation procedure for AF today is the pulmonary vein isolation (PVI). In PVI, the lesions are formed around the PV ostia with the aim of electrically isolating the PVs from the rest of the left atrium. The PVI came into existence because of the pioneering discovery by Haissaguerre et al. that some ectopic triggers from the PVs enter the atrium and maintains AF [41] (illustrated in **Figure 5**). Some studies also suggest that these focal triggers could initiate non-PV AF drivers as shown in **Figure 5**. More about these non-PV drivers are discussed in Section 3. PVI showed remarkable increase in success rate of AF treatment and hence was adopted as the standard procedure by clinicians across the globe. There was also improvement over the traditional PVI that proposed only lesions around PV ostia. A strategy called the circumferential ablation was introduced which defined the lesions around the antrum of the PVs as opposed to the ostia [42]. In addition to circumferential ablation, a linear lesion set was proposed, which appeared to produce better outcome in clinical studies. Some of these non-PV lesions consisted of roof line, lines at mitral isthmus, and lines in between the PV pairs. PVI is mostly the primary strategy, and linear lesions are mostly preferred as a strategy in addition to PVI. However, what ablation to perform on top of PVI is disputable and is decided mostly based on the patient's individual atrial and AF properties.

Catheter ablation treatment combined with antiarrhythmic drug therapy is followed widely today. However, the treatment is not completely successful. Many patients experience recurrence of AF after the first procedure. Multiple repetitions of the procedure have to be performed especially for persistent AF patients, to control the recurrence. After a single pro-

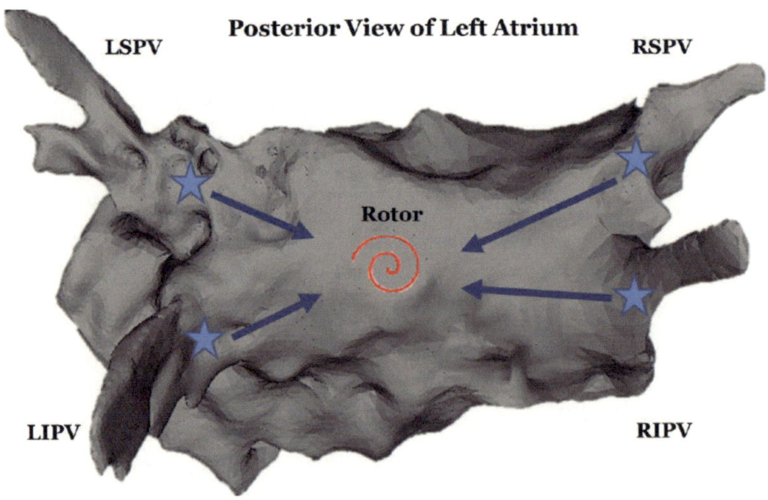

Figure 5. PV triggers initiating AF (posterior view): Figure illustrates the ectopic focal triggers originating from the PVs eventually initiating spiral waves in the LA wall, thus initiating and sustaining AF. LSPV: left superior pulmonary vein; RSPV: right superior pulmonary vein; LIPV: left inferior pulmonary vein; RIPV: right inferior pulmonary vein.

cedure, late recurrence of AF occurs between 11 and 29%, and after repeated procedures, it occurs between 7 and 24% [37]. A widely accepted reason for the recurrence is the reconnection of the PVs, however, there are also theories suggesting that the recurrence could be due to the arrhythmogenic sources (especially functional sources) existing outside the PVs, which are not addressed by the current catheter ablation procedure.

3. Computer-aided technologies for atrial fibrillation

The clinical DSS is largely used during an AF ablation procedure. In order to ablate different regions of the LA, it is necessary to have a visualization of both the atrium and the catheter's location. The fluoroscopy technique which produces a real-time image of the catheter and the atrial structures was used initially for visualization. However, fluoroscopy uses X-rays, and prolonged exposure is harmful for the patient as well as for the clinicians performing the procedure. In order to reduce the fluoroscopy time, a novel technology called the electroanatomic mapping was introduced. Electroanatomic mapping is a technique where the clinician maneuvers a mapping catheter across the LA endocardium and the computer produces a three-dimensional virtual map of the LA endocardium. This mesh structure displays the LA anatomic structures along with the PVs (the atrial structure shown in **Figure 5** is a mesh produced by such a mapping system). In addition, the electroanatomic mapping systems have the function to display the real-time catheter position on the mesh. This makes it possible for the clinician to ablate anywhere using the 3D mesh as the reference. Some electroanatomic mapping systems available in the market are "CARTO" by Biosense Webster Inc., "EnSite NaVx" by St. Jude Medical, and "Rhythmia" by Boston Scientific. Electroanatomic mapping systems not only produce the mesh structure, but also are capable of performing several other interesting functions that help clinicians to make ablation decisions. One such feature is the activation map. As the name "electroanatomic mapping" suggests, the map shows anatomy as well as the electrical activations in the form of a voltage map with color codes. This largely helps in treating atrial tachycardia, the clinician can see in the electroanatomic map and visualize where the earliest activation occurred, and then perform ablation accordingly. Further, the system displays the ablation lesions on the mesh with a unique color code that is varied based on the power delivered by the RF catheter. This helps the clinician to ensure that the tissue was sufficiently cauterized to stop the conduction at that location.

The mapping catheters that are used to construct the electroanatomic mesh are specialized diagnostic catheters known as a multipole diagnostic catheter (MPDC) (some types of MPDCs are shown in **Figure 6**). It consists of multiple nodes with voltage sensitive electrodes. These electrodes are arranged in a particular geometric shape which differs between different MPDC types. Some common MPDCs are Lasso and Pentaray both by Biosense Webster, FirMap (Abbott EP), Constellation (Boston scientific), Achieve (Medtronic), and Advisor (St. Jude Medical). A major feature of the MPDCs is that the electrodes can record the EGMs when they are placed in contact with the tissue. Hence, the MPDC is placed in different endocardial locations to build the mesh structure and also to obtain the EGMs. These EGMs can further be used to perform non-PV ablation. As stated earlier, PVI is not completely successful, and in order to improve the success, non-PV targets should be determined and ablated. For example,

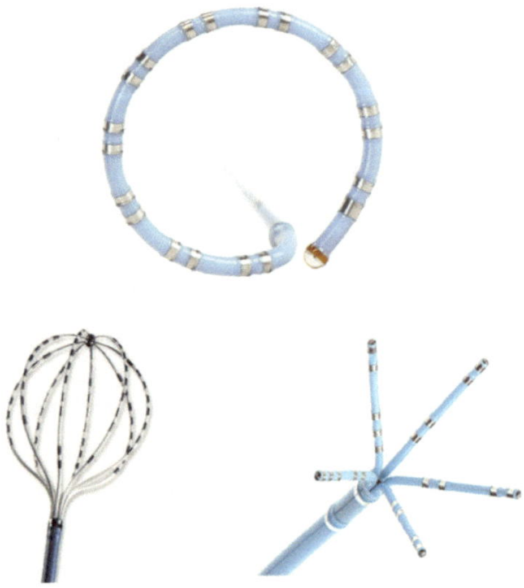

Figure 6. Different types of MPDCs: Figure shows the various types of MPDCs, which are used for generating electroanatomic maps and for recording information from the endocardium. The top one is a 20 unipole Lasso catheter, the bottom-left is a Basket catheter and the bottom-right one is a Pentaray catheter. Image reproduced from Ref. [33].

some studies showed the presence of slow conduction regions in the myocardium, which when ablated, terminated AF in their studies [43]. These sites can be identified by recording the EGMs, which, based on a specific definition, could be characterized as what is called as complex fractionated atrial electrograms (CFAEs). CFAE ablation was the first EGM-based (mechanistic) non-PV ablation, while all other strategies are anatomy based (nonmechanistic), in the sense that they do not require any functional quantities such as the EGMs to determine whether or not to ablate that site. Based on the above concept, some mapping systems were installed with a feature to automatically compute CFAE sites, and indicate them on the mesh, for the clinicians to make the ablation decision about CFAE. However, in current clinical practice, CFAE ablation is not very common, possibly because of some controversial results reported by some studies [37, 44]. This demonstrates the need for determining the "real" non-PV targets which play a role in AF maintenance. Traditionally, in AF studies performed in the past using physical experiments and computer simulations, several studies have demonstrated circular and spiral patterns of electrical waves propagating along the tissue during AF [45–48]. The AF spiral waves were termed as rotors which later gained more attention among researchers in the field. Rotors consist of a wavefront and a wavetail, and they may rotate about a functional center (**Figure 7**). The gap between the front and the tail is the wavelength of the rotor. A rotor propagates with a conduction velocity, and rotates following a periodic cycle length (the velocity vectors at the wavefront of a rotor are illustrated in **Figure 7**). Rotors can also form wave breaks that eventually lead to multiple chaotic spiral waves. Rotors were initially encountered only in animal studies. For the first time, they were claimed to be observed in human clinical studies by Narayan et al. [49]. In addition to finding rotors, their study also reports observation of some ectopic foci outside the PVs, and that they act as AF drivers. The technique that revealed the presence of rotors using the EGM in humans is called phase mapping [49]. According to this technique, the EGMs are collected simultaneously at

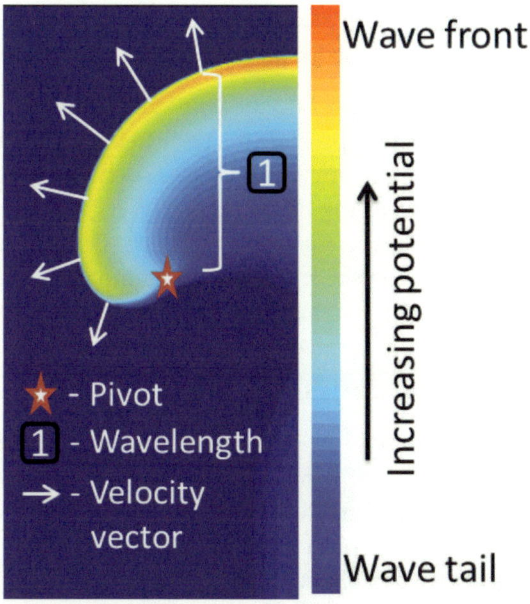

Figure 7. Propagation of a rotor wave: The different components of a rotor wave are illustrated in the figure. The arrows points in the direction of the wavefront propagation. Image recreated based on the work in reference [50].

different LA locations using a basket type MPDC (shown in **Figure 6**), and the signals are processed using Hilbert transform in order to obtain a map of the spatiotemporal variation of the signal phase. This phase map showed progressive change of phase in a circular pattern around a core called as the phase singular, thus demonstrating the characteristic of a rotor. The method of Hilbert transform that is used to obtain the phase map has also been used in different contexts of fibrillation in earlier studies [51, 52]. The algorithm/ablation procedure used by Narayan et al. was called focal impulse and rotor modulation (FIRM). Based on the outcome of the clinical studies on FIRM-guided ablation and several other follow-up studies, the FIRM algorithm was found to be effective, especially when combined with PVI [53]. The FIRM technology was later commercialized as a clinical diagnosis system for AF, now owned by Abbott Electrophysiology.

While whether or not the rotors are the primary AF drivers, is a topic still under investigation, developing novel algorithms for identifying and localizing rotors have been a critical area of research in the community. Several methods were introduced to help map rotors using engineering techniques in both time and frequency domain [54–58]. Some of these methods are specifically designed to use conventional MPDCs such as a Lasso catheter, aiming to outperform the limitations of the current EP systems available for identifying rotors.

As opposed to the time domain approach of phase mapping, there were also some frequency domain approaches, one of which is called the dominant frequency (DF) mapping. According to the DF mapping technique, the fast Fourier transform (FFT) of the signals at various locations is computed, and the highest frequency from the FFT plot at each location is considered as the DF for the respective location. When the DFs at various regions of the atrium were investigated, the frequency distribution showed organization and was said to have high values in the left atrium [50]. However, there are some studies suggesting that DF is not an effective method to analyze AF [37].

The workstations available today in the EP labs consists of all the components required to assist the clinicians during an ablation procedure, such as the electroanatomic mapping software, mapping and ablation catheters, imaging devices such as fluoroscopy and ultrasound, and other associated software such as the FIRM mapping, DF mapping, and CFAE mapping. Therefore, EP workstation is the best example of a clinical DSS, without which the ablation procedures is nearly impossible to perform today. This demonstrates the significance of clinical DSS not only in AF, but also in general clinical cardiac electrophysiology.

3.1. Developed methods of clinical decision making for AF

As discussed earlier, clinical DSSs play an important role in AF ablation treatment. This section presents a detailed discussion of some techniques and algorithms developed by our group that could be potentially implemented in a clinical DSS to assist a clinician for managing AF patients. A schematic diagram of the various EP systems along with the integration of one of the developed clinical DSS system is illustrated in **Figure 8**.

The role of clinical DSS in AF could be categorized into three important tasks:

- Detection of AF from the surface ECG for AF therapy management.
- Prediction of successful postcardioversion patients with persistent AF.
- Identification of successful ablation targets from EGM signals.

The above three tasks quite covers the necessary tasks required for AF management today. All the algorithms mentioned below were implemented in MATLAB (The MathWorks, Inc., Natick, MA, USA).

3.1.1. Detection of AF from surface ECG for AF therapy management

Rate control and rhythm control are two strategies for treatment of AF. The goal of rhythm control is to convert an arrhythmic condition to NSR, and that of rate control is to slow down the heart rate when it increases due to AF. Catheter ablation therapy is an example of rhythm control method. Although catheter ablation is a commonly preferred treatment, at an initial stage of AF, doctors recommend rate control therapy. It could be performed using rate control drugs or cardiac pacemakers.

Detection of AF is a crucial operation for providing timely and appropriate treatment for the patient. AF detection techniques mostly involve application of signal processing algorithms to ECG signals [59]. There are two major types of methods for detecting AF, first, by calculating the R-R interval (RRI), which represents the heart rate. Majority of the methods in the literature are based on RRI [60–68]. Another approach is by using RRI in combination with atrial activity (AA) analysis, which uses heart rate along with atrial ECG pattern. However, in rate controlled patients, the heart rate is externally controlled, in which case, the algorithms that are based on rate will fail to detect AF [69, 70]. Currently available methods working based

http://dx.doi.org/10.5772/65620

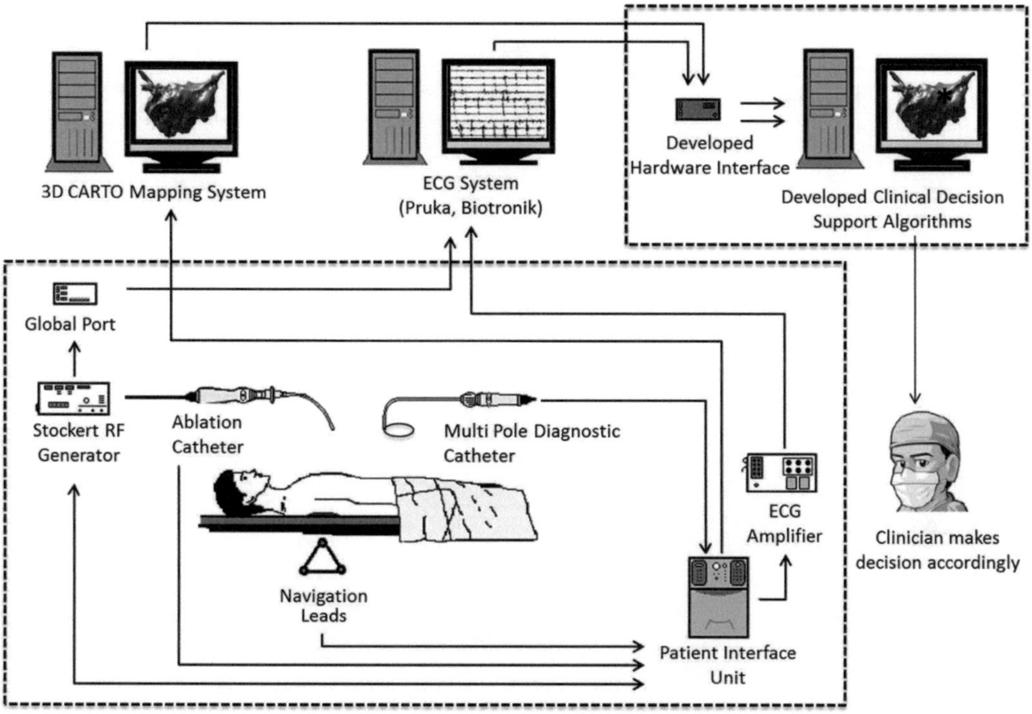

Figure 8. Schematic of a clinical DSS for AF: The figure shows a schematic of the different components of a typical EP laboratory, integrated with the developed clinical DSS algorithm. The computer screen of the developed DSS illustrates an example of ablation target localization, where the asterisk indicates the estimated rotor location as would be produced by the algorithm described in Section 3.1.3.

on AA exclusively, do not perform well [71]. AA analysis is more complicated in rate-controlled patients and could result in false diagnosis mainly because of the low voltage nature of the AA signals compared to the ventricle activities. The idea that the absence of P-waves is a major indicator of AF is used in most of the AF detection algorithms. However, ECG is a nonstationary signal and P-waves have relatively less amplitude, so the algorithms using P-wave detection encounter many challenges. In this section, we discuss a robust algorithm that we developed for automatic AF detection. The algorithm is independent of heart rate, and is suitable for rate-controlled patients with paroxysmal AF. The algorithm is capable of fast and reliable detection of AF by using minimum cardiac cycles (heart beats).

The algorithm essentially uses short ECG signals, and applies a feature extraction and machine learning approach to detect whether or not an abnormality exists in the signal. A block diagram of the developed system is shown in **Figure 9**.

The input signal is first subjected to preprocessing. The preprocessing step consists of a third-order Butterworth bandpass filter in order to reduce noise. The poles are designed to be at 0.5 and 50 Hz. For each heartbeat, nine features are extracted out of which three are statistical features and the rest are morphological features. The statistical features include variance, skewness, and kurtosis. The morphological features are calculated as the average amplitude

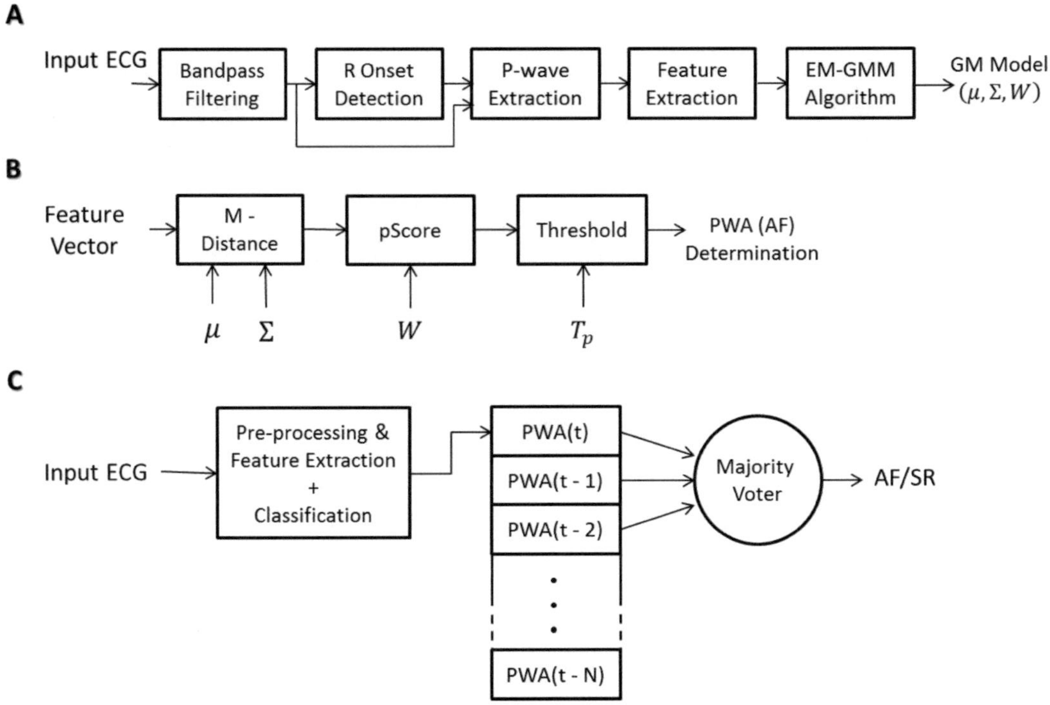

Figure 9. AF detection method: Figure shows the block diagram of the developed method of AF detection. PWA = P-wave absence, M-distance = Mahalanobis distance. A, Feature extraction and training; B, classification; C, majority voter post-processing.

of the P-wave at different intervals (i.e., first 20 ms or last 10, 20, 20, or 30 ms). A statistical model using a multivariate Gaussian mixture model (GMM) is created using the distribution of the NSR P-wave features. To generate the training model, the expectation-maximization (EM) algorithm is iteratively applied [72]. For the testing phase, the same preprocessing is performed and the same features are extracted, but now a majority vote of seven heart beats is employed in order to classify whether the test signal represents An NSR or AF. The algorithm is evaluated on the MIT-BIH AF Database from Physiobank [73]. The dataset includes 25 long-term (10 h) ECG recordings with AF (23 paroxysmal and 2 persistent) and contains 299 AF episodes (about 93.4 h). The proposed algorithm demonstrated that it is capable of classifying AF with a very high sensitivity of 98.08%. The sensitivity was highest among the compared algorithms (see **Table 1**). The specificity was 91.66% which had the second lowest classification error comparatively, which is a significant performance considering that the other methods are RRI-based approaches.

3.1.2. Prediction of successful postcardioversion patients with persistent AF

As discussed earlier, DCE cardioversion is one of the treatment options available, in which an electric shock is applied to the chest at certain intervals in order to restore NSR. This treatment however does not have a high long-term success rate, although it has more than 90% procedure success. A more well-defined method to evaluate the effectiveness, and hence

http://dx.doi.org/10.5772/65620

Algorithm	Year	Method	WL (seconds)	Se (%)	Sp (%)	PPV (%)	Err (%)
Moody et al.*	1983	RRI	60	93.58	–	85.92	–
				87.54	95.14	92.29	7.88
Cerutti et al.*	1997	RRI	90	93.3	–	94.4	–
				96.10	81.55	75.76	16.62
Tatento et al.*	2001	RRI	50	94.4	97.2	96.1	–
				91.20	96.08	90.32	5.32
Logan et al.*	2005	RRI	120	96	89	–	–
				87.30	90.31	85.72	10.89
Lake et al.	2011	RRI	12	91	94	–	–
Couceiro et al.*	2008	RRI + PWA	60	93.80	96.09	–	–
				96.58	82.66	78.76	11.77
Babaezaideh et al.*	2009	RRIRRI/PWA	>60	91	96	86	–
				89	96	88	–
Dash et al.†	2009	RRI	128 beats	94.4	95.1	–	–
Huang et al.†	2011	RRI	101 beats	96.1	98.1	–	–
Proposed algorithm	2014	PWA	1 beat	89.37	89.54	72.40	11.34
			7 beats	98.09	91.66	79.17	6.88

Unreported performance measures are displayed as a dash. Se = Sensitivity, Sp = Specificity, PPV = Positive predictive value, Err = Error rate.

*Additional algorithm evaluation completed by Larburu et al. is shown on the second row. Optimal window length (WL) was determined by Larburu et al.

†Results include additional processing for the purpose of ectopic beat filtering.

Table 1. Comparison of AF detection algorithms including additional evaluation performed by Larburu et al. [74].

predict the likelihood of maintaining NSR after cardioversion for patients who are about to undergo cardioversion, is important, so that the risks involved in cardioversion can be assessed [75]. If such a prediction can be performed, then the doctor could make a decision accordingly on whether to give the patient a cardioversion or not.

This section presents a novel computational method to perform signal analysis of AF patient ECG recorded before cardioversion and predict what the success of the treatment would be. A block diagram of the developed system is shown in **Figure 10**.

The method comprises preprocessing, extraction of features, classification, and then validation. The preprocessing is to remove the noise and the isoelectric line perturbations, for which a bandpass filter with cut off frequencies of 0.01 and 50Hz were applied. Following this, AA is extracted from the QRST complex using an average beat subtraction technique. There are a total of seven features extracted from the AA signals. The extracted features are calculated from the matching pursuit (MP) time-frequency representation of the AA signals [76]. A classifier based on quadratic discriminative analysis (QDA) is trained using the extracted features from the training data. The trained classifier was evaluated on an ECG data [77]

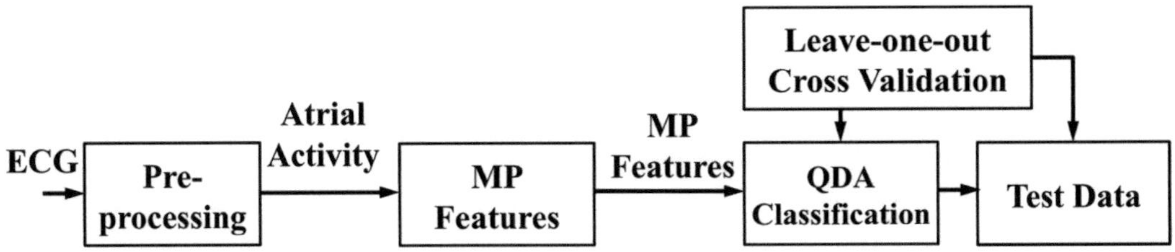

Figure 10. Prediction of cardioversion outcome: Figure shows the block diagram of the developed prediction method.

with 40 persistent AF patients who had a successful external DCE cardioversion therapy, but after 2-week follow-up, 20 patients had maintained NSR (AF-free) and 20 had a relapse of AF (AF-relapse). A leave-one-out cross-validation classification produced an outcome of 100% sensitivity and 95% specificity. Compared to the relevant methods in the literature (see **Table 2**), the proposed method resulted in the highest sensitivity and specificity values in predicting the success of DCE cardioversion in AF patients.

3.1.3. Identification of successful ablation targets from EGM signals

Catheter ablation is the most commonly preferred treatment for AF. However, the success rate of the procedure is only suboptimal due to recurrence of AF especially with persistent type patients. The arrhythmogenic rotors existing outside the PVs could be a potential target for ablation. However, in today's clinical practice there is no well-defined method to find the location of these rotors. Hence, a system that could estimate the rotor location and hence guide the clinician to the targets would be a significant clinical DSS for AF ablation in today's clinical scenario.

Method	Study size	Significance	Sensitivity	Specificity
P-wave duration, 1997 [78]	35	0.001	73%	71%
Heart rate variability, 2001 [79]	93	–	76%	90%
Fibrillatory rate, 2003 [80]	44	0.021	–	–
Clustering of RR intervals, 2004 [81]	66	0.034	–	–
P-wave duration, 2005 [82]	118	0.0001	72%	77%
P-wave duration, 2006 [83]	122,493	0.02	90%	21%
Fibrillatory rate, 2006 [84]	175	0.0001	79%	80%
Fibrillatory rate, 2006 [85]	54	0.002	–	–
Harmonic decay, 2006 [85]	54	0.0004	92%	47%
Sample entropy, 2006 [86]	66	0.02	–	–
Wavelet transform, 2007 [87]	30	–	100%	89%
P-wave dispersion, 2011 [88]	26	0.001	86%	95%
Wavelet sample entropy, 2008 [89]	40	–	95%	93%
Proposed MP-based method, 2014	40	0.005	100%	95%

Table 2. Comparison of signal processing methods.

The developed method is a novel probabilistic approach to localize rotors [90]. The relevant methods available in the literature for locating rotors involve deterministic, noniterative solutions using time-domain and frequency-domain characteristics [54–58]. The developed method uses a Bayesian filtering approach to search for the rotors by iteratively guiding an MPDC toward the center of a rotor. The algorithm was evaluated using a 2D realistic atrial tissue simulation. We developed a numerical simulation of a 10 cm × 10 cm 2D atrial tissue with a spatial resolution of 0.025 cm and sampling frequency of 500 Hz, using the Nygren human atrial cell model [91]. The numerical simulation was written using FORTRAN programming, and the visualization of the output was implemented in MATLAB. A single stable rotor was initiated and a standard 20 pole Lasso catheter (Biosense Webster, Diamond Bar, CA, USA) was simulated, from which the bipolar EGMs were obtained.

As shown in **Figure 11**, the method uses the discrete search space and some EGM characteristics as input, and gives the probability distribution of the presence of rotor in the search space, from which the rotor location can be estimated as the output. The 2D tissue is the bounded search space and it is discretized to form a grid, the coordinates of which is the first input to the algorithm. The center of the Lasso can be placed anywhere on this grid space. When a catheter is placed at a location, the following EGM characteristics are computed, which is the second input: the first activated bipole (FAB) and the rotor propagation ratio (RPR). FAB denotes the label number of the bipolar electrode of the Lasso that gets activated earliest by the rotor's wavefront. It is mathematically represented by Φ. RPR, represented by Φ, is the ratio of the two following characteristics: total conduction delay and cycle length, the definition of which can be found in the publication of our preliminary studies using both simulation and real clinical data [54].

The overall proposed idea is that the clinician places the catheter at any arbitrary endocardium location and records the EGMs. Then the system calculates FAB and RPR from these EGMs. The search space is discretized and now, both the inputs to the Bayesian algorithm are kept ready. The system first checks if the current catheter location is already a rotor center or not. This is performed using the EGM characteristics and the mathematical criterion, $\tau \simeq 1$, that is established for rotor convergence in our previous work [54]. If it is already a

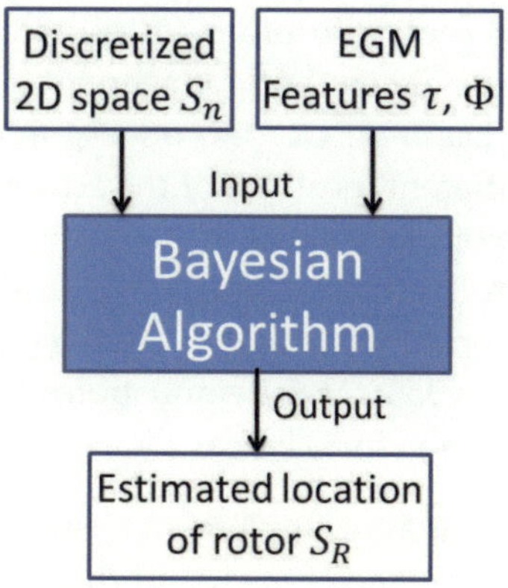

Figure 11. Overview of the guidance algorithm—The inputs are the search space and the two EGM characteristics, RPR (τ) and FAB (Φ) and the output is the estimated location of rotor.

rotor center, then, the clinician is advised to perform ablation, however, if it is not a rotor, i.e., if the convergence condition is not satisfied, then the inputs are provided to the developed algorithm to estimate a high probability location. The clinician then moves the catheter to this new location. This completes one iteration of the catheter-guidance algorithm. The EGMs are recorded again at the new location, and the convergence condition is checked again. If a rotor center is still not found, the new EGMs are processed by the algorithm to output a new estimate, and the catheter is moved by the clinician to this location. This process is repeated until a rotor is located, i.e., until the convergence condition is satisfied. The results of the developed algorithm demonstrate that the time taken to reach convergence is minimized during every iteration. This is mainly because of the updating steps of the recursive Bayesian filter, which tends to decrease the variance of the posterior distribution with increasing iterations.

The Bayesian algorithm uses the traditional Bayes theorem formulation which states that the posterior is proportional to the product of the prior and the likelihood. The posterior probability is nothing but the probability distribution of the presence of rotor in the search space. Here, the task is to determine the likelihood, and for that the EGM characteristics are used. The likelihood in our algorithm is defined as a function of two separate likelihood functions which are each a function of the features calculated from the local EGM recording. The prior is considered to be uniform distribution, meaning that the rotor could be present anywhere on the search space initially. However, in future, the prior could be tuned to any particular distribution according to clinicians' expertise and the information from cardiac anatomy. Finally, the algorithm uses the maximum *a posteriori* technique on the posterior distribution to determine the estimated location of a rotor center. This is the procedure during the first iteration; during the second one, the posterior from the previous step becomes the new prior in the Bayesian formulation, and the estimation is carried out again. This process continues until we converge.

Such an iterative framework makes the guidance to be adaptive, which could be much useful to tackle the dynamic nature of rotors. The results of our algorithm are highly promising. The algorithm was tested by placing the catheter in all the possible grid locations on the 2D simulated tissue. The algorithm achieved 100% convergence, and it took 3.37 ± 1.05 (mean ± sd) number of steps to find a rotor center. In order to assess the usefulness of the developed method, we compared it to a possible method for searching for rotors that could be used in current clinical practice using a Lasso MPDC. It is an unguided approach carried out by randomly placing the catheter at different locations of the atrium, and checking for convergence at each location. After a couple of placements, if the rotor is not found, the clinician might simply abort the manual search. We implemented this strategy on the simulation, with 20 iterations as the threshold. The convergence in the unguided case was only 34% and the number of steps, mean ± sd was 6.58 ± 3.72. This demonstrates the significance of the developed guidance strategy for implementation in a clinical setting.

Some examples of the catheter guidance implemented in MATLAB, is shown in **Figure 12**. The initial arbitrary location of the catheter is s1, and the catheter is advanced (as "dictated" by the algorithm) through s2, and finally converges at s3, which happen to be the rotor center.

http://dx.doi.org/10.5772/65620

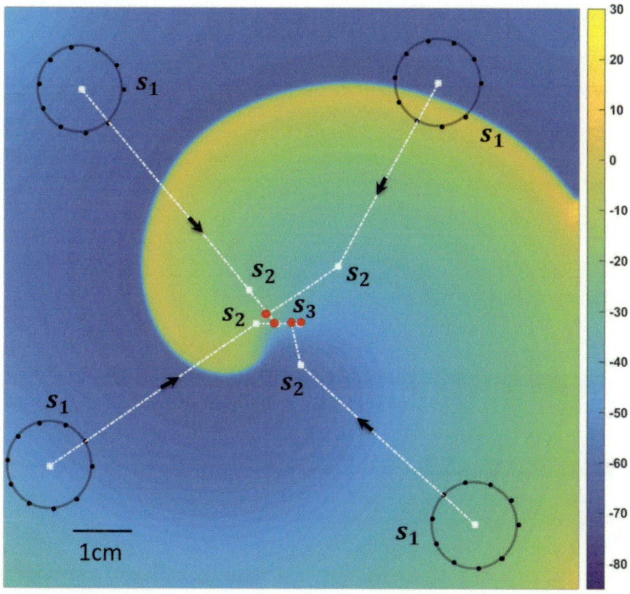

Figure 12. Some examples of the catheter-guidance paths using the proposed algorithm on the simulation—Each path is indicated from the first step, s1, to the rotor-convergence location in s3.

The algorithm's robustness can be clearly seen in the figure, with two major observations: First, the adaptive nature from the distance of the jump; the jump from s1 to s2 is always longer than the subsequent jumps, which means that the method tries to take shorter steps when it "feels" that it is getting close to a rotor center. The second observation is the adaptivity with respect to the direction; the direction of the path diverts toward the center of the rotor with increasing iterations. Additionally, it is also seen that the convergence points (red dots in the figure) are very close to the center (according to the developed simulation). The developed algorithm however is only a preliminary design and has to be improvised in future to tackle practical scenarios such as heterogeneous wave propagation, rotors with different cycle lengths, rotors with meandering center, etc.

4. Conclusion

This chapter reviewed some of the clinical decision support systems that have been developed and used in the therapy management of AF patient. Specifically, we discussed methods for detection of AF episodes from surface ECG signals, prediction of the success of DCE cardioversion from ECG signals, and identification of ablation targets for AF catheter ablation. The clinical DSS development is taking place in the right pace, the research field is witnessing promising methods that could turn into reliable clinical DSS technologies to assist the clinicians in the process of AF treatment and management in order to enhance the health of millions of patients afflicted by this debilitating rhythm disorder so that they can live longer and more fulfilling lives.

Acknowledgements

A part of the work was funded by the National Institutes of Health R15HL127663 grant to Dr. Ghoraani.

Conflict of interest

The authors declare no conflict of interests.

Author details

Prasanth Ganesan[1], Mark Sterling[2], Steven Ladavich[3] and Behnaz Ghoraani[1*]

*Address all correspondence to: bghoraani@ieee.org

1 Department of Computer and Electrical Engineering, Florida Atlantic University, Boca Raton, Florida, USA

2 Department of Computer Science, Nazarbayev University, Astana, Republic of Kazakhstan

3 Department of Biomedical Engineering, Rochester Institute of Technology, Rochester, New York, USA

References

[1] Turban E. Decision Support and Expert Systems: Management Support Systems. Prentice Hall PTR Upper Saddle River, NJ, USA; 1990.

[2] Raymond RC. Use of the time-sharing computer in business planning and budgeting. Management Science. 1966;12(8):B-363–B-381.

[3] Turban E. The use of mathematical models in plant maintenance decision making. Management Science. 1967;13(6):B-342–B-358.

[4] Shortliffe E. Computer-Based Medical Consultations: MYCIN. vol. 2. American Elsevier Publishing Company, Inc. 52 Vanderbilt Avenue, New York, NY 10017; 2012.

[5] Ancelin C, Le P, De Saint-Quentin S, Villatte N. EXPRESS: an expert system to perform system safety studies. In: Artificial Intelligence and Other Innovative Computer Applications in the Nuclear Industry. Springer US; 1988. pp. 761–768.

[6] Engelbart DC. Augmenting human intellect: a conceptual framework (1962). PACKER, Randall and JORDAN, Ken Multimedia from Wagner to Virtual Reality. New York: WW Norton & Company; 2001. pp. 64–90.

[7] Power DJ. Decision support systems: a historical overview. In: Handbook on Decision Support Systems 1. Springer Berlin Heidelberg; 2008. pp. 121–140.

[8] Power DJ, Sharda R, Burstein F. Decision Support Systems. Wiley Online Library. John Wiley & Sons, Ltd, US; 2015.

[9] Ferguson RL, Jones CH. A computer aided decision system. Management Science. 1969;15(10):B-550–B-561.

[10] McKenney JL, Scott MM. Management Decision Systems: Computer-Based Support for Decision Making. Harvard Business School Press Boston, MA, USA; 1984.

[11] Power DJ. Decision Support Basics. Business Expert Press, LLC, 222 East 46th Street, New York, NY 10017; 2009.

[12] Slagle JR. A heuristic program that solves symbolic integration problems in freshman calculus. Journal of the ACM (JACM). 1963;10(4):507–520.

[13] Little JDC. BRANDAID: A marketing-mix model, part 1: structure. Operations Research. 1975;23(4):628–655.

[14] Lindsay RK, Buchanan BG, Feigenbaum EA, Lederberg J. DENDRAL: a case study of the first expert system for scientific hypothesis formation. Artificial Intelligence. 1993;61(2):209–261.

[15] Shim JP, Warkentin M, Courtney JF, Power DJ, Sharda R, Carlsson C. Past, present, and future of decision support technology. Decision Support Systems. 2002;33(2):111–126.

[16] Berner ES. Clinical Decision Support Systems. Springer Science+Business Media, LLC, 233 Spring Street, New York, NY 10013, USA; 2007.

[17] Collen MF, McCray AT. Decision support systems (DSS). In: The History of Medical Informatics in the United States. Springer-Verlag London Ltd, London; 2015. pp. 685–722.

[18] Sadegh-Zadeh K. Clinical decision support systems. In: Handbook of Analytic Philosophy of Medicine. Springer; 2015. pp. 705–722.

[19] Giger ML. Computer-aided diagnosis. RSNA Categorical Course in Physics; 1993. Volume 6915, pp. 283–298.

[20] van Ginneken B, Novak CL. Computer-aided diagnosis. In: Proceedings of SPIE vol. 8315; 2012. pp. 831501–83 1511.

[21] Kaplan B. Evaluating informatics applications clinical decision support systems literature review. International Journal of Medical Informatics. 2001;64(1):15–37.

[22] Bron EE, Smits M, Van Der Flier WM, Vrenken H, Barkhof F, Scheltens P, et al. Standardized evaluation of algorithms for computer-aided diagnosis of dementia based on structural MRI: the CADDementia challenge. NeuroImage. 2015;111:562–579.

[23] Doi K. Current status and future potential of computer-aided diagnosis in medical imaging. The British Journal of Radiology. 2014; 78, pages s3–s19.

[24] Doi K. Computer-aided diagnosis in medical imaging: historical review, current status and future potential. Computerized Medical Imaging and Graphics. 2007;31(4):198–211.

[25] Acharya UR, Sudarshan VK, Adeli H, Santhosh J, Koh JEW, Adeli A. Computer-aided diagnosis of depression using EEG signals. European Neurology. 2015;73(5–6):329–336.

[26] Huynh B, Drukker K, Giger M. MO-DE-207B-06: Computer-aided diagnosis of breast ultrasound images using transfer learning from deep convolutional neural networks. Medical Physics. 2016;43(6):3705–3705.

[27] Hirschauer TJ, Adeli H, Buford JA. Computer-aided diagnosis of Parkinsons disease using enhanced probabilistic neural network. Journal of Medical Systems. 2015;39(11):1–12.

[28] Mozaffarian D, Benjamin EJ, Go AS, Arnett DK, Blaha MJ, Cushman M, et al. Heart disease and stroke statistics update a report from the American Heart Association. Circulation. 2015;131(4):e29–e322.

[29] Chugh SS, Roth GA, Gillum RF, Mensah GA. Global burden of atrial fibrillation in developed and developing nations. Global Heart. 2014;9(1):113–119.

[30] Issa Z, Miller JM, Zipes DP. Clinical Arrhythmology and Electrophysiology: A Companion to Braunwald's Heart Disease: Expert Consult: online and print. Elsevier Saunders, 1600 John F. Kennedy Bld. Ste 1800, Philadelphia, PA 19103-2899; 2012.

[31] Hurst JW. Naming of the waves in the ECG, with a brief account of their genesis. Circulation. 1998;98(18):1937–1942.

[32] Hlaing T, DiMino T, Kowey PR, Yan G. ECG repolarization waves: their genesis and clinical implications. Annals of Noninvasive Electrocardiology. 2005;10(2):211–223.

[33] Ganesan P. Characterization of cardiac electrogram signals during atrial fibrillation. Thesis, Rochester Institute of Technology. 2015; Accessed fromhttp://scholarworks.rit.edu/theses/8760

[34] Atkielski A, Wikimedia. Sinus Rhythm Labels; 2007. Available from: https://upload.wikimedia.org/wikipedia/commons/9/9e/SinusRhythmLabels.svg

[35] Houghton A, Gray D. Making Sense of the ECG: A Hands-On Guide. CRC Press, Taylor & Francis Group, 6000 Broken Sound Parkway NW, Duite 300, Boca Raton, FL 33487–2742; 2014.

[36] Fenton FH, Cherry EM, Glass L. Cardiac arrhythmia. Scholarpedia. 2008;3(7):1665.

[37] Calkins H, Kuck KH, Cappato R, Brugada J, Camm AJ, Chen SA, et al. 2012 HRS/EHRA/ECAS Expert Consensus Statement on Catheter and Surgical Ablation of Atrial Fibrillation: Recommendations for Patient Selection, Procedural Techniques, Patient Management and Follow-up, Definitions, Endpoints, and Research Trial Design: A report of the Heart Rhythm Society (HRS) Task Force on Catheter and Surgical

[87] Watson JN, Addison PS, Uchaipichat N, Shah AS, Grubb NR. Wavelet transform analysis predicts outcome of DC cardioversion for atrial fibrillation patients. Computers in Biology and Medicine. 2007;37(4):517–523.

[88] Basar N, Görel OM, Ozcan F, Ozlu MF, Yesilay AB, Cagli K, et al. Diagnostic accuracy of P-wave dispersion in prediction of maintenance of sinus rhythm after external cardioversion of atrial fibrillation/atriyal fibrilasyonun eksternal kardiyoversiyondan sonra sinüs ritminin korunmasini öngörmede P dalga dispersiyonunun tanisal degeri. Anadulu Kardiyoloji Dergisi: AKD. 2011;11(1):34.

[89] Alcaraz R, Rieta JJ. A non-invasive method to predict electrical cardioversion outcome of persistent atrial fibrillation. Medical and Biological Engineering and Computing. 2008;46(7):625–635.

[90] Ganesan P, Salmin AJ, Cherry EM, Ghoraani B. Development of a novel probabilistic algorithm for localization of rotors during atrial fibrillation. In: 2016 38th Annual International Conference of the IEEE Engineering in Medicine and Biology Society (EMBC). IEEE. 2016; pp. 493–496.

[91] Nygren A, Fiset C, Firek L, Clark JW, Lindblad DS, Clark RB, et al. Mathematical model of an adult human atrial cell the role of k+ currents in repolarization. Circulation Research. 1998;82(1):63–81.

http://dx.doi.org/5772/65038

$$B_i = \frac{\text{lm} / \text{Dm}}{\text{le} / \text{De}} \tag{10}$$

The Biot number measures the ratio of internal diffusion and external diffusion and can be approximated by the ratio of the thickness between the inner membrane (lm) and outer diffusion layer (le) for a constant diffusion constant D. Previous studies indicate that the biosensor achieves the best sensitivity at high Thiele modulus and high Biot number, that is, under the conditions where the reaction is in internal diffusion control with minimal external diffusion. To minimize external serum diffusion, the pipette blood volume can be controlled based on the geometric design of the reaction region.

3. Application

3.1. Enzymatic determination of serum cholesterol

Methods for determining serum cholesterol levels have been developed for prepared aqueous reagents (**Figure 2**) [11]. In the first step, the cholesterol ester is converted to free cholesterol and fatty acids using the cholesterol esterase (CE) enzyme. The free cholesterol is then converted to electro-active species hydrogen peroxide and cholest-4-en-3-one using the cholesterol oxidase (CO) enzyme. Hydroxide is an electron-donating species that can be used to generate an electrical current to quantify the amount of cholesterol in the blood serum. The determination scheme is shown below.

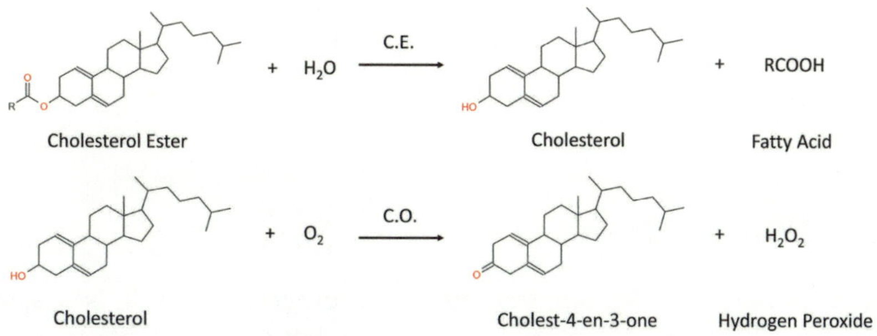

Figure 2. Enzymatic reaction for the quantification of cholesterol. In the first step, cholesterol ester is converted to free cholesterol and fatty acid through hydrolysis by the cholesterol esterase (CE) enzyme. In the second step, free cholesterol is converted to cholest-4-en-3-one and the electron-donating species hydrogen peroxide by the cholesterol oxidase (CO) enzyme.

3.2. Modeling multienzyme systems

To model the biosensor kinetics for cholesterol determination, a multienzyme model is constructed based on the one-enzyme model. Assume the biosensor is operated under internal diffusion control, that is, Biot number is infinite, and the serum diffusion layer thickness is small compared with the membrane thickness. The biosensor kinetics is simulated only in the membrane region.

3.2.1. Multienzyme reaction-diffusion equation

The conversion of cholesterol ester to hydroxide is a two-step enzymatic reaction and thus can be captured using a multienzyme reaction-diffusion equation. In non-dimensionalized form

$$\frac{\partial[S1]}{\partial T}=\frac{\partial^2[S1]}{\partial X^2}-(\phi 1)^2\frac{[S2]}{1+[S2]} \tag{11}$$

$$\frac{\partial[S2]}{\partial T}=\frac{\partial^2[S2]}{\partial X^2}-(\phi 2)^2\frac{[S2]}{1+[S2]}+(\phi 1)^2\frac{[S1]\left(\frac{Ks1}{Ks2}\right)}{1+[S1]} \tag{12}$$

$$\frac{\partial[P]}{\partial T}=D\frac{\partial^2[P]}{\partial X^2}+(\phi 2)^2\frac{[S2]}{1+[S2]} \tag{13}$$

[S1] = cholesterol ester, [S2] = cholesterol, and [P] = hydrogen peroxide

$\varphi 1$ = cholesterol esterase Thiele modulus

$\varphi 2$ = cholesterol oxidase Thiele modulus

ks1 (cholesterol esterase catalytic constant) = 1.9×10^{-5} [M]

ks2 (cholesterol oxidase catalytic constant) = 3.5×10^{-4} [M]

V_{max} = 30 u*mg for both enzymes

3.2.2. Boundary and initial conditions

The multienzyme reaction-diffusion equation for cholesterol analysis is a system partial differential equation, and to solve the equation, six boundary conditions and six initial conditions are required.

3.2.2.1. Boundary conditions 1 and 2

Since the cholesterol ester and free cholesterol are nonreactive at the electrode surface, their flux is zero:

$$\left.\frac{\partial[S1]}{\partial x}\right|_{x=0}=\left.\frac{\partial[S2]}{\partial x}\right|_{x=0}=0 \tag{14}$$

3.2.2.2. Boundary condition 3

Since hydrogen peroxide is consumed very fast, thus there is zero concentration at the electrode surface:

$$P\big|_{x=0} = 0 \tag{15}$$

3.2.2.3. Boundary conditions 4–6

Assume the concentration of cholesterol ester at the top of the membrane maintains constant concentration and the concentration of cholesterol and hydrogen peroxide are zero:

$$S_1\big|_{x=\mathrm{lm}} = S_O \tag{16}$$

$$S_2\big|_{x=\mathrm{lm}} = 0 \tag{17}$$

$$P\big|_{x=\mathrm{lm}} = 0 \tag{18}$$

3.2.3. Initial condition

At the initial time point, there is only cholesterol ester S1 on top of the sensing membrane with a concentration S0. As the reaction has yet to start, there is no cholesterol S2 or hydrogen peroxide P presented in the membrane:

$$\text{At } t = 0 \;\; \text{S1} = \text{S0} \;\; X \geq 1 \tag{19}$$

$$\text{S2} = 0 \;\; 0 \leq X < 1 \tag{20}$$

$$\text{P} = 0 \qquad \forall X \tag{21}$$

3.3. MATLAB simulation

The biosensor performance for multienzyme reaction cholesterol determination is simulated by solving a system of partial differential equations using MATLAB. The system of partial differential equations is casted into matrix form and solved using the MATLAB function PDEPE by assuming slab geometry. All units are non-dimensionalized. Note that $X = 1$ is the top of the membrane and $X = 0$ is the side of sensing electrode. For the simplified model, the Thiele modulus for both CE and CO is 1.

The solution of the system reaction-diffusion equation for cholesterol analysis is shown in **Figures 3–5**. The concentration profile shows that only 25% of the cholesterol ester has been converted to cholesterol at steady-state time and maintains at a constant concentration. On the other hand, the free cholesterol achieves 100% conversion to hydrogen peroxide. This suggests that the cholesterol ester conversion is the rate-limiting step. Interestingly, the hydrogen peroxide concentration reaches a maximum value toward the middle of the membrane and decreases on both ends, possibly due to higher mean cholesterol ester and cholesterol concentration in the middle region.

The current density plot shows that the current density reaches steady state at time 2T (17 seconds) correlating with the steady concentration of cholesterol ester and cholesterol concentration at this time point (**Figure 6**). Due to low cholesterol ester conversion, the cholesterol concentration at steady state is low, 0.0028 (0.5 μM). The current density plot also shows that the biosensor signal reaches a steady current at 2T (17 seconds) with a current magnitude of 0.0032 (0.64 μA/(cm^2)).

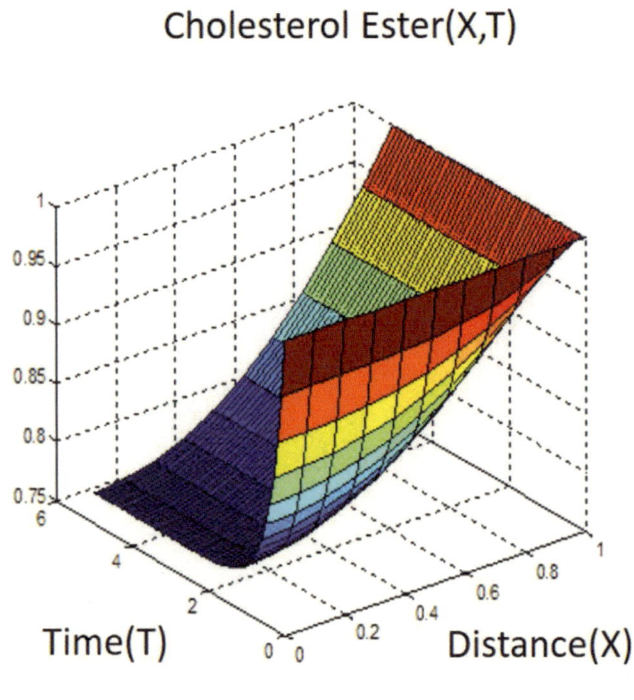

Figure 3. The concentration profile of cholesterol ester. The concentration profile shows that only 25% of the cholesterol ester has been converted to cholesterol at steady-state time and maintains at a constant concentration.

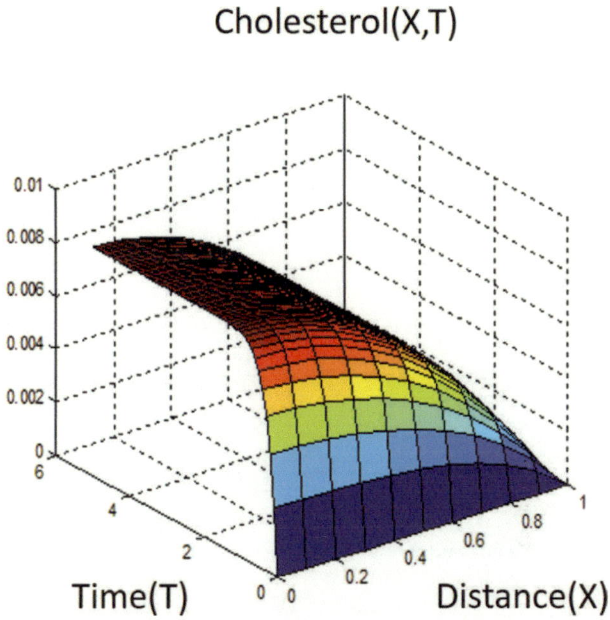

Figure 4. The concentration profile of free cholesterol. The free cholesterol achieves 100% conversion to hydrogen peroxide, suggesting that the cholesterol ester conversion is the rate-limiting step.

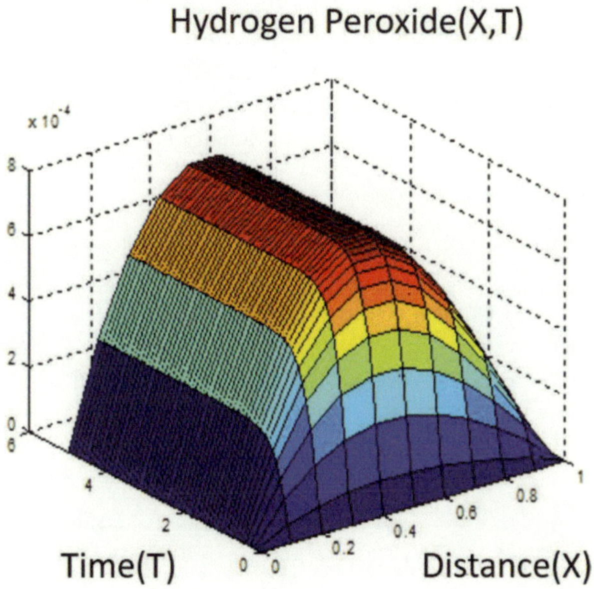

Figure 5. The concentration profile of the reaction product hydrogen peroxide. The hydrogen peroxide concentration reaches a maximum value toward the middle of the membrane and decreases on both ends, possibly due to higher mean cholesterol ester and cholesterol concentration in the middle region.

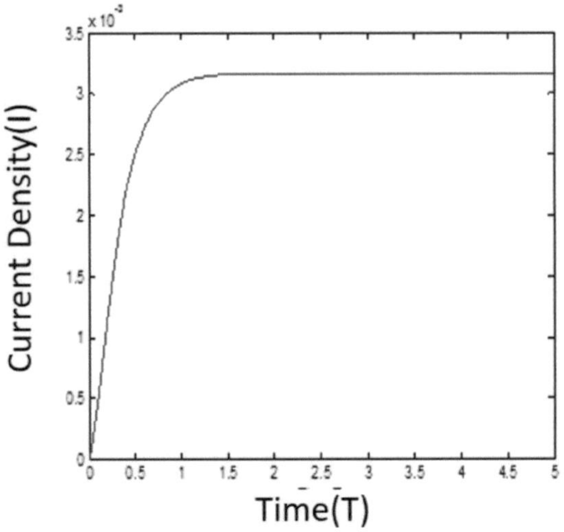

Figure 6. Plot of current density as a function of time derived from hydrogen peroxide reaction profile (**Figure 5**) at $X = 0$.

3.4. Biosensor performance characterization

3.4.1. Substrate-current activity relationship

The current-substrate calibration curve is constructed by simulating the steady-state current at 2T and varying the concentration of cholesterol ester from 1 to 10 S. The plot shows that the biosensor has high sensitivity and is linear at low substrate concentration (<1 S unit) and the current density continues to increase and gradually reaches a plateau at high substrate concentration (> 1 S unit). The maximum current density is 0.064 (12.8 μA/(cm^2)) (**Figure 7**).

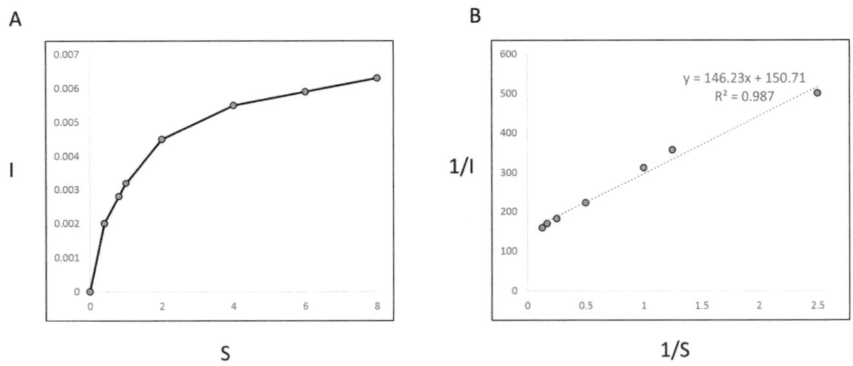

Figure 7. Characterization of biosensor performance using substrate-current activity relationship. (A) The maximum current density is predicted at different substrate concentrations. Note that the substrate-current activity relationship obeys the Michaelis-Menten kinetic equation. (B) Inverse linear plot of the inverse current and substrate showed high linearity ($R^2 = 0.987$).

To quantitatively model how current density varies with substrate concentration, a mathematical model was constructed. Here, we observed that substrate-current activity relationship obeys the Michaelis-Menten kinetic equation. Specifically,

$$J = \frac{a[S]}{b+[S]} \tag{22}$$

J is the dimensionless current density, $[S]$ is the cholesterol ester substrate concentration, and a and b are undetermined variables. At low substrate concentration ($[S] \ll 1$), the equation can be approximated by a linear equation with the slope proportional to the ratio of a and b:

$$J = \frac{a}{b}[S] \tag{23}$$

At high substrate concentration, the current density is constant, corresponding to maximum current density:

$$J = J_{\max} = a \tag{24}$$

The two variables can be solved by the inverse linear plot:

$$\frac{1}{J} = \frac{b+[S]}{a[S]} = \frac{b}{a}[S] + \frac{1}{a} \tag{25}$$

By curve fitting, we determine $a = 0.0066$ and $b = 0.965$. Thus, we have recovered the substrate-current activity relationship:

$$J = \frac{0.0066[S]}{0.965+[S]} \tag{26}$$

3.4.2. Sensitivity

The sensitivity of a biosensor signal can be defined as the unit increases in current density per unit increase in substrate concentration at the steady-state condition. High sensitivity is often required to differentiate between normal and pathological readings for a biosensor measurement. From the substrate-current activity relationship, the sensitivity can be expressed as the derivative of current density J with respect to $[S]$. To determine the optimal sensitivity, we calculate the second derivatives of the sensitivity expression at small S concentrations:

$$\frac{d^2J}{dS^2}=\frac{2a[S]}{(b+[S])^3}-\frac{2a}{(b+[S])^2}\cong\frac{2a}{b+[S]^2}\left(\frac{[S]}{b}-1\right) \quad (27)$$

Thus, we find that the substrate concentration $[S]$ at b = 0.965 yields the greatest sensitivity based on the current density output.

3.4.3. *Measurement time*

The measurement time is another important element in biosensor design. For a point-of-care biosensor, it determines how fast the patient can retrieve the test results after the serum has been applied to the test strip. For an amperometric biosensor, the measurement time is determined by how fast the current achieves steady state. In our example, the measurement time is approximated at 2T or 17 seconds.

3.4.4. *Measurement range*

The measurement range is defined as the substrate concentration range where the substrate-current activity relationship is linear. A broad measurement range is preferable to be able to differentiate normal from pathological condition as well as pathological severity. As the calibration curve often plateaus out at higher substrate concentration, it becomes harder to provide an accurate reading at this region. In our example, the linear region is at $[S] < 2$ (38 μM).

3.5. Biosensor optimization

Since the behavior of the reaction-diffusion equation is controlled by two Thiele moduli φ1 and φ2 of CE and CO, it is possible to optimize biosensor response using these two parameters. From Eqs. (11) and (13), the conversion rate of cholesterol ester and the production rate of hydrogen peroxide are proportional to $\varphi1^2$ and $\varphi2^2$, respectively. From the computational simulation, we observed that Thiele modulus 1 = 1 at $S = 1$ only achieved a 25% cholesterol ester conversion rate. By increasing the Thiele moduli 1–5, the system was able to achieve full cholesterol ester conversion at 1T (8.5 seconds). Similarly, by increasing the Thiele moduli 2–5, the steady current attained a maximum value 0.05 (10 $\mu A/(cm^2)$). The results showed a 25-fold increase in sensitivity from the original value of 0.007 to 0.05, and the maximum current increased from 0.006 (1.2 $\mu A/(cm^2)$) to 0.55 (0.1 $mA/(cm^2)$) (**Table 1**).

φ1	φ2	Sensitivity (*dJ*/*dS*)	Measurement range (*S*)	Measurement time (*T*)
1	1	0.0068	1	1
5	5	0.053	1	1
8	16	0.05	20	1

Table 1. Biosensor optimization using the Thiele modulus.

3.6. Biosensor model validation

The biosensor simulation result was compared with real-time experimental data [12]. The biosensor system consisted of a planar gold electrode modified with immobilized enzyme peroxidase, an insoluble mediator, layers of acetate cellulose, and the enzyme cholesterol oxidase in a buffer solution. Furthermore, all the cholesterol in the ester form was pretreated with cholesterol esterase to convert it to free cholesterol. The experiment showed that the linear range is up to 40 μM. We applied the optimization techniques to completely convert and linearize the cholesterol ester calibration up to 2S or 38 μM using a steady-state current. The optimized Thiele moduli were found to be Thiele modulus 1 = 4 and Thiele modulus 2 = 5, respectively. The membrane thickness was chosen at 0.1 um to match the maximum current in the experiment 70 nA and assumed that the reaction area diameter was 5mm. The simulation results showed excellent agreement with the experimental data. The calibration curve showed that the current response was linear up to 50 μM with a sensitivity of 0.5 nA/μM, which was close to the experiment values of the maximum range 40μM and sensitivity 0.6 nA/μM (**Figure 8**).

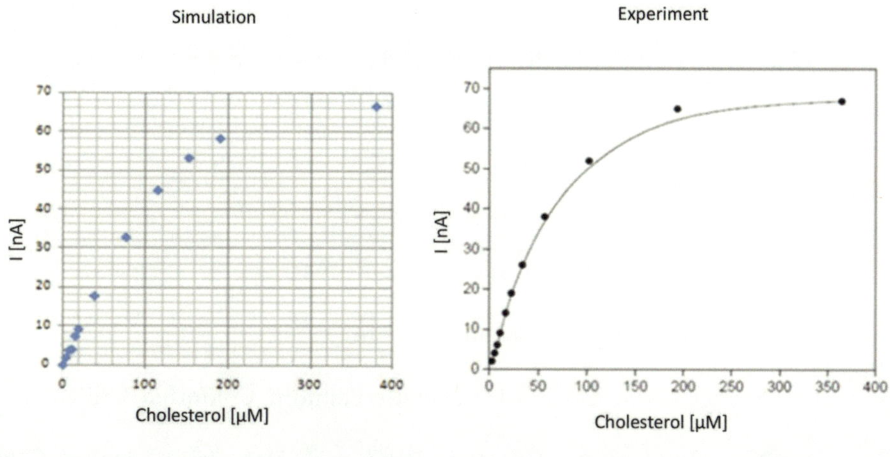

Figure 8. Biosensor model validation. The biosensor current response of cholesterol input predicted by the enzymatic diffusion equation is compared with that derived from the experiment. (A) Biosensor current response by mathematical simulation. Simulation parameters: l = 0.1, cholesterol esterase = 0.029 mg, cholesterol oxidase = 0.21mg, and the Biot number = ∞. (B) Biosensor current response by experimentation. Planar gold electrode modified with immobilized enzyme peroxidase, an insoluble mediator, layers of acetate cellulose, and the enzyme cholesterol oxidase in a buffer solution.

4. Conclusion

We have constructed a mathematical model to simulate biosensor kinetics for cholesterol determination. By monitoring the steady current from the current density plot, the measurement time can be determined, and the current-substrate calibration can be constructed at the steady-state time point. The maximum range is the maximum concentration of cholesterol ester in the linear region. The characteristic substrate-current activity relationship obeys Michaelis-Menten kinetics, and the equation can be determined by the sensitivity and maximum current density. Through mathematical analysis of system parameters, the optimal enzyme composition is shown to be the minimum amount of enzymes that can achieve total conversion of cholesterol ester as well as produce the highest possible steady-state current. Finally, the model was validated by comparing the results with real-time biosensor data. The free parameters such as membrane thickness or reaction area can be scaled to match specific design criteria or scale-up operation. Several potential improvements for the biosensor model include incorporating a serum diffusion layer by reducing the Biot number to produce a more realistic simulation, generalizing the multienzyme formulation and simulating the biosensor response under different amplification methods. Finally, we anticipated that the computer-aided model could be applied to simulate other multienzyme systems such as glucose or triglyceride determination as well as any other point-of-care diagnostic application.

Acknowledgements

We thank Dr. Elliot Landaw at UCLA for the helpful discussion of the materials.

Author details

Yu-Chen Lo[1*], Ren Gui[2], Hiroshi Honda[2] and Jorge Z. Torres[3]

*Address all correspondence to: bennylo@stanford.edu

1 Department of Bioengineering, Stanford University, Stanford, California, United States

2 Department of Bioengineering, Northwestern Polytechnic University, Fremont, California, United States

3 Department of Chemistry and Biochemistry, University of California, Los Angeles, California, United States

References

[1] Kavey RE, Daniels SR, Lauer RM, Atkins DL, Hayman LL, Taubert K, et al. American Heart Association guidelines for primary prevention of atherosclerotic cardiovascular disease beginning in childhood. Circulation. 2003;107(11):1562-6. PubMed PMID: 12654618.

[2] Romero MR, Ahumada F, Garay F, Baruzzi AM. Amperometric biosensor for direct blood lactate detection. Analytical Chemistry. 2010;82(13):5568-72. doi: 10.1021/ac1004426. PubMed PMID: 20518470.

[3] Kwan RC, Leung HF, Hon PY, Cheung HC, Hirota K, Renneberg R. Amperometric biosensor for determining human salivary phosphate. Analytical Biochemistry. 2005;343(2):263-7. doi: 10.1016/j.ab.2005.05.021. PubMed PMID: 15993373.

[4] Tarasov A, Gray DW, Tsai MY, Shields N, Montrose A, Creedon N, et al. A potentiometric biosensor for rapid on-site disease diagnostics. Biosensors and Bioelectronics. 2016;79:669-78. doi: 10.1016/j.bios.2015.12.086. PubMed PMID: 26765531.

[5] Shtelzer S, Braun S. An optical biosensor based upon glucose oxidase immobilized in sol-gel silicate matrix. Biotechnology and Applied Biochemistry. 1994;19(Pt 3):293-305. PubMed PMID: 8031505.

[6] Zhao J, Yan Y, Zhu L, Li X, Li G. An amperometric biosensor for the detection of hydrogen peroxide released from human breast cancer cells. Biosensors and Bioelectronics. 2013;41:815-9. doi: 10.1016/j.bios.2012.10.019. PubMed PMID: 23122755.

[7] Bishop ML, Fody EP, Schoeff LE. Clinical Chemistry: Principles, Procedures, Correlations. 5th ed. Philadelphia: Lippincott Williams & Wilkins; 2005. xxvi, 730 p.

[8] Mao CJ, Chen XB, Niu HL, Song JM, Zhang SY, Cui RJ. A novel enzymatic hydrogen peroxide biosensor based on Ag/C nanocables. Biosensors and Bioelectronics. 2012;31(1):544-7. doi: 10.1016/j.bios.2011.10.001. PubMed PMID: 22024593.

[9] Cornish-Bowden A, Whitman CP. A century of Michaelis-Menten kinetics. Introduction. FEBS Letters. 2013;587(17):2711. doi: 10.1016/j.febslet.2013.07.035. PubMed PMID: 23899672.

[10] Monica TJ, Andersen DC, Goochee CF. A mathematical model of sialylation of N-linked oligosaccharides in the trans-Golgi network. Glycobiology. 1997;7(4):515-21. PubMed PMID: 9184832.

[11] Roeschlau P, Bernt E, Gruber W. Enzymatic determination of total cholesterol in serum. Zeitschrift für Klinische Chemie und Klinische Biochemie. 1974;12(5):226. PubMed PMID: 4440114.

[12] Katrlik J, Valach M, Jantosova L. Interference free amperometric biosensor for direct cholesterol determination, ACTA Facultatis Pharmaceutiae Universitatis Comenianae, Tomas, LII; 2005.

Chapter 7

Computer-Aided Diagnosis in Neuroimaging

Francisco J. Martínez-Murcia,

Juan Manuel Górriz and Javier Ramírez

Additional information is available at the end of the chapter

http://dx.doi.org/10.5772/64980

Abstract

This chapter is intended to provide an overview to the most used methods for computer-aided diagnosis in neuroimaging and its application to neurodegenerative diseases. The fundamental preprocessing steps, and how they are applied to different image modalities, will be thoroughly presented. We introduce a number of widely used neuroimaging analysis algorithms, together with a wide overview on the recent advances in brain imaging processing. Finally, we provide a general conclusion on the state of the art in brain imaging processing and possible future developments.

Keywords: neuroimaging, VBM, feature extraction, CT, MRI, PET, SPECT, machine learning, classification

1. Introduction

Neuroimaging has meant a major breakthrough for the diagnosis and treatment of neurodegenerative diseases. Not so long ago, biomedical signal processing was limited to filtering, modelling or spectral analysis, prior to visual inspection. In the past decades, a number of powerful mathematical and statistical tools have been developed and evolved together with an increasing development and use of neuroimaging. Structural modalities such as computed tomography (CT) or the widely known magnetic resonance imaging (MRI), and later functional imaging techniques such as positron emission tomography (PET) and single photon emission computed tomography (SPECT) provide unprecedented insight in the internals of the brain, allowing the study of the structural and functional changes that can be linked to neurodegenerative diseases. This means a huge amount of data where automatic tools can help to identify patterns, reduce noise and enhance our knowledge of the brain functioning.

Computer-aided diagnosis (CAD) systems in neuroimaging include a variety of methods that range from preprocessing of the images (just after acquisition) to advanced machine-learning algorithms to identify disease-related patterns. Algorithms used in the reconstruction of medical imaging, such as the tomographic reconstruction (TR) or the filtered back-projection (FBP) lay outside the scope of this chapter, focused on the application of CAD systems to neuroimaging.

This chapter starts with an exposition of the preprocessing methods used in different neuroimaging modalities, including registration, normalization and segmentation. We provide references on the algorithms behind well-known pieces of software such as statistical parametric mapping (SPM) [1], FreeSurfer [2] or the FMRIB Software Library (FSL) [3]. Later, the most used computer-aided diagnosis systems in psychiatry, psychology and neurology are described. These include SPM [1] and voxel-based morphometry (VBM) [4], voxels as features (VAFs) [5] and how the computation of regions of interest (ROIs) work in semiquantitative analysis. In the next section, new advances in neuroimaging analysis are presented, starting with the basis of machine learning and classification, including support vector machines (SVMs) [5–8], but also logistic regression [9, 10] or classifier ensembles [11, 12]. Given the characteristics of neuroimaging data, where we study large, possibly correlated, data, the extraction of higher-level features is essential. Therefore, in the last section, we provide an introduction to commonly used image decomposition algorithms such as principal component analysis (PCA) [8, 13–18] and independent component analysis (ICA) [19–22]. Finally, other recent feature extraction algorithms including spatial and statistical methods such as texture analysis [23–31], morphological tools [31–33] or artificial neural networks [34–40] are presented.

2. Preprocessing

Preprocessing of the neurological images is a fundamental step in CAD systems as it ensures that all the images, either structural or functional, are comparable. We consider a preprocessing step, an algorithm that, applied after the acquisition and reconstruction of the images–usually a machine-dependent procedure–is intended to produce directly comparable images that represent a certain magnitude. The number and type of procedures to follow in preprocessing differs from one modality to another, although normalization and smoothing are used throughout all of them (see **Figure 1**).

2.1. Spatial normalization or registration

The anatomy of every subject's brain is slightly different in shape and size. In order to compare images of different subjects, we need to eliminate these particularities and transform the images so that the subsequent group analysis or comparison can be performed. To do so, the individual images are mapped from their individual subject space (current anatomy) to a reference space, a common anatomical reference that allows the comparison. This procedure is known as *spatial normalization* or *registration*.

http://dx.doi.org/10.5772/64980

There are a number of algorithms used in image registration, but the procedure usually involves the computation of a series of parameters to map the source images to a template that works as a common anatomical reference (see Section 2.1.2 for an overview on registration algorithms). The most widely used template is the Montreal Neurological Institute (MNI) template.

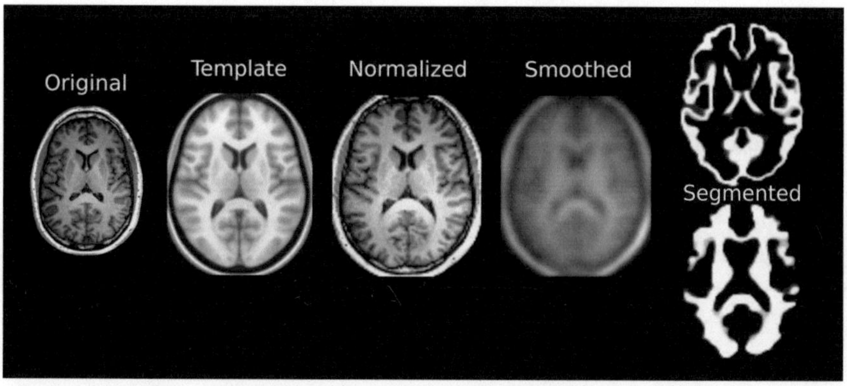

Figure 1. Example of the pipeline followed in structural MRI preprocessing, comprising spatial normalization, smoothing and segmentation.

2.1.1. *The MNI space and template*

The MNI space is the most widely used space for brain registration and was recently adopted by the International Consortium for Brain Mapping (ICBM) as its standard template. It defines a standard three-dimensional (3D) coordinate system (also known as 'atlas'), which is used to map the location of brain structures independently of the size and shape of each subject's brain.

The MNI space was intended to replace the Talairach space, a system based on a dissected and photographed brain for the Talairach and Tournoux atlas. In contrast to this, the MNI created a new template that was approximately matched to the Talairach brain but using a set of normal MRI scans. The current standard MNI template is the ICBM152 [41], which is the average of 152 normal MRI scans that have been matched to an older version of the MNI template using a nine-parameter affine transform.

2.1.2. *Registration algorithms*

Algorithms used in registration can be categorized in *linear* transformations (being the *affine* transform the most complex) and *non-rigid* or elastic transformations. Affine transformations are applied as a matrix multiplication and include terms for translation, scale, rotation, shear, squeeze and so on. These lineal transformations are applied globally to the image and therefore do not account for local geometric differences. Most neuroimaging software includes some kind of affine registration, including FreeSurfer [2], FSL (via package FLIRT) [3] or Elastix.

The estimation of the parameters is performed via the optimization of a given cost function, the minimum-squared difference between the source image and the template being the most basic. Modern software include more refined functions, for example, Tukey's biweight function (in mri_robust_template of FreeSurfer) [11], or the mutual information (in FLIRT) [42], that operate under a high-complexity schema involving local and global multiresolution optimization. When working with images of the same modality, the preferred cost function is the minimum-squared difference between the source image and the template, whereas in the case of multimodal registration, the maximization of the mutual information is preferred.

Non-rigid transformations can apply local transformation to align the target image to the template. Many of these non-rigid transformations are applied as a local fine-tuning after a previous affine transformation, although some of them use higher-complexity models that do not need this previous step. Some non-rigid transformations include radial basis functions (RBFs) (thin plate or surface splines, multiquadrics and compactly supported transformations), physical continuum models and large deformation models (diffeomorphisms). Of these, the most popular are diffeomorphic transformations, which feature the estimation and application of a warp field, and they are used in SPM (default) [1], FreeSurfer [2], FSL (FNIRT) [3], Elastix or ANTs.

2.1.3. Co-registration

Sometimes, we use different modalities, usually a functional and a structural image, for the same subject. It would be therefore very useful that these two (or even more) different images spatially match each other, so that any processing can be fit to any of them and applied to all. Since functional images have low resolution, the procedure for performing spatial normalization frequently involves co-registration to the structural image, which has a higher level of detail. Then the spatial normalization (or registration) parameters are estimated on the structural image and applied to all the co-registered maps. In the context of low-resolution functional imaging, affine co-registration to the structural image is preferred.

2.2. Smoothing

Despite the spatial normalization applied to the images, differences between subjects are still a problem that can reduce the signal-to-noise ratio (SNR) of the neuroimaging data. This problem increases as the number of subjects increases. To increase the SNR, it is recommended to filter out the highest frequencies, that is, applying a *smoothing*. Smoothing removes the smallest scale changes between voxels, making the detection of large-scale changes easier.

On the other hand, smoothing the images lowers its resolution. Smoothing is usually applied using a 3D Gaussian kernel to the image, determined by its full-width at half maximum (FWHM) parameter, which is the diameter of the smoothing kernel at half of its height. The choice of the size of the kernel is therefore of fundamental importance, and it depends on the signal to be detected. A small kernel will make our further processing confound noise with activation signal, but a larger kernel can parse out significant signal. As a general rule, the size of the kernel should be smaller than the activation to be detected.

http://dx.doi.org/10.5772/64980

2.3. Functional MRI-specific steps

The acquisition of functional MRI (fMRI) involves a more complex preprocessing of the images, given its dynamic features. fMRI studies acquire a long sequence of low-resolution MRI images that contain a magnitude known as blood-oxygen-level-dependent (BOLD) contrast. This sequence of three-dimensional volumes is combined into a four-dimensional (4D) volume that conceptually works similar to a video. In this context, the outcome can be much more affected by the subject motion. Therefore, procedures such as slice-timing correction and motion correction are mandatory in fMRI.

2.3.1. Slice-timing correction

In fMRI, the scanner acquires each slice within a single brain volume at different times. Different methods are used to acquire the slices: descending order (top to down), ascending order (bottom to up) and interleaved (the slices are acquired in a certain sequence). The time interval between one slice and another is usually small, but after acquiring a whole brain volume, there might be a difference of several seconds between the first and the last acquisition.

To compensate for the time differences between slice acquisition within a single volume, a *slice-timing correction* is performed by temporally interpolating the slices so that the resulting volume is approximately equivalent to acquiring the whole brain at the same time point. These time differences are especially important in event-driven experimental design, where timing is very relevant. Linear, quadratic or spline functions are used to interpolate the slices.

2.3.2. Motion correction

Motion correction, also known as *realignment*, accounts for the undesirable effect of head movement during the acquisition of the data. It is almost impossible for a subject to lie perfectly still during the acquisition of an fMRI sequence, and even the small movements can lead to variation in the BOLD values that, if uncorrected, can lead to activation of false positives.

The correction of this problem usually uses a rigid-body transformation similar to those used in registration. In this case, a model characterized by six parameters that account for translation and rotation is frequently used. The parameter estimation is performed by minimizing a cost function, such as correlation or mutual information, between the volumes and a reference time volume, usually the mean image of all time points.

Sometimes, the movement of the head is so fast that motion correction cannot correct its effects. In that case, the most used approach is to eliminate the images acquired during that fast movement, using an artefact detection algorithm that identifies large variations between images at adjacent time points.

2.4. Intensity normalization

Most functional neuroimaging modalities, in contrast to unitless structural MRI images, are the representation of the distribution of a certain contrast over the brain. There exist a larger number of sources of variability that can affect the final values: contrast uptake, radiotracer decay time, metabolism, and so on. In order to establish comparisons between subjects, an *intensity normalization* procedure is required.

Intensity normalization methods are to be linear in nature, since it is essential to maintain the intensity ratio between brain regions, acting on the whole brain. In its simplest form, it consists of a division by a constant. This parameter is often estimated [6, 7] as the average value of the 95th bin of the histogram of the image, that is, the average of the 5% higher-intensity values, in what is known as the *normalization to the maximum*. Another approach, called *integral normalization*, estimates this parameter as the sum of all values of the image. A more complex approach requires *a priori* knowledge of the distribution of intensity in a normal subject. This is designed so that the whole image is divided by the binding potential (BP) [43], a specific-to-non-specific ratio between the intensities in areas where the tracer should be concentred and the non-specific areas.

Then, we have general linear transformations, defined as $Y = aX + b$. These procedures use estimates of the probability density function (PDF) of the source images and then estimate the parameters a and b, which transform their original PDF to an expected range. Methods to estimate the PDF parameters range from the simplest, non-parametric histogram [44] to more advanced estimates such as an analysis of covariance (ANCOVA) approach used in SPM [44, 45], or parametric estimates involving the Gaussian or the more general alpha-stable distribution [46], which has been recently tested with great success.

Structural modalities also suffer from some sources of intensity variability, for example, magnetic field inhomogeneity, noise, evolution of the scanners, and so on. Field inhomogeneity causes distortions in both geometry and intensity of the MR images [47], usually addressed via increasing the strength of the gradient magnetic field or preprocessing. Intensity variability is especially noticeable in multicentre-imaging studies, where images should share certain characteristics. To improve the homogeneity of a set of structural images acquired at different locations, the use of quantitative MRI images has been recently proposed [48]. In contrast to typical unitless $T1$-weighted images, quantitative imaging can provide neuroimaging biomarkers for myelination, water and iron levels that are absolute measures comparable across imaging sites and time points.

2.5. Segmentation

Segmentation, mostly of structural MRI images, involves a series of algorithms aimed at constructing maps of the distribution of different tissues. The general approach is to separate the image in three different maps containing grey matter (GM), white matter (WM) and cerebrospinal fluid (CSF), although some software can also output data for bone, soft tissue or very detailed functional regions and subregions [49–51]. The procedure is applied after all aforementioned steps, including field inhomogeneity correction, which is essential for a correct segmentation. Here, we provide insight on the most used algorithms for segmentation

http://dx.doi.org/10.5772/64980

2.5.1. Statistical parametric mapping

In SPM, the segmentation procedure uses an expectation-maximization (EM) algorithm to obtain the parameters corresponding to a mixture of Gaussians that represents the tissue classes. Afterwards, an affine transformation is applied using tissue probability maps that are in the ICBM/MNI space. It currently takes normalized MRI images and extracts up to six maps: GM, WM, CSF, bone, soft tissue and air/background.

2.5.2. FMRIB software library

Two algorithms are used in FSL to perform segmentation: the FMRIB Automated Segmentation Tool (FAST) and the FMRIB Integrated Registration and Segmentation Tool (FIRST).

FAST is based on a hidden Markov random field model optimized through the EM algorithm. It firstly registers the brain volume to the MNI space and then segments the volume into three tissue classes (GM, WM and CSF). Skull-stripped versions of the anatomical image are needed.

On the other hand, FIRST is intended to extract subcortical structures of the brain characterized by parameters of surface meshes and point distribution models located in a database, built using manually segmented data. The source images are matched to the database, and the most probable structure is extracted based on the shape of the image.

2.5.3. FreeSurfer

FreeSurfer uses surfaces to perform posterior analysis, such as cortical thickness estimation. Therefore, the main aim of the command reckon_all, which performs most preprocessing steps, is not to obtain new image maps containing tissues, but surfaces that identify the different areas in the brain.

After registration to the MNI305 space, voxels are classified into white mater and other based on their location, intensity and local neighbourhood intensities. Afterwards, an estimation of the bias field is performed using these selected voxels, to correct the image. Next, the skull is stripped using a deformable template model [49]. The hemispheres are separated using cutting planes based on the expected MNI305 location of the corpus callosum and pons, and several algorithms that detect these shapes in the source images. The surfaces for each hemisphere are estimated first using the outside of the white matter mass, and then refined to follow the intensity gradients between WM and GM, and GM and CSF, called the pial surface, which will allow the estimation of cortical thickness [50].

FreeSurfer also implements a volume-based stream designed to obtain cortical and subcortical tissue volumes and label them. This stream performs a different, pathology-insensitive affine registration to the MNI305 space, followed by an initial volumetric labelling. Then, the intensity bias is corrected, and a new non-linear alignment to a MNI305 atlas is performed. The labelling process is a very complex one and is more thoroughly explained in Ref. [51].

3. Basic analyses

After performing a preprocessing of the source images, many procedures can be applied to extract the information required for clinical practice. In this section, we focus on those analyses that are more extended in clinical practice. These are currently preferred by medical staff, since they are easily interpretable and require little knowledge of computer science. Nevertheless, they are computer-aided systems that yield significant information to assist in the procedure of diagnosis. In later sections, we develop the application of more advanced systems that make use of machine learning to help in the same procedure.

3.1. Analysis of regions of interest (ROIs)

The analysis of *regions of interest (ROIs)* is the most basic computationally aided analysis of neuroimaging. It involves either purely manual or computer-assisted delimitation of regions in both structural and functional imaging and a posterior analysis of the delimited volumes.

A number of analyses can be performed on these regions, depending on the image modality. In the case of structural MRI, a frequent approach is the estimation of the volume of cortical and subcortical structures, called *morphometry*. The delimitation of ROIs is often performed automatically and then manually refined and allows the quantification of diseases that alter the normal distribution and size of GM and WM. This is the case of brain atrophy, a common issue in dementia, or brain tumours.

This ROI analysis is hardly used in fMRI, but very extended in nuclear imaging (PET or SPECT). Since the maps obtained with these techniques quantify the uptake of certain drugs, the total uptake can be obtained as the sum of intensities inside the drawn volume. However, the most used measure in these modalities is a ratio between the intensities in specific and non-specific areas, especially with drugs that bind to specific targets such as dopamine, amyloid plaques, and so on.

3.1.1. Cortical thickness

A specific case of a fully computer-assisted ROI analysis is the *cortical thickness* measure performed in FreeSurfer [50]. As aforementioned, once the GM-WM and GM-CSF surfaces have been estimated, the amount of GM in a direction perpendicular to the surface can be estimated. Combined with the subcortical segmentation algorithms, this allows to a very powerful estimation of the average cortical thickness by anatomical region. Thus, per region GM differences such as atrophy or hypertrophy can be characterized, making it perhaps the most widely used method in neuroscience.

3.2. Voxel-wise analyses

To overcome the time-consuming procedure of the traditional analysis of ROIs, several algorithms that act at the voxel level have been proposed. These include the statistical parametric mapping (SPM), a voxel-based morphometry (VBM) or the first machine-learning approach in this chapter, called voxel as features (VAF) (see **Figure 2**).

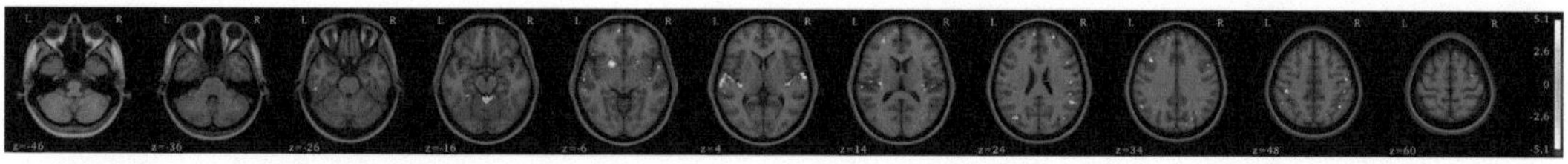

Figure 2. Example of a voxel-based morphometry output. Significant areas ($p < 0.05, |t| > 2.56$) in a comparison of autism-affected patients and healthy controls are highlighted.

3.2.1. Statistical parametric mapping (SPM)

Statistical parametric mapping (SPM) was proposed by Friston et al. [45] to automatically examine differences in brain activity during functional-imaging studies involving fMRI or PET. The technique can be applied to both single images (PET) and time series (fMRI), and the idea behind it is construct a general linear model (GLM) to describe the variability in the data in terms of experimental and confounding effects.

The level of activation is assessed at a voxel level using univariate statistics, and featuring a correction for type I errors (false positives), due to the problem of multiple comparisons. In the case of time series analysis, a linear convolution of the voxel signal with an estimation of the hemodynamic response is performed, and then the activation is tested against the analysed task.

The representation of the activation is frequently presented as an overlay of the Z-scores obtained for each voxel after the multiple comparisons correction on a structural image. The Z-score–or standard score–is the signed number of standard deviations an observation is above the mean. The resulting maps allow a visual inspection of the active brain areas, which can later be related to a certain disease or task.

3.2.2. Voxel-based morphometry (VBM)

Voxel-based morphometry (VBM) is the application of SPM to structural MRI images [4]. The principle behind VBM is the registration to a template, and then a smoothing of the structural image so that the smaller anatomical differences between subjects are reduced. Finally, a GLM is applied voxel-wise to all the images, in order to obtain a Z-score map that highlights the areas where the differences are greater.

As commented in Section 2.2, the size of the smoothing kernel is an important parameter. A small kernel will lead to artefacts in the Z-maps, including misalignment of brain structures, differences in folding patterns or misclassification of tissue types. On the other hand, a larger kernel will not be able to detect smaller regions.

Newer algorithms expand the idea behind VBM using multivariate approaches, to reveal different patterns. These algorithms include an independent component analysis (ICA) decomposition of the dataset and conversion to Z-scores, called source-based morphometry [52] and a multidimensional tensor-based morphometry [53].

3.2.3. Voxels as features (VAF)

Voxel-as-features (VAFs) is another voxel-wise approach proposed in Ref. [5] for the diagnosis of Alzheimer's disease using functional imaging. It can be considered the first machine-learning approach in this chapter, since it features a linear support vector machine (SVM) classifier whose input features are the intensities of all voxels in the images. It has been used in many works [6, 13, 25, 32, 33] as a baseline and an estimation of the performance achieved by expert physicians by means of visual analysis.

Additionally, some improvements can be done over the raw VAF, for example, using statistical hypothesis testing to obtain the most significant voxels, thus reducing the computational load and increasing the accuracy. The weight vector of the linear SVM can be inversely transformed to the dimension of the original images, and therefore provide a visual map that reflects the most influential voxels, in a similar way to the Z-maps of SPM and VBM.

4. Advances in brain image analysis

The application of new machine-learning techniques in CAD systems is a current trend. Works on this topic have increased exponentially in the past 10 years, and it is expected to grow even more. Machine learning explores the study and construction of algorithms that can learn from and make predictions on data, and therefore it is very useful in neuroimaging.

Two approaches exist in machine learning. *Supervised learning* explores the patterns that lead to a certain outcome, for example, the brain activation patterns that are related to a certain disease. On the other hand, *unsupervised learning* explores the underlying structure of the data. Machine learning in CAD is mostly based on supervised learning, since it is focused on the prediction and analysis of patterns related to a certain disease.

In its simplest form, a machine-learning pipeline for neuroimaging consists of a single *classifier*, just as the VAF approach that we mentioned. However, classifiers can improve their detection power if higher-level features are extracted from the data, for example, features that represent the distribution of the voxel intensities, the texture of the images or the sources of variance of the maps. This is known as *feature extraction*, and the most common technique is *image decomposition*.

4.1. Classification in neuroimaging

We mentioned that the simplest approach to machine learning is classification. Classification basically is induction, that is, using a set of samples extracted from the real world from which we know their class (also known as label or category), and build a model that can identify the class of new samples that were never seen.

Statistical classification is a fertile field, and many classification algorithms are being developed at the moment. A wide range of strategies exist, among them are the following: *instance-based methods*, where the new samples are classified by a measure of similarity with known samples;

hyperplane-based methods, where a multidimensional function that weights the input features produces a score that identifies the class; *decision trees,* where the information is encoded in hierarchical nodes that test one feature at a time; *classifier ensembles, artificial neural networks* and many others.

Hyperplane-based methods are perhaps the most extended in neuroimaging and among them, by far, *support vector machines (SVM)* [6–8]. They offer high accuracy in high-dimensional spaces and can be expanded with the use of kernels to tackle non-linearly separable data. Furthermore, they are very robust to overfitting (unlike decision trees) and therefore more generalizable. Other frequent methods include the hyperplane-based *logistic regression* [9, 10]—and its multiclass version, the *Softmax classifier*–decision trees and *random forests* [54–56], and ensembles of neural networks [34] or ensembles of SVM [11, 12].

4.1.1. Support vector machines (SVM)

Support vector machines (SVM) have been widely used in neuroimaging [5–8] and other high-dimensional problems due to their overfitting robustness. In its linear version, training the classifier is equivalent to finding the coefficient vector $\vec{w}$ that defines the separation hyperplane:

$$(\vec{w}\vec{x}_i - b) = 0 \tag{1}$$

so that the distance between the hyperplane and the nearest point $\vec{x}_i$ is maximized. That way, the problem reduces to minimize the loss function (based on the Hinge loss):

$$\left[\frac{1}{n}\sum_{i=1}^{n}\max[0, y_i(\vec{w}\vec{x}_i - b)]\right] + \lambda \parallel \vec{w} \parallel^2 \tag{2}$$

where y_i is the class of the i-th training sample, b is the bias so that $b/\|\vec{w}\|$ is the offset of the hyperplane from the origin in the direction of $\vec{w}$, and λ is the regularization term, used to keep the coefficients in $\vec{w}$ as small as possible. Many methods exist to perform this optimization, for example, gradient descent or primal and dual loss (using quadratic programming).

Despite the fact that SVMs are mostly used in its linear form, an extension to non-linearly separable problems can be made using the kernel trick. By using kernels, we can implicitly transform data to a higher-dimensional space, but without needing to work directly in that transformed space, simply replacing all dot products in the SVM computation with the kernel. A kernel is a function $K: \mathbb{R}^N \times \mathbb{R}^N \rightarrow \mathbb{R}$ so that $K(\vec{x}_i, \vec{x}_j) = \langle\phi(\vec{x}_i), \phi(\vec{x}_j)\rangle_M$, where $\langle\cdot,\cdot\rangle_M$ is the dot product in $\mathbb{R}^M$ and $\phi(\vec{x}_i)$ is a function that transform $\vec{x}_i$ to that higher-dimensional space. Some common kernel functions are the polynomial kernel $K(\vec{x}_i, \vec{x}_j) = (\gamma\langle\vec{x}_i, \vec{x}_j\rangle + r)^d$ or the radial basis function (RBF) $K(\vec{x}_i, \vec{x}_j) = \exp\left(-\gamma\left(|\vec{x}_i - \vec{x}_j|^2\right)\right)$.

4.1.2. *Ensembles of classifiers*

Ensembles of classifiers are a recent approach to machine learning in which, instead of choosing the best classification algorithm, we train and test different classifiers with different properties, and then combine their outputs to obtain the prediction. In the simplest technique, called *bagging*, we combined the results of the classifiers by voting. This is the strategy used in most neuroimaging works, for example in [11] where the brain was divided into subvolumes and a classifier was assigned to each one. In *boosting* weights are assigned to training samples, and then varied so that new classifiers focus on the samples where previous classifiers failed. Finally, in *stacking*, the outputs of individual classifiers are used as features in a new classifier that combines them. This was the approach used in *spatial component analysis (SCA)* [12], where an ensemble of M SVM was trained on M anatomically defined regions, and their outputs were combined to define a new decision function based on Bayesian networks.

4.2. Image decomposition

Signal decomposition algorithms are the first feature extraction algorithms that we will deal with. They are aimed at modelling a set of samples as a linear combination of latent variables. These latent variables or components can be thought of as the basis of an n-dimensional space where each sample is projected and represented as an n-dimensional vector. In a general case applied to our neuroimaging data, the source images $\mathbf{X}$ can be modelled as

$$\mathbf{X} = s_0 \overrightarrow{\boldsymbol{w}_0} + s_1 \overrightarrow{\boldsymbol{w}_1} + \cdots + s_N \overrightarrow{\boldsymbol{w}_N} + \epsilon = \vec{\boldsymbol{s}}\boldsymbol{W} + \epsilon \qquad (3)$$

where s_i is the coordinate (or component score) of the current image in the ith dimension of the new space defined by all the base vectors $\overrightarrow{\boldsymbol{w}_i}$ (component loadings), and ϵ is the error of the estimation. **Figure 3** shows an illustration of the process.

Signal decomposition techniques are widely used in many applications, ranging from one-dimensional signals such as audio or electroencephalography (EEG) to multidimensional arrays, and are frequently applied as feature reduction to overcome the *small sample-size problem*, that is, the loss of statistical power due to a larger number of features compared to the number of samples.

4.2.1. *Principal component analysis (PCA)*

Principal component analysis (PCA) is a decomposition method where each component (here known as principal components) is intended to model a portion of the variance. The order of the components is set so that the greatest variance in the component space comes to lie on the first coordinate, the second greatest variance on the second coordinate, and so on. The set of principal component loadings, $\mathbf{W}$, is the set of eigenvectors obtained when applying the eigenvalue decomposition of the covariance matrix of the signal, that is, $\mathbf{X}^T\mathbf{X}$. It is not uncommon for neuroimaging specialist to refer to these eigenvectors as *eigenbrains*.

http://dx.doi.org/10.5772/64980

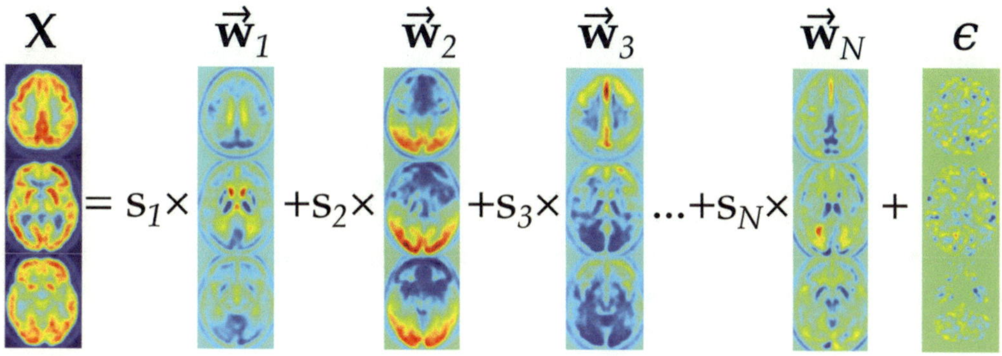

Figure 3. Illustration of a decomposition procedure of a PET-FDG brain image using PCA.

The most frequent approach to compute PCA on a given dataset is by using the singular value decomposition (SVD). This performs the decomposition of **X** in eigenvalues and eigenvectors in the form

$$\mathbf{X} = \mathbf{U}\boldsymbol{\Sigma}\mathbf{W}^{\mathrm{T}} \tag{4}$$

Here, **U** and **W** are square matrices, respectively, containing n and p orthogonal unit vectors of length n and p, known as left and right singular vectors of **X**; and **Σ**is an n-by-p rectangular diagonal matrix that contains the singular values of **X**. When compared to the eigenvector factorization of $\mathbf{X}^{\mathrm{T}}\mathbf{X}$, it is patent that the right singular vectors **X** of are equivalent to the eigenvectors of $\mathbf{X}^{\mathrm{T}}\mathbf{X}$, while **Σ**, the singular values of **X**, are equal to the square roots of the eigenvalues of $\mathbf{X}^{\mathrm{T}}\mathbf{X}$, therefore, the set of principal component scores **S** of **X** in the principal component space can be performed as

$$\mathbf{S} = \mathbf{X}\mathbf{W} \tag{5}$$

As can be seen here, PCA does not account for the noise independently, but it integrates it in the model as another source of variance. The component-loading matrix can be truncated (i.e., only the first m components are used) to reduce the dimension of the principal component space, which is its most used application.

PCA has been used in many neuroimaging works, mainly used for feature reduction in a classification pipeline of nuclear imaging [13–15], but also in structural MRI [16, 17], functional MRI [18] or EEG signals [8].

4.2.2. Independent component analysis (ICA)

Independent component analysis (ICA) performs a decomposition of the source images, but, unlike PCA, it assumes that the components are non-Gaussian and statistically independent from each other. Independence of the components is assessed via either the minimization of the mutual information or checking the non-Gaussianity of the components (motivated by the central limit theorem).

There exist a number of algorithms that implement ICA, from which the most extended are FastICA [57] and InfoMax [58], although other alternatives, such as CuBICA, JADE or TDSEP, are available. Most algorithms use an initial data preprocessing involving centring (create a zero mean signal by subtracting the mean), whitening and dimensionality reduction (with eigenvalue decomposition, SVD or PCA). Afterwards, the algorithm performs a decomposition of each of the m components by minimizing the cost function based on the independence criteria, usually the InfoMax, the Kullback-Leibler divergence or maximum entropy in the case of mutual information algorithms and kurtosis or negentropy for the non-Gaussianity-based algorithms. Most ICA algorithms require the number of sources m as an input.

The terms used in ICA vary from the ones used in PCA decomposition, although they roughly represent the same concepts. It is all based on a mixing model, where the original data **X**, known as mixed signal, is considered a mixture of several unmixed sources **S**, and therefore the matrix **W** that projects **X** to the ICA space **S** is known as the unmixing matrix.

A basic version of the FastICA algorithm is intended to find a unit vector $\vec{w}_p$ for the pth component so that the projection $\vec{w}_p^T\vec{x}$ maximizes non-Gaussianity, measured using an approximation of negentropy $J(\vec{w}_p^T\vec{x})$. To do so, first, we initialize the weight vector $\vec{w}_p$ to random. Then, using the derivative of the negentropy estimates, we perform the update:

$$\vec{w}_p^{+} = \mathrm{E}\{\vec{x}g(\vec{w}_p\vec{x})\} - \mathrm{E}\{g(\vec{w}_p\vec{x})\}\vec{w}_p \tag{6}$$

$$\vec{w}_p = \vec{w}_p^{+} / \| \vec{w}_p^{+} \| \tag{7}$$

This is performed for all components and iterated until convergence. The outputs $\vec{w}_1^T\vec{x}, \ldots, \vec{w}_n^T\vec{x}$ must be decorrelated after each iteration to prevent different vectors from converging to the same maxima. This is achieved, after pooling all $\vec{w}_1, \vec{w}_2, \ldots \vec{w}_n$ to the unmixing matrix **w** in a matricial form, using the alternative found in [57]

$$\mathbf{W} = \mathbf{W} / \sqrt{\| \mathbf{W}\mathbf{W}^T \|} \tag{8}$$

and repeating

$$\mathbf{W} = \frac{3}{2}\mathbf{W} - \frac{1}{2}\mathbf{W}\mathbf{W}^T\mathbf{W} \tag{9}$$

http://dx.doi.org/10.5772/64980

until convergence.

Many neuroimaging works have also applied ICA for feature extraction and reduction in classification pipelines [19, 20], but its main application today is in the processing of EEG signals [21, 22].

4.3. Other feature extraction techniques

In this section, we address feature extraction techniques other than the aforementioned decomposition algorithms. The philosophy behind them is still to provide higher-level features that allow a feature space reduction to overcome the small sample-size problem, but they are intended to extract and quantify information that otherwise would not be available.

4.3.1. Texture analysis

Texture analysis is any procedure intended to classify and quantify the spatial variation of voxel intensity throughout the image. In neuroimaging, they are more commonly used to classify images or to segment them (which can be also considered a form of classification). Depending on the number of variable studies, we can divide the methodology into first-, second- and higher-order statistical texture analysis. In *first-order statistics*, only voxel intensity values are considered, and values such as average, variance, kurtosis or frequency (histogram) of intensity values are computed.

Second-order statistical texture analysis is by far the most popular form. It is based on the probability of finding a pair of grey level at a certain distance and orientation on a certain image. Most algorithms are based in the grey level co-occurrence matrix (GLCM), in which is known as *Haralick texture analysis* [59]. The GLCM can be thought of as a representation of the frequency of the adjacent pixel variations in a certain spatial direction and distance. For a three-dimensional $n \times m \times k$ brain image $\mathbf{I}$ and two different grey levels i and j, at a given offset Δ the co-occurrence value is defined as

$$\mathbf{C}_\Delta(i,j) = \sum_{p=(1,1,1)}^{(n,m,k)} \begin{cases} 1, & \text{if } \mathbf{I}(p) = i, \mathbf{I}(p+\Delta) = j \\ 0, & \text{otherwise} \end{cases} \tag{10}$$

where $p = (x, y, z)$ is the spatial position where $x = 1 \ldots n, y = 1, \ldots m, z = 1, \ldots k$, and $\Delta = (d_x, d_y, d_z)$ is the offset vector, which accounts for the direction and distance between voxels. The size of the GLCM matrix $\mathbf{C}_\Delta$ whose elements were defined before depends on the number of grey levels used in the image posterization, usually 8 or 16. Twelve Haralick texture features were proposed in [59] using a normalized co-occurrence matrix $\mathbf{P}_\Delta = \mathbf{C}_\Delta / \sum_{i,j} \mathbf{C}_\Delta(i,j)$ however, many more have been developed throughout the years. We provide formulas for energy $(\sum_{i,j} \{\mathbf{P}_\Delta(i,j)\}^2)$ entropy $(-\sum_{i,j} \mathbf{P}_\Delta(i,j) \log \mathbf{P}_\Delta(i,j))$ or contrast $(\sum_{i,j} |i-j|^2 \mathbf{P}_\Delta(i,j))$ among others. A 3D co-occurrence matrix was used for the analysis of MRI [23], segmentation [24] and analysis of SPECT images [25].

Higher-order analyses include the grey-level run length method (GLRLM) [26] that computes the number of grey-level runs of various run lengths. Each grey-level run is a set of consecutive and collinear voxels having the same grey-level value. Other texture-based feature extraction methods that have been applied in neuroimaging are the wavelet transform [27], the Fourier transform, used for segmentation [28] and characterization of MRI images [29], or local binary patterns (LBPs) [30, 31].

4.3.2. *Spherical brain mapping (SBM)*

The *spherical brain mapping (SBM)* is a framework that performs feature reduction of neuroimaging from three-dimensional volumes to two-dimensional maps representing a certain feature [32]. This is done by establishing a spherical coordinate system centred at the anterior commissure (AC) and defining a mapping vector $\vec{v}_{\theta,\varphi}$ at an elevation (θ) and azimuth (ϕ) angles. The sets of voxels $V_{\theta,\varphi}$ crossed by this vector are used to compute a value such as the average, variance or entropy, in each coordinate, and finally these values are used as pixels in a two-dimensional map representing that amount. This converts million-voxels volumes to several-thousand images, which achieves a significant computational load reduction as well. Maps for average, entropy or kurtosis of an MRI image are shown in **Figure 4**.

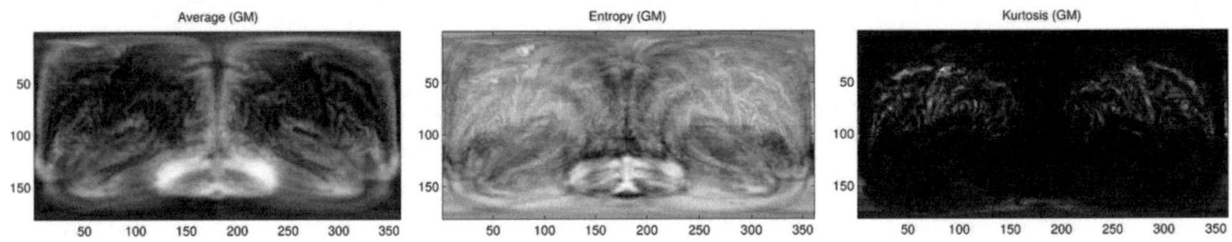

Figure 4. Example of the average, entropy and kurtosis maps generated by SBM.

An extension using volumetric LBP was recently proposed [31], and another utility that uses hidden Markov models to compute the path in the direction (θ,ϕ) using similar-intensity measures was later proposed [33].

4.3.3. *Artificial neural networks (ANN)*

Artificial neural networks (ANN) were inspired by the analysis of biological neural networks in the second half of the twentieth century, but then diverged from their original goal and now are a diverse area of research in machine learning. ANNs are composed by neurons, which model the behaviour of biological neurons by adding up the input signals x_i, using different weightings w_i and producing an output by means of an activation function $f(x)$. Over the time, activation functions such as sigmoid or tan$h$ have been used, although nowadays the most common is rectified linear unit (ReLU), that computes the function $f(x) = \max(0, x)$ (see **Figure 5**).

The architecture of an ANN is a series of interconnected layers containing neurons. The perceptron, one of the most basic approaches, comprises an input layer (no neurons), a hidden layer (composed by n neurons connected with all inputs and all neurons in the output layers) and one output layer. ANNs have been proven to be universal approximators. This means that given any continuous function $f(x)$, and some error $\epsilon > 0$, there exist an ANN $g(x)$ with at least one hidden layer such that $|f(x) - g(x)| < \epsilon$. The addition of more layers (a deeper network) allows the ANN to gain more abstract knowledge in the training process, especially in convolutional networks, where different types of layers coexist. In these networks, the deeper the ANN is, the more abstract the internal representation of the data will be.

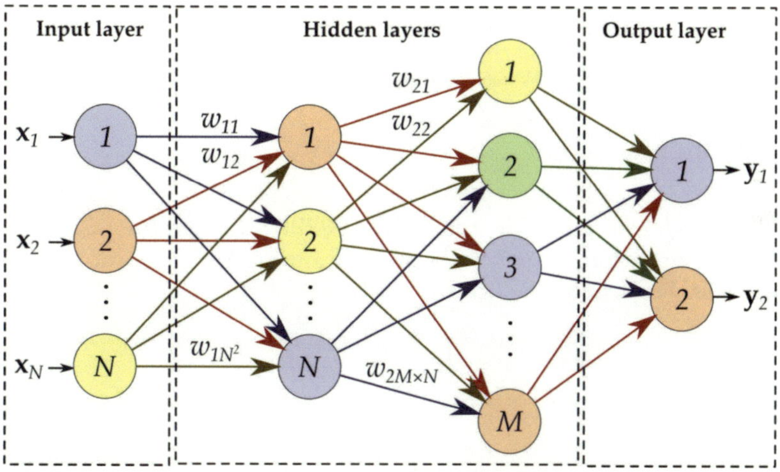

Figure 5. Illustration of the architecture of a perceptron with two hidden layers.

The field is extremely vast and there exist countless architectures, but the most common when applying them to neuroimaging are the *multilayer perceptron* [34] and *self-organizing maps* (SOMs) for segmentation [35] and pattern recognition in functional imaging [36], and more recently *convolutional networks*, which are the base of deep learning, used in segmentation [37], feature extraction [39] and classification [38, 40].

5. Conclusions

Computer-aided diagnosis systems are currently a thriving area of research. The bases are already established and contained in widely used software such as SPM or FreeSurfer. The neuroimaging community already uses these in their daily work, both at research and at clinical practice, with great benefit for the patients. These pieces of software usually include preprocessing (registration, intensity normalization, segmentation, etc.) and posterior automated procedures, such as ROI analysis, VBM or SPM, just like we saw in Sections 2 and 3.

In addition to this, state-of-the-art CAD systems involve the use of advanced techniques to characterize neuroimaging data. The field is still being developed and relevant breakthroughs are still to be made. Advances are being made in a daily basis, with the development of new image modalities involving highly specific radiotracers, advanced registration, correction of inhomogeneities or application of existing machine learning and large data algorithms.

In this review, we have revealed a tendency towards fully automated tools capable of processing neuroimaging data, extract information and even predict the likelihood of having a specific condition. It is very likely that neuroimaging techniques will continue to increase its resolution and usage, and in this scenario the amount of data available will grow exponentially. CAD systems involving most of the topics that we covered in this chapter will be therefore crucial in clinical practice to provide understanding of all available information, otherwise intractable. Only this way can we address a major challenge: to discover meaningful patterns related to behaviour or diseases that ultimately help us to understand how the brain works.

Acknowledgements

This work was partially supported by the MINECO/FEDER under the TEC2015-64718-R and the Consejería de Innovación, Ciencia y Empresa (Junta de Andalucía, Spain) under the P11-TIC-7103 Excellence Project.

Author details

Francisco J. Martínez-Murcia, Juan Manuel Górriz* and Javier Ramírez

*Address all correspondence to: gorriz@ugr.es

Department of Signal Theory, Networking and Communications, University of Granada, Granada, Spain

References

[1] Penny W, Friston K, Ashburner J, Kiebel S, Nichols T, editors. Statistical Parametric Mapping: The Analysis of Functional Brain Images. 1st ed. London: Academic Press; 2006. 656 p.

[2] Reuter M, Rosas HD, Fischl B: Highly accurate inverse consistent registration: a robust approach. Neuroimage. 2010;53(4):1181–1196. DOI: 10.1016/j.neuroimage.2010.07.020.

[3] Smith SM, Jenkinson M, Woolrich MW, Beckmann CF, Behrens TEJ, Johansen-Berg H, Bannister PR, De Luca M, Drobnjak I, Flitney DE, Niazy R, Saunders J, Vickers J, Zhang Y, De Stefano N, Brady JM, Matthews PM: Advances in functional and structural MR image analysis and implementation as FSL. NeuroImage. 2004;23(S1):208–219. DOI: 10.1016/j.neuroimage.2004.07.051.

[4] Ashburner J, Friston KJ: Voxel-based morphometry—the methods. NeuroImage. 2000;11(6):805–821. DOI: 10.1006/nimg.2000.0582.

[5] Stoeckel J, Ayache N, Malandain G, Koulibaly PM, Ebmeier KP, Darcourt J. Automatic classification of SPECT images of Alzheimer's disease patients and control subjects. In: Medical Image Computing and Computer-Assisted Intervention—MICCAI 2004; September 26–29, 2004; Saint-Malo, France. Springer Berlin Heidelberg; 2004. p. 654–662. DOI: 10.1007/978-3-540-30136-3_80.

[6] Salas-Gonzalez D, Górriz JM, Ramírez J, López M, Illan IA, Segovia F, Puntonet CG, Gómez-Río M: Analysis of SPECT brain images for the diagnosis of Alzheimer's disease using moments and support vector machines. Neuroscience Letters. 2009;461(1):60–64. DOI: 10.1016/j.neulet.2009.05.056.

[7] Martínez-Murcia FJ, Górriz JM, Ramírez J, Puntonet CG, Salas-González D: Computer aided diagnosis tool for Alzheimer's disease based on Mann–Whitney–Wilcoxon U-test. Expert Systems with Applications. 2012;39(10):9676–9685. DOI: 10.1016/j.eswa.2012.02.153.

[8] Baumgartner R, Ryner L, Richter W, Summers R, Jarmasz M, Somorjai R: Comparison of two exploratory data analysis methods for fMRI: fuzzy clustering vs. principal component analysis. Magnetic Resonance Imaging. 2000;18(1):89–94. DOI: 10.1016/S0730-725X(99)00102-2.

[9] Ryali S, Supekar K, Abrams DA, Menon V: Sparse logistic regression for whole-brain classification of fMRI data. Neuroimage. 2010;51(2):752–764. DOI: 10.1016/j.neuroimage.2010.02.040.

[10] Dickerson BC, Goncharova I, Sullivan MP, Forchetti C, Wilson RS, Bennett DA, Beckett LA, de Toledo-Morrell L: MRI-derived entorhinal and hippocampal atrophy in incipient and very mild Alzheimer's disease. Neurobiology of Aging. 2001;22(5):747–754. DOI: 10.1016/S0197-4580(01)00271-8.

[11] Gorriz JM, Ramirez J, Lassl A, Salas-Gonzalez D, Lang EW, Puntonet CG, Alvarez I, Lopez M, Gomez-Rio M: Automatic computer aided diagnosis tool using component-based SVM. In: 2008 IEEE Nuclear Science Symposium Conference Record; October 19–25, 2008; Dresden, Germany. IEEE; 2008. p. 4392–4395. DOI: 10.1109/NSSMIC.2008.4774255cc.

[12] Illán IA, Górriz JM, Ramírez J, Meyer-Baese A: Spatial component analysis of MRI data for Alzheimer's disease diagnosis: a Bayesian network approach. Frontiers in Computational Neuroscience. 2014;8:00156. DOI: 10.3389/fncom.2014.00156.

[13] López M, Ramírez J, Górriz JM, Álvarez I, Salas-Gonzalez D, Segovia F, Chaves R, Padilla P, Gómez-Río M: Principal component analysis-based techniques and supervised classification schemes for the early detection of Alzheimer's disease. Neurocomputing. 2011;74(8):1260–1271. DOI: 10.1016/j.neucom.2010.06.025.

[14] Hansen LK, Larsen J, Nielsen FÅ, Strother SC, Rostrup E, Savoy R, Lang N, Sidtis J, Svarer C, Paulson OB: Generalizable patterns in neuroimaging: how many principal components? Neuroimage. 1999;9(5):534–544. DOI: 10.1006/nimg.1998.0425.

[15] Friston KJ, Frith CD, Liddle PF, Frackowiak RSJ: Functional connectivity: the principal-component analysis of large (PET) data sets. Journal of Cerebral Blood Flow and Metabolism. 1993;13(1):5–14. DOI: 10.1038/jcbfm.1993.4.

[16] Ung H, Brown JE, Johnson KA, Younger J, Hush J, Mackey S: Multivariate classification of structural MRI data detects chronic low back pain. Cerebral Cortex. 2012. DOI: 10.1093/cercor/bhs378.

[17] Khedher L, Ramírez J, Górriz JM, Brahim A, Segovia F: Early diagnosis of Alzheimer's disease based on partial least squares, principal component analysis and support vector machine using segmented MRI images. Neurocomputing. 2015;151(1):139–150. DOI: 10.1016/j.neucom.2014.09.072.

[18] Subasi A, Gursoy MI: EEG signal classification using PCA, ICA, LDA and support vector machines. Expert Systems with Applications. 2010;37(12):8659–8666. DOI: 10.1016/j.eswa.2010.06.065.

[19] Illán IA, Górriz JM, Ramírez J, Salas-Gonzalez D, López MM, Segovia F, Chaves R, Gómez-Rio M, Puntonet CG: 18F-FDG PET imaging analysis for computer aided Alzheimer's diagnosis. Information Sciences. 2011;181(4):903–916. DOI: 10.1016/j.ins.2010.10.027.

[20] Calhoun VD, Adali T, Pearlson GD, Pekar JJ: A method for making group inferences from functional MRI data using independent component analysis. Human Brain Mapping. 2001;14(3):140–151. DOI: 10.1002/hbm.1048.

[21] Delorme A, Makeig S: EEGLAB: an open source toolbox for analysis of single-trial EEG dynamics including independent component analysis. Journal of Neuroscience Methods. 2004;131(1):9–21. DOI: 10.1016/j.jneumeth.2003.10.009.

[22] Mammone N, La Foresta F, Morabito FC: Automatic artifact rejection from multichannel scalp EEG by wavelet ICA. IEEE Sensors Journal. 2011;12(3):533–542. DOI: 10.1109/JSEN.2011.2115236.

[23] Kovalev VA, Kruggel F, Gertz HJ, von Cramon DY: Three-dimensional texture analysis of MRI brain datasets. IEEE Transactions on Medical Imaging. 2001;20(5):424–433. DOI: 10.1109/42.925295.

[24] Kruggel F, Paul JS, Gertz HJ: Texture-based segmentation of diffuse lesions of the brain's white matter. NeuroImage. 2008;39(3):987–996. DOI: 10.1016/j.neuroimage.2007.09.058.

[25] Martinez-Murcia FJ, Górriz JM, Ramírez J, Moreno-Caballero M, Gómez-Río M: Parametrization of textural patterns in I-123-ioflupane imaging for the automatic detection of Parkinsonism. Medical Physics. 2014;41(1):012502. DOI: 10.1118/1.4845115.

[26] Galloway MM: Texture analysis using gray level run lengths. Computer Graphics and Image Processing. 1975;4(2):172–179. DOI: doi:10.1016/S0146-664X(75)80008-6.

[27] El-Dahshan EA, Hosny T, Salem ABM: Hybrid intelligent techniques for MRI brain images classification. Digital Signal Processing. 2010;20(2):433–441. DOI: 10.1016/j.dsp.2009.07.002.

[28] Székely G, Kelemen A, Brechbühler C, Gerig G: Segmentation of 2-D and 3-D objects from MRI volume data using constrained elastic deformations of flexible Fourier contour and surface models. Medical Image Analysis. 1996;1(1):19–34. DOI: 10.1016/S1361-8415(01)80003-7.

[29] Wedeen VJ, Reese TG, Tuch DS, Weigel MR, Dou JG, Weiskoff RM, Chessler D. Mapping fiber orientation spectra in cerebral white matter with Fourier-transform diffusion MRI. In: Proceedings of the 8th Annual Meeting of ISMRM; Denver: 2000. p. 82.

[30] Unay D, Ekin A, Cetin M, Jasinschi R, Ercil A. Robustness of local binary patterns in brain MR image analysis. In: 2007 29th Annual International Conference of the IEEE Engineering in Medicine and Biology Society; August 22–26, 2007; Lyon. IEEE; 2007. p. 2098–2101. DOI: 10.1109/IEMBS.2007.4352735.

[31] Martinez-Murcia FJ, Ortiz A, Górriz JM, Ramírez J, Illán IA. A volumetric radial LBP projection of MRI brain images for the diagnosis of Alzheimer's disease. In: International Work-Conference on the Interplay Between Natural and Artificial Computation, IWINAC 2015; June 1–5, 2015; Elche, Spain. Berlin: Springer International Publishing; 2015. p. 19–28. DOI: 10.1007/978-3-319-18914-7_3.

[32] Martínez-Murcia FJ, Górriz JM, Ramírez J, Ortiz A: A spherical brain mapping of MR images for the detection of Alzheimer's disease. Current Alzheimer Research. 2016;13(5):575–588. DOI: 10.2174/1567205013666160314145158.

[33] Martínez-Murcia FJ, Górriz JM, Ramírez J, Ortiz A: A structural parametrization of the brain using hidden Markov models-based paths in Alzheimer's disease. International Journal of Neural Systems. 2016;26(6):1650024. DOI: 10.1142/S0129065716500246.

[34] Liu J, Shang S, Zheng K, Wen JR: Multi-view ensemble learning for dementia diagnosis from neuroimaging: an artificial neural network approach. Neurocomputing. 2016;195:112–116. DOI: 10.1016/j.neucom.2015.09.119.

[35] Reddick WE, Glass JO, Cook EN, Elkin TD: Automated segmentation and classification of multispectral magnetic resonance images of brain using artificial neural networks. IEEE Transactions on Medical Imaging. 2002;16(6):911–918. DOI: 10.1109/42.650887.

[36] Wiggins JL, Peltier SJ, Ashinoff S, Weng SJ, Carrasco M, Welsh RC, Lord C, Monk CS: Using a self-organizing map algorithm to detect age-related changes in functional connectivity during rest in autism spectrum disorders. Brain Research. 2011;1380:187–197. DOI: 10.1016/j.brainres.2010.10.102.

[37] Moeskops P, Viergever MA, Mendrik AM, de Vries LS: Automatic segmentation of MR brain images with a convolutional neural network. IEEE Transactions on Medical Imaging. 2016;35(5):1252–1261. DOI: 10.1109/TMI.2016.2548501.

[38] Plis SM, Hjelm DR, Salakhutdinov R, Allen EA, Bockholt HJ, Long JD, Johnson HJ, Paulsen JS, Turner JA, Calhoun VD: Deep learning for neuroimaging: a validation study. Frontiers in Neuroscience. 2014;8(00229). DOI: 10.3389/fnins. 2014.00229.

[39] Suka HI, Lee SW, Shen D: Hierarchical feature representation and multimodal fusion with deep learning for AD/MCI diagnosis. Neuroimage. 2014;101:569–582. DOI: 10.1016/j.neuroimage.2014.06.077.

[40] Ortiz A, Martínez-Murcia FJ, García-Tarifa MJ, Lozano F, Górriz JM, Ramírez J. Automated diagnosis of Parkinsonian syndromes by deep sparse filtering-based features. In: Innovation in Medicine and Healthcare 2016; Springer International Publishing; 2016. p. 249–258. DOI: 10.1007/978-3-319-39687-3_24.

[41] Mazziotta J, Toga A, Evans A, Fox P, Lancaster J, Zilles K, Woods R, Paus T, Simpson G, Pike B, Holmes C, Collins L, Thompson P, MacDonald D, Iacoboni M, Schormann T, Amunts K, Palomero-Gallagher N, Geyer S, Parsons L, Narr K, Kabani N, Le Goualher G, Boomsma D, Cannon T, Kawashima R, Mazoyer B: A probabilistic atlas and reference system for the human brain: International Consortium for Brain Mapping (ICBM). Philosophical Transactions of the Royal Society of London B: Biological Sciences. 2001;356(1412):1293–1322. DOI: 10.1098/rstb.2001.0915.

[42] Jenkinson M, Smith S: A global optimisation method for robust affine registration of brain images. Medical Image Analysis. 2001;5(2):143–156. DOI: 10.1016/ S1361-8415(01)00036-6.

[43] Scherfler C, Seppi K, Donnemiller E, Goebel G, Brenneis C, Virgolini I, Wenning GK, Poewe W: Voxel-wise analysis of [123I]β-CIT SPECT differentiates the Parkinson variant of multiple system atrophy from idiopathic Parkinson's disease. Brain. 2005;128(7):1605–1612. DOI: 10.1093/brain/awh485.

[44] Arndt S, Cizadlo T, O'Leary D, Gold S. Andreasen NC: Normalizing counts and cerebral blood flow intensity in functional imaging studies of the human brain. Neuroimage. 1996;3(3):175–184. DOI: 10.1006/nimg.1996.0019.

[45] Friston KJ, Holmes AP, Worsley KJ, Poline JP, Frith CD: Statistical parametric maps in functional imaging: a general linear approach. Human Brain Mapping. 1994;2(4):189–210. DOI: 10.1002/hbm.460020402.

[46] Salas-Gonzalez D, Górriz JM, Ramírez J, Illán IA, Lang EW: Linear intensity normalization of FP-CIT SPECT brain images using the α-stable distribution. NeuroImage. 2013;65(15):449–455. DOI: 10.1016/j.neuroimage.2012.10.005.

[47] Chang H, Fitzpatrick JM: A technique for accurate magnetic resonance imaging in the presence of field inhomogeneities. IEEE Transactions on Medical Imaging. 2002;11(3): 319–329. DOI: 10.1109/42.158935S.

[48] Weiskopf N, Suckling J, Williams G, Correia MM, Inkster B, Tait R, Ooi C, Bullmore ET, Lutti A: Quantitative multi-parameter mapping of R1, PD*, MT, and R2* at 3T: a multi-center validation. Frontiers in Neuroscience. 2013;7. DOI: 10.3389/fnins.2013.00095.

[49] Ségonne F, Dale AM, Busa E, Glessner M, Salat D, Hahn HK, Fischl B: A hybrid approach to the skull stripping problem in MRI. Neuroimage. 2004;22(3):1060–1075. DOI: 10.1016/j.neuroimage.2004.03.032.

[50] Dale AM, Fischl B, Sereno MI: Cortical surface-based analysis: I. Segmentation and surface reconstruction. Neuroimage. 1999;9(2):179–194. DOI: 10.1006/nimg.1998.0395.

[51] Fischl B, Salat DH, Busa E, Albert M, Dieterich M, Haselgrove C, van der Kouwe A, Killiany R, Kennedy D, Klaveness S, Montillo A, Makris N, Rosen B, Dale AM: Whole brain segmentation: automated labeling of neuroanatomical structures in the human brain. Neuron. 2022;33(3):341–355. DOI: 10.1016/S0896-6273(02)00569-X.

[52] Xu L, Groth KM, Pearlson G, Schretlen DJ, Calhoun VD: Source-based morphometry: the use of independent component analysis to identify gray matter differences with application to schizophrenia. Human Brain Mapping. 2009;30(3):711–724. DOI: 10.1002/hbm.20540.

[53] Bossa M, Zacur E, Olmos S, ADNI: Tensor-based morphometry with stationary velocity field diffeomorphic registration: application to ADNI. Neuroimage. 2010;51(3):956–969. DOI: 10.1016/j.neuroimage.2010.02.061.

[54] Artaechevarria X, Munoz-Barrutia A, Ortiz-de-Solorzano C: Combination strategies in multi-atlas image segmentation: application to brain MR data. IEEE Transactions on Medical Imaging. 2009;28(8):1266–1277. DOI: 10.1109/TMI.2009.2014372.

[55] Salas-Gonzalez D, Górriz JM, Ramírez J, López M, álvarez I, Segovia F, Chaves R, Puntonet CG: Computer-aided diagnosis of Alzheimer's disease using support vector machines and classification trees. Physics in Medicine and Biology. 2010;55(10):2807. DOI: 10.1088/0031-9155/55/10/002.

[56] Ramírez J, Górriz JM, Segovia F, Chaves R, Salas-Gonzalez D, López M, álvarez I, Padilla P: Computer aided diagnosis system for the Alzheimer's disease based on partial least squares and random forest SPECT image classification. Neuroscience Letters. 2010;472(2):99–103. DOI: 10.1016/j.neulet.2010.01.056.

[57] Hyvärinen A, Oja E: Independent component analysis: algorithms and applications. Neural Networks. 2000;13(4–5):411–430. DOI: 10.1016/S0893-6080(00)00026-5.

[58] Lee TW, Girolami M, Sejnowski TJ: Independent component analysis using an extended infomax algorithm for mixed subgaussian and supergaussian sources. Neural Computation. 1999;11(2):417–441. DOI: 10.1162/089976699300016719.

[59] Haralick RM: Statistical and structural approaches to texture. Proceedings of the IEEE. 1979;67(5):786–804. DOI: 10.1109/PROC.1979.11328.